Captain Paul Watson

DEATH OF A WHALE

THE CHALLENGE OF ANTI-WHALING ACTIVISTS AND INDIGENOUS RIGHTS

Groundswell Books
Summertown, Tennessee

Library of Congress Cataloging-in-Publication Data available upon request.

We chose to print this title on sustainably harvested paper stock certified by the Forest Stewardship Council, an independent auditor of responsible forestry practices. For more information, visit us.fsc.org.

Printed in the United States of America

Groundswell Books
an imprint of BPC
PO Box 99
Summertown, TN 38483
888-260-8458
bookpubco.com

ISBN: 978-1-57067-401-3

25 24 23 22 21   1 2 3 4 5 6 7 8 9

Dedicated to the memory of **Alberta "Binki" Thompson.** The words Koditcheeot hitÁktÁkxe are in the language of the Ko-Ditch-ee-ot, which means "people living at the cape" or "cape dwellers." The name Makah was mistakenly applied to the tribe during treaty negotiations with the US government, as officials misunderstood the Salish names other tribes called them. HitÁktÁkxe means "power," as in the type of power an individual spiritually receives. Alberta "Binki" Thompson was a Makah woman who was given the power to defend the *che-che-wid*, which is the Ko-Ditch-ee-ot word for "gray whale."

This book is also dedicated to the two women who were arrested and injured while defending the whales from the Makah whalers, Erin Abbott and Julie Woodyer.

CONTENTS

Preface

began writing this book in 1999, but in 2000, after writing six chapters, I decided to sit on it because this is history, and I felt that some time had to pass before the book could be properly completed. It is now twenty-two years since that one whale died in May 1999, and although the controversy continues, the issue can be now viewed in a more sobering light.

In writing this book, I of course realize that I may be throwing gasoline on the embers of that controversy, but I do feel it is time to relate the story of Sea Shepherd's opposition to the killing of whales by the Makah Nation of the Pacific Northwest of the United States. I led that opposition, and in doing so, I knew I would be inviting criticism and condemnation, including accusations of racism and ethnocentrism.

The perception by many was that we were opposing the cultural practices of a small Native American tribe. We were accused of being insensitive to the traditions of the Makah and even of being insensitive to American Native culture in general. We were not. The issue was complex, and it was not a simple cowboy-and-Indian fantasy that the Seattle media tried to make it into. It was, in fact, about two completely different points of view, and those points of view were not defined by race or culture.

It was a clash between people who wanted to kill whales and people who opposed the killing of whales. There were Makah tribal members who wanted to kill whales and Makah tribal members who opposed the killing of whales. In fact, there were people in both camps from various and diverse backgrounds. There were Native Americans plus non-Native Americans on both sides. There were conservationists on both sides. There were people sympathetic to Native American culture and traditions opposing the killing of the whales, and there were people who were engaged in defending whales who were also supporting the Makah position that they had the legal right to kill whales.

Because of my longtime association with the causes of Native American rights, I lost a few friends over this campaign, and in some circles I was labeled anti-Native. Although that did cause me some concern, it all came down to the fact that I had no choice but to defend the whales from their would-be killers, no matter what justification these killers might wish to use to defend the activity.

Since 1975, I have sworn to defend whales and dolphins from any and all humans intent upon killing them and to do so without discrimination as to the culture, race, or economic position of those intent upon doing so. Quite simply, I equate the killing of cetaceans with murder, and for murder there can be no justification.

My reason for intervening was simple: There are internationally agreed-upon regulations dealing with whaling and, specifically, with Indigenous whaling operations. The Makah whalers were not in compliance with those regulations.

It was my position then, as it is today, that we had no choice but to do the campaign. Failure to oppose whaling would entail discrimination on our part. We could not treat the Makah whalers any differently than the Faroese, Icelandic, Norwegian, or Japanese whalers. The Faroese claimed Indigenous rights and yet we opposed them. The Japanese, although supporting the Makah position that killing whales was an Indigenous right, have banned the Indigenous Ainu people of Japan from killing whales.

It has always been my position that Sea Shepherd must act to oppose any whaling activity that is conducted outside of the authority of the International Whaling Commission, no matter by whom, where, or for what reason. It would have been hypocritical and, frankly, quite racist for us to have exempted the Makah whalers. We also knew that the whalers did not represent the views of all the Makah people, many of whom were opposed to killing whales, especially many of the elders.

We initiated the campaign for the whales in accordance with our objectives to intervene against unlawful whaling activities. I stand by that position twenty-six years later, just as I did when we first became involved in the campaign in 1995. This is my account of real events, told to the best of my recollection. As such, I stand by this book and the story of our successful campaign to oppose and stop the plan by the Makah whalers and the Makah tribal council to resurrect the whaling operations that they had ended almost a century earlier.

Foreword

by Robert Hunter

The late Robert Lorne Hunter was the author of *Occupied Canada*. This widely acclaimed book about injustices to Native Canadians was the recipient of the Canadian Governor General's Literary Award for Non-fiction in 1991. Hunter was also a cofounder and the first president of Greenpeace Foundation. Before his death in 2005, Hunter was the ecology reporter for *Citytv* in Toronto. His book *Red Blood*, published in 1999, was a humorous account of his experiences working with Native Canadians as a public relations writer for the Kwakiutl Band in British Columbia and his participation in the campaign, along with the *Sea Shepherd* crew and me, to seize the replica of Columbus's ship, the *Santa Maria*.

Hunter wrote this foreword originally for the June 3–10, 1999, issue of the Vancouver weekly newsmagazine the *Georgia Straight*.

RED TIDE

Environmentalists were a lot sadder during the last two weeks of May, more disillusioned than they've been in a long time.

But everybody lost something—Natives most definitely included—when the Makah went over to the Dark Side and killed a gray whale near Neah Bay, despite the best efforts of groups like the Sea Shepherd Conservation Society and the West Coast Anti-Whaling Society.

It was an uneven tussle. The Makah had the US Coast Guard on their side, thanks to the backing of the hypocritical US government itself, with our own Canadian fisheries minister, David Anderson, slinking around in the background, issuing special permits to clear the way should the novice whalers have to chase a large wounded animal into Canadian waters.

When I saw footage of young, wet-suit-clad Makah "warriors" standing on the body of the dead whale, giving exultant clenched-fist power salutes as though they had accomplished a great thing, I seriously thought, "Maybe there isn't any hope for this planet."

What heroic, noble warriors, stuff of legends, throwing a spear into an unsuspecting three-year-old gray whale (a child whale that had probably been petted by humans while down in the wintering lagoons of the Baja Peninsula), then pumping it full of lead with a .50 caliber rifle and cheering in victory as it slowly, agonizingly convulsed in a soup of blood and piss while back at home Native kids waved signs saying, "Kill the Whales!"

A fabulous cultural and spiritual renaissance in the making.

So much for one of the abiding myths of the environmental movement, namely that the Natives could be counted on to treat nature with more respect than the white man. Some activists have long argued that environmentalists should support all Native land claims because the Aboriginals will automatically do a better job of preserving the wilderness than the rest of us.

Well, what we green types lost when the Makah's .50 caliber opened up was not just one whale but the one remaining spark of collective innocence we still enjoyed: our naïve assumption about the inherent eco-nobility—indeed, the superiority—of our Aboriginal brothers and sisters.

The Makah didn't just blow holes in the whale; they also blew apart one of the best public relations gigs going: namely, the notion, fortified by modern books, television, and movies alike, that Natives are automatically the Good Guys when it comes to the environment. In the movie *Free Willy*, the Native guy had to be on the whale's side, as any other position would have confused the audience.

Oh well, another lovely hippie fantasy bites the dust.

Of course, it has always been racial stereotyping to make any presumption about all North American Indian people. There are thousands of little Palestine-like Aboriginal enclaves on the continent where the First Nations have been penned up, all of them arguably distinct cultures in their own right, even when they are members of a scattered tribe. Killing whales is not suddenly an "Indian thing." Members of BC's Gitxsan and Wet'suwet'en peoples, for instance, traveled to Neah Bay to try to talk sense into the Makah leadership.

They failed, but they tried—the point being that not all Natives can be tarred with the Makah brush. Still, the killing stirred up such visceral feelings on both sides of the border that it has to be a public relations disaster for the Makah, the US Coast Guard, and our own acquiescent Canadian federal fisheries minister.

To the extent that the killing stirs up anti-Native feelings, it is bad all around for harmony, mutual respect, and enlightened politics. Racists are chortling over their twelve packs, and liberals can only cringe. After all, with a vicious stab and a burst of heavy-caliber fire, the Makah have squandered the goodwill of environmentalists, people who have generally stood steadfast at the shoulders of Native activists for the past few decades, and who, at the very least, have been solicitous—some might even say obsequious—in the presence of Native leaders, who they have been conditioned to regard as natural allies.

And indeed, hardcore anti-logging people tell me that the support of Natives is absolutely vital in the struggle to save the remaining old-growth forests in Canada. So don't expect to see a sudden official rift between ecofreaks and Natives. Their interests and struggles will continue to overlap, and alliances will go on—no doubt because they must—but an element of implicit trust is gone forever.

Native spirituality itself has taken a hit, because the Makah falsely played up their spirituality from the start until almost the finish, when an Inuit butcher had to be flown in to cut up the whale's body. Who can believe for a moment in any "traditional" ritual that involves towing a ceremonial canoe from one pod of migrating whales to another with powerful outboard engines until a small-enough victim can be isolated, then using a .50 caliber rifle to kill the whale, high-pressure air hoses to float it, and a diesel-powered fish boat to tow the carcass to shore, where a chainsaw and a forklift wait?

As for the spirituality of it all, blood sacrifices are pretty much out of vogue among the rest of the world's religions. And what is the religion of the Makah, anyway?

When I was in Neah Bay last October, having dinner as a member of the media in a community hall full of Makah tribal members, a white-haired old woman got up and offered a blessing in the name of "our Lord Jesus Christ." Virtually everyone bowed, most clasping their hands in prayer. Looked like Christians to me. So when did attacking a harmless sea mammal with high-caliber weaponry become an act of redemption?

Spiritual posturing aside, the truth is that the Makah—who have promised not to sell their catch—have had a secret agenda all along. Documents obtained by the Sea Shepherd Conservation Society through the US Freedom of Information Act on October 2, 1998, show that as far back as 1995, Makah officials, meaning the leadership of the tribal council, were talking behind closed doors with American federal officials about nothing less than a commercial whaling operation.

The documents include email correspondence between US National Marine Fisheries Service people and notes from meetings that were taken by Michael F. Tillman, the deputy US commissioner to the International Whaling Commission. A memo dated April 27, 1995, and hand addressed to "MFT" (Tillman) from "RLB" (identified by Sea Shepherd as Robert L. Brownell of the NMFS) makes it clear that Makah representatives were "planning to operate a processing plant so as to sell to markets outside the US. The Makah have started discussions with Japan and Norway about selling their whale products to both countries. The plant could be used to process the catches of other tribes as well."

In the memo, Brownell defines "catches" as meaning gray whales, harbor seals, California sea lions, minke whales, small cetaceans, and, potentially, sea otters. Open Season.

If this seems all very underhanded, it certainly is no less devious than the machinations of Fisheries and Oceans Canada, which was accused by the Humane Society of Canada, after the latest obtained federal documents under the Access to Information Act, of fronting for Japanese whaling interests by aiding the Makah, with whom the Japanese want to do business.

Humane Society spokesman Michael O'Sullivan has filed formal complaints with the Convention on the International Trade in Endangered Species of Wild Fauna and Flora, fingering Fisheries Minister Anderson for illegally issuing a permit to export whale meat (should a whale be killed while in Canadian waters) and issuing a license to hunt whales without the permission of the International Whaling Commission, which is the only body with the power to approve such hunts. (Canada withdrew its membership in the IWC in the 1980s.)

Almost lost in the flurry of images of the dying whale was the original point of protests: namely that the IWC did not sanction a whale hunt by the Makah in the first place because the lubricious argument that they need the meat for subsistence (after living seventy years without it) has not been accepted by anybody—except, unfortunately, US vice president Al Gore and the US whaling commissioner, James Baker.

The US administration has bought the Makah's constitutional argument that whaling rights were never ceded in their treaty, which wouldn't be a problem except that the White House refuses to take the next step: recognize that the Makah, like the US itself, must be subject to binding international conservation laws—a hard case to make, for sure, with Japan and Norway and now the Makah themselves running amok.

The reentry of the Makah into the ranks of the world's whalers couldn't be coming at a worse time, with Japan having clearly decided to turn a blind eye to its internal trade in whale meat, which DNA testing of fish-market and supermarket samples by visiting eco groups has shown definitively to include flesh from among every species of whale, including the edge-of-extinction blue whale.

This means that the official IWC-ordered moratorium on the killing of all whales is being routinely ignored. We are almost back to the days of the Cold War, when Soviet whalers took anything and everything but lied about it in the records, so the whales seemed protected by quota systems but weren't.

Again, the IWC is showing itself to be toothless. Norway and Japan scheme tirelessly to dismantle the regulations that are all that is holding back a full-scale resumption of commercial whaling worldwide. Norway, meanwhile, hunts in open defiance of the IWC ban, and Japan uses a technical loophole in the agreement to continue killing minke whales for "scientific research," with the meat somehow ending up in Japanese markets and restaurants.

On top of continued human hunting, whales in general are facing threats to their survival related to climate change and attendant changing ocean conditions. On the East Coast, the endangered right whale's tiny population of about 350, which was slowly but steadily recovering, has lost its momentum and is liable to start shrinking again soon. Reasons: fishnets, poisons, and shipping lanes passing through their birthing grounds.

So far during this spring's Pacific migration (1999) from Mexico to the Bering Sea, at least seven gray whales have washed up along the West Coast, their body tissues saturated with industrial contaminants. Any "sustainable" killing of whales, Aboriginal or otherwise, has to factor in the possibility of catastrophic population decline in the not-too-distant future, even without hunting, as temperatures climb, disrupting the ocean's ecosystem upon which the whales depend.

Further proof that these are rotten times to be starting up a whale hunt: The Pacific killer whale (*Orcinus orca*) has just been added to Canada's endangered species list—and this without any hunting, or even capture, of the creatures for decades. The problems: habitat destruction, toxins, less food. The world's whales—along with their entire ecosystem —are under enough stress already without being hunted. It is as simple as that.

The residents of Neah Bay had a party the night before the kill. In current political terms, the Makah have managed to isolate themselves so thoroughly that they have become the eco-Serbs of the West Coast. They have also thrown a whale-sized monkey wrench into ongoing treaty negotiations in British Columbia, with the Nuu-chah-nulth unwisely slapping "whaling rights" on the table at the very moment BC political leaders are denouncing the very idea of whaling off provincial shores. If this were a game, you'd have to move any other Vancouver Island land claims to the back of the board.

All I know is that as a writer who used to work as a public relations advisor to the Nimpkish Band at Alert Bay, and as the author of a history of Canada from the Native point of view, I'm glad I'm not on deck as a Native flack or negotiator having to deal with the backlash that is going to be felt. If I were advising my old bosses now—or any other Native group—I'd say, "Keep your heads low, minimize demands, look innocent. Makah who?"

And I do know this, as a longtime supporter of various Native causes who has always been in favor of the most generous land-claims settlements possible, I can no longer offer my blanket support. The moral and ethical ground just got a whole lot stickier. If the price of the Nuu-chah-nulth achieving self-determination, for instance, is the enshrinement of their right to kill whales, then fuck 'em.

I'd be happy to see Coast Guard boats out there—both Canadian and American—protecting the whales for a change instead of the whalers. And if it takes cops with guns to keep humans with guns at bay, so be it. Keep your mad-dog humans on a chain, I say, until the whales have safely passed.

CHAPTER 1

The Spirit of Aumanil

Paul, your wisdom and concern is acknowledged by myself and the elders. May the Great Spirit bless you for all your work.

KHOT-LA-CHA (CHIEF SIMON BAKER), SQUAMISH, CAPILANO RESERVE

I have always been a strong and active advocate of Aboriginal Indigenous rights. I am, however, also a wildlife conservationist, and occasionally my advocacy for wildlife brings me into conflict with many different cultures, ethnic groups, and nationalities. My priority is always the interest of wildlife and endangered and threatened species over the interests and demands of humans, any group of humans, without discrimination.

I am Métis and a direct descendent of chief Henri Membertou (1490–1560), the *sakmow* (grand chief) of the Mi'kmaq First Nations in sixteenth-century Acadia. (My lineage is outlined on page 237.) The European side of my family are Acadian and have lived in Acadia (presently Prince Edward Island, Nova Scotia, and New Brunswick) since the mid-sixteenth century.

I was born in the traditional lands of the Senecas. The Senecas were one of the five nations of the Iroquois, along with the Mohawk, Oneida, Onondaga, and Cayuga. The Senecas established two communities on the northern shores of Lake Ontario, the village of Ganatsekwyagon

1

near the mouth of the Rouge River and the village of Teiaiagon on the banks of the Humber. The name originates from the Iroquois word *tkaronto*, meaning "where there are trees standing in the water."

My father met my mother, Annamarie Larsen, in Toronto, where I was born. When I was six years old, I returned with my parents to New Brunswick. I was raised in the fishing community of St. Andrews by-the-Sea, New Brunswick, just across the water from the state of Maine. At an early age, I was familiar with the local Passamaquoddy Band across the water near Eastport and spent time exploring the woods, river, and bays on both sides of the border.

At the age of ten, I had jumped into wildlife-protection activities when a young beaver that I regularly played with was killed in a leg-hold trap. I began to sabotage traplines, both Native and white. I wore snowshoes backward to confuse the trappers. I did not see how the ownership of those cruel devices made any difference to the victims. It was a great joy to me to release ensnared animals. Over the next few years, I freed dozens of cats, dogs, seagulls, beavers, and a young fawn from the grotesque contraptions that I then threw into the river or ponds. I was never caught, and it was a source of amusement for me to listen to the complaints of the trappers over the mysterious disappearance of their hardware. No one suspected a child.

It was at this age that I discovered the books of Grey Owl when I read *Sajo and the Beaver People*. Archie Belany, an Englishman who lived as an Indian with his Mohawk wife, Anahareo, championed the beaver. They were both very much role models for me. I also discovered *Roots of Heaven* by Romain Gary, and I was fascinated and inspired by Gary's character Morel, who waged war against elephant hunters.

I knew at a very young age what it was I wished to do with my life. I could think of nothing more satisfying than protecting animals and championing the cause of Indians.

As a North American with Native heritage, I have been well educated in the history of conquest and genocide that has spawned the nations of Canada, the United States, and Mexico. I suffer from no illusions here. I was raised in poverty and I have seen the poverty of numerous reservations. I have also had a lifelong association with many Native communities.

I held no illusions about the horrific destruction caused by the bloody fur trade, the damage it did to wildlife populations, and the disruption it had caused to First Nations people, turning them from relatively respectful hunters into pawns of the Hudson Bay Company, virtual slaves to the company store who each year slaughtered more and more of the beaver, the fox, the mink, the deer, and the wolf so that they could strive for the material status enjoyed by the white man.

Still, I saw that the Indian had been drafted to service the trap-lines in exchange for the pittance paid to them, while the fur industry reaped massive profits from the coldly cruel, gory labor of the Indian. I saw the beaver and the Indian as victims of an economic system that exploited both without thought to the future of either.

My commitment to Native rights has not been the typical liberal approach of sympathy and patronization. I have never seen Native people as special but simply as an Aboriginal people who have suffered from an unjust conquest at the hands of generations of primarily European conquerors. It was my objection to that injustice that led me into an indisputably active role in fighting for Native rights.

In 1972, I became one of the first members of the British Columbia Association of Non-Status Indians. I still carry my membership card from that date, signed by the president of the association, Irene MacDonald, and the secretary, K. Maracle. As a reporter for the Vancouver alternative weekly the *Georgia Straight*, I did an investigative project into the death of a Chilcotin Indian named Fred Quilt. A coroner's jury had ruled his death accidental. My writings, among others, and pressure from the BC Association of Non-Status Indians, led to further inquiries until it was finally determined that Quilt had been beaten to death by mounted police officers. The two officers involved were not charged but were transferred out of the province.

That same year, as a journalist, I covered the United Nations Conference on Environment and Development held in Sweden. Environment, conservation, Third World struggles, and Native rights were my primary journalistic concerns as I worked on ships to support myself and to finance my studies in communications at Simon Fraser University in Burnaby, British Columbia.

Also in 1972, after a trip as a crew member on a Norwegian merchant ship to South Africa, I submitted an article about a South African prisoner on Robben Island. My story was rejected by numerous publications. No one wanted to hear about an anti-apartheid terrorist and a convicted felon. My story ran only in the *Georgia Straight*. The "terrorist" was Nelson Mandela.

Nelson Mandela's life has always been an inspiration to me. The very idea that Nelson Mandela would one day be president of South Africa was unthinkable and thus impossible, yet the impossible became possible.

To this day, I firmly believe that the answer to a seemingly impossible problem is to find the impossible solution. There are three virtues that will assist in finding that answer: passion, backed up by courage and imagination.

On Friday, March 9, 1973, David Garrick, Al Anderson, Steve Whalen, and I set off from Vancouver in Al's Datsun pickup. We arrived in Pine Ridge on March 13 and boldly attempted to drive into the village of Wounded Knee a few hours later.

Two miles from the village, we ran smack into a fully armed FBI roadblock. We were told to step out of the vehicle with our hands in the air as the agents searched the car. They found an ax and two hunting knives, and David Garrick and I were promptly arrested and charged with possession of offensive weapons. We were then driven back to Pine Ridge and tossed into the jail for a few hours before being released and told to return to Canada.

We quickly discovered from reporters that Wounded Knee was surrounded by numerous federal agents, including fourteen armored personnel carriers. I had no intention of returning to Vancouver. Al Anderson and Steve Whalen decided to go home, leaving David and me behind. The two of us allied ourselves with Dewy Brave Heart in the town of Calico, and he helped us to get into the village. I attempted the long hike from Calico over the hills by myself during the night. It was a longer hike than I expected and much colder. When I got close to the FBI patrols, I crawled over the ground with tumbleweeds tied to my back. Unfortunately, I was spotted, arrested a second time, driven back to Pine Ridge, and charged with being a foreign national in an emergency area. This time I was given two hours to leave the reservation and return home.

As I left the jail, I noticed reporters in a line in front of the Bureau of Indian Affairs office. One of them told me they were waiting to apply for a day pass to enter Wounded Knee. I decided to join the line, and when I reached the desk, I told them I was a reporter for the *Vancouver Sun* and the *Georgia Straight*. I had my *Georgia Straight* press card with me and told them that they could call Robert Hunter at the *Vancouver Sun* to verify my reporting for that paper.

Bob covered me, and the BIA public relations guy handed me a day pass.

I caught a ride with another reporter. We drove without incident through the roadblock, and I found myself in the village of Wounded Knee. I reported to Stan Holder, the head of American Indian Movement (AIM) security, and told him I would like to stay as a volunteer. He asked me if I had any skills. I said I was a medic, and he assigned me to the building designated as the hospital.

Thus I served as a volunteer assistant medic for AIM at the siege of Wounded Knee. As others my age fought in Vietnam, I found my initiation into combat in the hills of South Dakota. As a Canadian, I did not need to worry about the draft, but I always felt that it would have been so difficult to have been forced to choose, as so many young Americans of my generation had to do.

Fortunately, I never had to use a gun; however, I was a target. Night after night of flare-illuminated and tracer-bullet-streaked skies, I dove into the snow or lay in soggy ditches to avoid the intense fire of tens of thousands of rounds searching for living targets.

David Garrick attempted from a different direction and successfully passed the roadblock, although he and a few others were fired at by some of chief Dick Wilson's Guardians of the Oglala Nation (GOONS).

I distinctly remember the cold, clear night when I found myself running along with a group carrying supplies toward Red Arrow bunker, where a wounded defender of Wounded Knee reportedly lay bleeding from a gunshot wound. Three armed warriors accompanied us. A few hundred yards away, rifle flashes erupted from a nearby hill and .50 caliber bullets began ripping up the road. Suddenly, Rocky Madrid fell, groaning with pain, an M-16 bullet between his ribs. I assisted in bringing Rocky back to our makeshift hospital, where I witnessed Leonard Crow Dog remove the bullet with a knife and plug the wound with freshly chewed sage root.

Over the next few weeks, I assisted Crow Dog, Doc Rosen, and the other medics in treating bullet wounds in a conflict that wounded forty-six Natives and one US marshal and killed two AIM warriors, Buddy Lamont and Frank Clearwater.

In Wounded Knee I met quite a few Vietnam veterans, and they wondered why they had gone to war in a foreign land when their own land remained under the power of the same military whose uniform they had worn. They were appreciative of the experience, however, for because of it, they had the skills to hold Wounded Knee from their former commanders. They were entrenched and dug in for whatever was needed to maintain the stand against the United States government.

On March 16, 1973, I was given the honor of citizenship within the independent Oglala Nation of Wounded Knee. I would be accepted by the Brave Heart family at Calico a few weeks later. In Wounded Knee I had undergone a vision quest in an Inipi ceremony under the guidance of the great Brule *wicasa wakan* (holy man), Wallace Black Elk. I took the name of the Sung'manitu and became Grey Wolf Clear Water, warrior brother to the Oglala Lakota Nation of Wounded Knee. Neither the Lakota nor Black Elk gave me this name. It came to me in my vision dream. David took the name of Two Deer Lone Eagle, and he also became a warrior brother to the Oglala Lakota Nation of Wounded Knee.

We could not have felt more honored if we had received the Victoria Cross, because at Wounded Knee we were soldiers in a war that actually meant something. My elation at the time was due to feeling that I was a part of something great and unique. Later, I realized that although I had served at Wounded Knee, I was still culturally a *wasicu* (not one of the people). The sacred hoop of the Lakota did not encompass me, yet the Lakota hoop was just one of many sacred hoops, and not all of these hoops were of the reality of humans, although all of the hoops, of all cultures of all beings, were connected. This I learned at Wounded Knee.

I also saw that the hoops of man were dissolving. The Lakota reality, centered on the sacred circle, was transforming into the perceptions centered on the square and the rectangle, from circular teepee to rectangular house, from the great circle of the unfettered plains to the squared patchwork of the barbed wire imprisoned fields. The land once free was now enslaved, owned, and brutalized. The only free frontier left was the domain of the landless—the oceans.

The vision quest had given me a path to follow. I had seen a wolf running in the vision. I had seen a bison struck with an arrow. The arrow had a string attached to it. I had seen myself turn upon the man who shot the bison, and I ran him down and pounced upon him like a wolf. After the chase, I remember seeing my wolfish face reflected back to me in the still, clear waters of a pond.

My vision told me that mine was a solitary spirit. I was free to pursue my own way in life, owing my allegiance to the tribes not of the people. My vision told me to follow the wounded bison, but I could not explain the arrow with the string. Most importantly, my vision told me to follow the voice that said, "Do not allow any person or spirit to force you from your path. If all the people in the world are against you, you must not stray, you must not yield, but keep to the path and dog the one who shot the bison until he is slain or you live no longer."

The only problem was that I did not understand what the bison was and who the slayer of the bison might be.

I left Wounded Knee as a person reborn. I had found myself, and I had learned the most important lessons of my life: courage under fire, commitment to a just cause, and, most importantly, an understanding that a warrior must fight for his beliefs against overwhelming odds, without concern for victory or defeat. The only concern is to do what is right and what is just, simply because it is the only course that can be taken. There can be no compromise with injustice.

American Indian Movement leader Russell Means also said something that has stayed with me all of my life. Although we were heavily outnumbered and the odds of us winning in that confrontation were zero, his view was that we should not worry about the odds against us nor be concerned about winning or losing. We were there because it was the right thing to do, the right place to do it, and the right time to do it.

David and I left Wounded Knee before the federal forces moved in. Many others were also leaving because food inside was becoming scarce. It was decided that only combatants would remain. David and I had agreed to be AIM soldiers, and our orders were to pull out. We did so reluctantly, but we did not question the wisdom of our leadership. Russell Means, Dennis Banks, Pedro Bissonette, and Stan Holder were brave men, and we knew that they knew that although they appreciated our humble help, this was not our place, nor was it our time.

Pedro Bissonette signed and stamped our passports and shook our hands when we left the hospital after paying our respects to Russell Means, Crow Dog, Black Elk, and Stan Holder, thanking them for allowing us to serve with them.

Pedro was a very kind man and a nonviolent activist. He was personally opposed to using a gun, although he had bowed to the decision of his people to pick up the gun. When he was killed on the reservation not long after the confrontation at Wounded Knee, I knew that the US marshal who shot him lied when he said it was self-defense. Pedro would never have raised a gun.

Getting past the government troops was the most dangerous experience we encountered after weeks of life-threatening situations. We were almost run down and crushed by an armored personnel carrier as we lay burrowed under the snow to avoid a patrol, and we crawled on our bellies so close to an FBI camp that we could hear the special agents talking around the campfire.

When we finally reached the village of Calico, we were frozen, tired, and faced with the prospect of getting off the reservation without being spotted by the GOONS. If not for Dewey Brave Heart and his family at Calico, we would most likely have been caught. He hid us in a remote cabin for a few days, and when things were relatively quiet, he drove us to the northern boundary of the reservation where we were able to hitchhike to Rapid City.

It was exactly a year later that Robert (Bob) Hunter approached me and asked if I would like to join him in a campaign to save whales. I had known Bob since 1971, when we had sailed together on the first Don't Make a Wave Committee voyages to protest nuclear testing in the Alaskan Aleutian Islands. We renamed our two ships: the *Phyllis Cormack* (an 85-foot halibut seiner) became the *Greenpeace* and the *Edgewater Fortune* (the 150-foot ex-Canadian minesweeper) became the *Greenpeace Too*. In 1972, we changed the name of the Don't Make a Wave Committee to the Greenpeace Foundation and I became one of its founding directors.

At Wounded Knee, David Garrick and I were representing Greenpeace. When we had sailed to Amchitka, we had been presented with the flag of the Kwakwaka'wakw (Kwakiutl) Nation as we stopped at Alert Bay en route to the Aleutians.

It was our belief that a strong environmental movement needed a strong alliance with Indigenous communities. The Kwakwaka'wakw had supported us on the Amchitka campaign, and we in turn supported the Oglala Lakota at Wounded Knee.

During our time in Wounded Knee, I regularly called Bob Hunter in Vancouver. He was a columnist for the *Vancouver Sun*. My pretense to the Bureau of Indian Affairs was therefore not really a fraud.

There was only one phone from Wounded Knee and the calls were free. The US government paid the bill to keep it from being cut off because, of course, they were monitoring every conversation. Courtesy of the FBI, the *Vancouver Sun* carried exclusive, almost daily coverage of the Wounded Knee standoff in Hunter's daily column.

When Hunter showed me the footage of Russian and Japanese whalers, I was startled to see the harpoon line snake out from the killing ship until it struck the whale in a shower of blood and gore. It was my vision. The bison was the whale, for the whale is to the ocean what the bison is to the sea of prairie grass. The arrow was the harpoon, and there was an instant revelation that this was the path my vision meant for me.

My vision told me to follow the way of the wolf in pursuing my path, and I have done so with steadfast stubbornness for nearly fifty years. That is the power of a vision quest. It is a commitment for life, and once shown the way, there is no turning off the path, at least not if the spirit guiding you is that of the Sung'manitu Wakan.

The vision had given this wasicu a nation. The Whale nation, the tribes of Cetacea. Their enemies became my enemies. Their murderers were those I would oppose. It was a wonderful gift, and I have never regretted having received it, for it has given me great freedom of the spirit and a sense of belonging, of knowing who I am and what I must do.

It has also given me protection. For more than four and a half decades, I have waged war on whalers without suffering a serious injury to my crews or to myself and without causing a single injury to the enemy we oppose.

But we have hurt them financially. We have sunk their ships, sabotaged their factories, destroyed their equipment, and saved their prey from their insidious and deadly harpoons.

But the greatest joy has been in coming to know my people of the sea. It did not take me long.

In 1975, during the first Greenpeace voyage to save the whales, I had four close and intimate experiences with whales. Two of those experiences were profoundly tragic and two were intensely exciting and joyful. It was the year before, in 1974, that I had my first real close encounter with a whale.

It was while we were preparing and organizing for our campaign to confront the Russians in the autumn of 1974. I knew that I wanted to do all that I could to protect these great creatures, but they were still mythical to me, unreal and distant. I needed to get close to them, and since there was only one candidate in the city of Vancouver at the time, I decided to get acquainted with Skana, a captive orca held by the Vancouver Aquarium.

It was at midnight on a moonlit night that I went over the wall, clad only in a bathing suit, crept across the concrete deck, and slipped into the cold waters of Skana's pool cell. It was slightly eerie having my body dangling in the pool, knowing that this great predator was swimming beneath me. I still had not seen her. It was just a calm, deserted swimming pool. There were no security guards, but I did not want to risk calling out her name. Suddenly, a whoosh of expelled air announced her presence behind me. I turned, but she was gone again, and then she was beside me, her snout only inches from my face.

It occurred to me that this would mark a very unusual activity in her schedule, and she might not be as friendly outside the observation of her trainer and the aquarium staff. This whale could swallow me whole, and no one would have known the difference. I would have just disappeared, since not a soul knew that I was here. Curiously, despite this, I did not feel any fear. I reached out and touched her face, and she responded by rolling over to allow me to stroke her throat. At one point she opened her formidable mouth, and to demonstrate my trust in her, I passed my hand over her pointed teeth and patted her soft pink tongue. Her mouth closed slowly and I felt her teeth press lightly against my skin, and then she released me.

We spent the next few hours swimming about, and I was able to hold on to her dorsal as she propelled me around the pool. I was careful to stay on the inside of her body, away from the wall. I was wary that such a large creature might be unaware of how fragile we humans are, and she might have accidentally collided with the wall of the pool. Despite my concerns, it always seemed that she was aware of where I was at all times, and she was being cautious to avoid causing me any injury.

It was absolutely amazing. This great being allowed me to play with her, to touch her and to bond with her, a creature from the wild who also happened to be the most powerful and largest carnivore on Earth. What other predator would have indulged me like this? And what a different psychology she possessed, so alien to that of our own. My kind had imprisoned her, and yet she bore me no malice. She did not greet me with anger, nor did she vent her frustrations on me.

In May of 1975, I was given the opportunity to compare the behavior of wild orcas to my experience with Skana. We were returning from the Queen Charlotte Islands on board the *Greenpeace V* when captain John Cormack spotted an oncoming pod of orcas. They were entering a narrow strait just south of Bella Bella.

I asked John to stop the ship, and he let me dive into the water wearing a wet suit. I swam away from the ship and placed myself directly into the path of the approaching whales. Some of the crew thought that I was being very foolish, and I was inclined to agree with them. Just having your head sticking above the water gives you a seal's-eye view of what an advancing gang of orcas looks like. The awful image of serving myself for lunch came immediately to mind. These were the damn bikers of the cetacean world, for Christ's sake, and here I was voluntarily placing myself in their path.

I could hear the "whoosh, whoosh" of their expelled breath, and I could see their ebony scimitar-shaped dorsal fins cleaving the water and cutting a very sharp path through the sea toward me. When the entire pod submerged, I found the silence of their disappearance to be more intimidating. My legs tingled as they dangled in the inky blackness of the strait, and my imagination was almost on the point of panic with images of severed limbs and my own lifeblood spilling into the sea.

This morbid fantasy was shattered by a thunderous "whoosh" as a large orca, much larger than Skana, emerged from the sea, and I felt the warm spray splashing my face. The great black mandala of its huge body simply poured by me as I squinted through the rainbow haze of the descending droplets of whale exhalation. The dorsal, as high as I am tall, suddenly ascended from the brine and arched skyward. Without thinking, I thrust out my hand, kicked my flippers, and found myself grasping the firm yet soft, warm, towering fin of the orca. As if I had just grabbed a passing train, I found myself pulled from the sea to be born alongside this incredible flesh-and-blood locomotive as it dove again, taking me with him into the depths.

I held on for over a minute before my head broke the surface. I had just enough time to catch my breath and then we were under the surface again, a cacophony of clicks and whistles surrounding me, a glimpse of white to my side, and then back to the surface again. It was as if the whale did not even notice my presence. I was just an uninvited hitchhiker out for a free ride. It was exhilarating. It was magical.

And it was quickly over as I felt the orca tremble and a ripple run through its mighty body. I found myself tumbling in his wake—feeling exhilarated yet rejected and immensely sad.

I had touched an orca in the wild. I had actually taken a ride upon the back of a whale. It is an experience so very difficult to describe. This ferocious creature that ate sea lions for breakfast had allowed me to touch it and live. I could not imagine doing this with a lion, a grizzly bear, or a crocodile, all of which are mere dwarfs compared to the orca.

When I returned to the *Greenpeace V*, John Cormack told me I was crazy, but he had a little twinkle in his eye as he said it. The old fisherman knew a thing or two, of that I was certain. "You know, when I was a kid, and that was a few years ago," said John with a chuckle, "I remember my first time up this coast, and there were many more whales than there are today. When some of these fishermen say there are too many whales, they have no idea what the hell they are talking about. It will never be like it was. No, sir, it never will be like that again."

I knew in my heart that he was right.

A few weeks later, off the Oregon coast, we came across a large fin whale cow with her calf. Greenpeace photographer Rex Weyler and I took off in a Zodiac to take pictures of her. As her massive body moved swiftly through the sea, I stood up in the inflatable. When we came alongside her, I simply stepped out onto her back. Rex pulled away, and I found myself surfing on the back of a whale. Her calf emerged to my right side. The calf's eye scanned me, no doubt wondering what this thing standing on its mother's back could be. It all happened very fast. The whale's gargantuan tail rose out of the water and smacked the surface so hard I could feel a shock wave. Rex pulled alongside me, and I dove from the whale's back into the inflatable and away from her.

"She was not very happy with that," Rex shouted above the outboard.

"No, she wasn't, but she gave me a warning, and it was not the sort of warning to ignore," I replied.

I felt somewhat guilty about harassing her and the calf like that, but the feeling of being so close to such a marvelous creature surpassed any other concern. I knew it would be something I would never do again. But I had felt her, very much aware that beneath my feet was another reality, a different perception, an alien culture, and I yearned to understand her, to glimpse the world through her perceptions, to see and hear the world with her eyes and ears.

These great creatures were transforming my own perceptions. No longer were they abstract objects; instead, they were shaping themselves before my eyes into beings, each possessing an individual personality and radiating uniqueness. I looked upon them with envy, respect, and, most of all, with love.

In life they were giving me a joy I had never before experienced. To those of you reading this who have swum with the whales and the dolphins, you know what I mean. You and I share something special and very rare, for we have seen what it is like to be in the presence of a being far greater than ourselves, more powerful, more intelligent, more sensitive, more perceptive, and profoundly more aware. Here was the god/goddess of the sea, the very material gist of the wisdom and strength of Poseidon, Neptune, Aegir, or Sedna.

But within the same month that the living whales filled my heart with joy, the deaths of two whales drained that joy from me. It was Saturday, June 21, 1975, and our little boat was some sixty miles off the northern coast of California. It was there that we discovered the Soviet whaling fleet in full pursuit of a pod of sperm whales. We could see them from the distance, and as we moved closer, David Garrick spotted something in the water. It was a red flag attached to a float that was attached to a body. It was a young sperm whale, only twenty-five feet in length, five feet under the regulation size ruled by the IWC, a mere youngster.

I dove over the side and swam to the whale, pulling myself onto the floating warm body as it bobbed upon the slight chop of the sea. She was dead, but only recently so. The frayed rope attached to the deeply embedded harpoon flowed from the wound, the fibers stained scarlet as they undulated with the swell. I reached over and my fingers felt the blood oozing from the awful puncture in her lower side. The blood was hot and sticky, and I felt nauseated.

I crawled along her sleek, firm body to her square head and looked deep into her eye, now slowly glazing over with the finality of her death. After my recent experience with the orca and the mother fin, I felt a deep rage rising up inside me, anger like nothing that I had ever experienced before. Why? For what? How could they? The evil, filthy, stinking bastards. In accordance with the primitive emotions of my species, my thoughts turned to revenge. I wanted to kill the bastards who had done this. It was anger just short of madness, and the intensity of it, the frustration of it, nearly overwhelmed me.

Slowly, softly, my fingers reached forward, and I gently closed the eye of the whale child as tears dripped down my cheek. A shout from my crewmates caused me to turn, and I saw a Soviet kill boat bearing down on me with her water hose spitting high-pressure brine. I glared at their crew, ignoring the warnings from my mates, but I knew that I was helpless against them. I slid from the corpse of the bleeding whale into the sea and swam back to the boat, where, frustrated beyond measure, we watched the Soviet whalers lash the tail alongside their craft and pull away to deliver their victim into the ravenous rear-end slipway of the *Dalniy Vostok*, the factory ship.

All that morning we documented death. At last we saw a harpoon boat in pursuit of a pod of sperm whales. Bob Hunter and I, in a fourteen-foot Zodiac, roared off in pursuit of the killers. What I would experience within the next hour would change my life radically. It was my epiphany and my emergence into the tribe of Cetacea. Little did I know that the person who woke that morning would awaken the next morning with a completely different worldview, a different reality.

Out of this tragedy I found rebirth and discovered a purpose. It would be in this purpose that I would find both satisfaction and joy. However, this is a story that I will relate later on in this book, at a time more appropriate for the telling. But I never lost my gratitude to the Oglala Lakota and AIM for granting me a constructive path for my life. I never forgot my debt to those who made it possible for me to experience, follow, and live a vision quest. It was a great gift.

In 1989, I stood with Kayapo warriors on the banks of the Xingu River in Amazonia to oppose the construction of a dam financed by the World Bank. It was there that I met chief Paulinho Paiakan and attended a special dance of Kayapo warriors, where my friend Simon Dick of the Kwakiutl performed a bear dance and shot an arrow into the sky, and to the amazement of the Kayapo and all of us, except for Simon, it did not fall back to Earth again.

Returning from Brazil, I met with Chief Paiakan at the home of Dr. David Suzuki, where we made plans to raise funds to purchase an airplane for the chief to enable him to patrol his land. David asked my friend Al "Jet" Johnson to assist, and in July 1989, he located a

Cessna U206F in Houston, where he flew it himself to Belem, Brazil, and stayed in Brazil as Paiakan's personal volunteer pilot for the next five months. Chief Paiakan gave me a Kayapo feathered headdress for my assistance.

In 1992, I was once again in Brazil, this time to attend the United Nations Conference on Environment and Development in Rio de Janeiro. I was hoping to meet up with Chief Paiakan again. He was expected to address the conference.

Unfortunately, the government of Brazil did not want to see the Kayapo chief disrupting their international party. Days before he was to arrive, a story broke that Chief Paiakan and his wife, Erikran, had abducted, raped, and tortured a sixteen-year-old white girl. My first reaction was that the timing was suspiciously convenient. Nonetheless, Paiakan's environmentalist allies dropped their support for him, as if he carried the plague. A few ecofeminist groups slammed him in the media, and *Veja*, the largest newsmagazine in Brazil, featured Paiakan's face on their cover with the banner headline screaming "Savage." Dr. David Suzuki, his wife, Tara Cullis, Canadian environmentalist Elizabeth May, and I were among the very few that defended him and called the story a lie.

After the conference was over and Chief Paiakan was denied his opportunity to talk to the world forum, the story was revealed to have been fabricated. The "victim" was the daughter of a rich landowner who wanted the Kayapo out of the way. There was not a shred of evidence, and despite the *Veja* story that stated she was tortured in a car and the seats were drenched in her blood, the car was located by more objective journalists and not a drop of blood was found.

Strangely, for such a heinous crime, there was no trial and the scandal disappeared as fast as it had arisen. *Veja* did not run a follow-up. Brazil got what it wanted and had been able to keep Chief Paiakan and his concerns for the rainforests of Amazonia from becoming embarrassing.

This illustrated what I had known for years: The media dictates truth. People are easily manipulated by the media, and without mastering the spin over that of your adversary, perceptions could easily turn against your position, casting you in a far different light than what was true and what you intended.

In 1991, I had been given another opportunity to serve with the First Nations once again. This time I contributed my ship and crew to the Gitxsan and Wet'suwet'en Nations of British Columbia. My ship the *Sea Shepherd* was temporarily renamed the *Aligat* (the Gitxsan word for "warrior"), and we boarded a crew of fourteen Gitxsan and Wet'suwet'en at Nassau in the Bahamas in early December. We were off to celebrate the quincentennial of the voyage of Christopher Columbus in a truly Indian manner. I placed myself under the command of chief Wii Seeks, and he asked me to set a course for San Salvador Island, where there was a large memorial commemorating the landing site of Columbus.

I stayed on board my ship and sent a boat ashore with Wii Seeks and his people, along with Peter Brown and Dinah Elissat, who accompanied them to document their actions onshore. Arriving on the site, they pulled down the Spanish and Canadian flags and raised the flag of the Gitxsan and Wet'suwet'en. They removed the bronze commemorative plaque and returned to the ship, and we immediately set sail for the Caribbean island nation of Turks and Caicos. It was there that we picked up my friend Bob Hunter, who was now working as a reporter for Citytv in Toronto. With him was Ron George, the newly elected leader of the National Indian Brotherhood, to whom Wii Seeks turned over his leadership.

We departed from Turks and Caicos to set out for our objective of intercepting the *Nina*, the *Pinta*, and the *Santa Maria*, the three replica caravels sailing in a reenactment voyage of the Columbus adventure of five hundred years before.

As the *Aligat* entered the waters near Puerto Rico, the United States Coast Guard joined the Spanish warship guarding the three replica caravels. In an attempt to avoid us, the ships ran dark along the coast of the Virgin Islands until we spotted them in the morning. The United States Coast Guard escorted the caravels through the reef, but the Spanish naval escort turned to blockade our approach, steaming toward our ship at full speed. I smiled because I had played this game a few times before, and if I could outbluff a Soviet frigate as I did off Siberia in 1981, I could certainly take on the Spaniards.

I found myself playing chicken with the Spanish warship. Dinah Elissat of Citytv in Toronto was on board, camera rolling as the Spanish vessel bore down upon us. As she said later, "It was great television." It was especially so when the Spaniards veered off first and we sped by, on toward the *Santa Maria*. With the Coast Guard blocking us, the *Nina*, *Pinta*, and *Santa Maria* entered the marina.

We thought we had failed, but Bob Hunter and Eagle clan wing chief Art Loring rallied the Indian crew. Joined by some of my crew, they seized the *Santa Maria*.

All hell broke loose. The Coast Guard joined marina security guards and were shortly followed by the FBI and the San Juan police tactical squad, complete with SWAT team snipers. Most importantly, the media arrived, and the more powerful weapons, the cameras, became trained on the rifles of the marksmen.

On board the *Santa Maria*, our crew was dressed in traditional regalia and wore war paint. The intention was to intimidate the Spanish crew, and it worked. They were clearly confused and did not know what to do about the Indian boarding crew.

Chief Wii Seeks and Ron George approached the captain of the *Santa Maria* and requested an audience with the Spanish consul to Puerto Rico. When the consul arrived, they laid down their terms for releasing the *Santa Maria*.

The cameras had neutralized the guns. The US government was not about to have a bunch of Canadian Indians slaughtered for protesting five hundred years of injustice. The police wisely decided to see if negotiations would work, and we were sure that the phone lines were buzzing between the Spanish and the Americans. A few hours later, the Spanish consul agreed to sign a written apology on behalf of Spain for five hundred years of unlawful occupation and agreed to fly the Gitxsan flag on the *Santa Maria*.

Wii Seeks and his warriors returned to our ship in police cars, courtesy of the chief of police, who then invited all of us out to a Chinese dinner, his treat. It was a very bizarre ending for the day. In the morning, we were pirates with sniper rifles aimed at our hearts. In the evening, we were clinking glasses and singing with San Juan's finest over Chinese food.

But we had made our point, and the next day, Wii Seeks took his people home in time for Christmas as we set out on the thousand-mile return voyage north to Key West, Florida, to prepare for a campaign against poachers off the Pacific coast of Costa Rica.

That voyage had cost me personally. I could not justify an Indian-rights voyage utilizing Sea Shepherd funds, so the expenses had exhausted my savings some $20,000. I felt it was well spent. It was a great adventure in good company, and we had succeeded in raining on the Columbus celebratory parade.

Robert Hunter wrote a wonderfully humorous account of this campaign a few years later in his book *Red Blood*. It was also an inspiration to some of my non-Indian crew members. The tribe adopted Jimmy Liebling, a young man from Maryland who boarded the *Santa Maria* with the Gitxsan. Another young woman from Alberta, Suniva Bronson, a staunch vegan and feminist, joined the Indians occupying Gustafsen Lake in British Columbia a few years later. She was shot and wounded in the arm, arrested, and sent to prison for a few months for her stand.

This is not to say that I always saw eye to eye with all Indian communities. In 1993, I opposed the Champagne and Aishihik plan to exterminate wolves in the Yukon. I met with the tribal council near Whitehorse, where we were told that as white people we did not have the right to oppose the advice of the elders, who, in their wisdom, decided the wolves must be eliminated.

The council kept dismissing us as white imperialists and racists for opposing their plans, and they expected us to go away like most good, guilt-ridden liberal types. I informed them that I was not buying any of their bullshit and that their elders were wrong to advocate total extermination. And, besides, they were Christians who shared the same cultural values as the surrounding white hunters and trappers who all hated wolves, and it was the wolf to whom we owed allegiance, not the Champagne and Aishihik.

We did not back down to their bogus charge of racism. What was racist about opposing the total extermination of wolf packs? Nothing, of course, except such unsubstantiated accusations have become a tactic among many non-white cultures, and even a few white cultures, as a means of getting what they want.

Again in 1993, we butted heads with the Nuu-chah-nulth, this time on the west coast of Vancouver Island, when we opposed the clearcut logging plans of the forest industry. I had taken my ship the *Sirenian* into Tofino Harbor and had dispersed a crowd of angry loggers when I fired a blank shot of powder from my cannon, forcing them to dive for cover on the dock. Later in the day, I met with chief Francis Frank, his council, and other environmental groups and was horrified to hear the other environmental groups inform the Indians that they would abide by whatever decision the Indians would make. Despite my warnings that this would be a dire mistake, the other groups insisted that the Nuu-chah-nulth would never sell out the forests—after all, they were Indians, and Indians are the original environmentalists.

The Nuu-chah-nulth were very smart. They said nothing and allowed the white ecofreaks the opportunity to set up roadblocks, where hundreds were arrested and jailed. The political stakes were getting higher as the arrests approached a thousand people. By the end of the summer, the logging companies and the British Columbian government needed to put the issue to rest. They struck a deal with the Nuu-chah-nulth for money and jobs and, voila, after all their trials and tribulations, the eco-protestors had to capitulate to their promise to abide by whatever the Nuu-chah-nulth wanted.

The trees of Clayoquot began to fall, and I was resented for having my predictions proved correct. People don't like to have their illusions shattered and, unfortunately, many environmentalists did not want to recognize that Indians are like anyone else. They want the same things. They have to pay the same bills. And many will make the same compromises to maintain the luxuries of the twentieth century.

A year later, it was another community that wanted more of the pie, but this time the stakes were much higher. The threat was not against a local ecosystem in the Yukon or on Vancouver Island but would have consequences throughout the world's oceans.

As much as it pained me to decide, we really had no choice. After fighting to stop whaling for a quarter of a century, after going head to head with pirate whalers, Soviet, Japanese, Icelandic, Faroese, Spanish, Korean, and South African whalers, and after sinking seven outlaw whaling ships, how could I allow all of this effort to be overturned by watching an illegal whale hunt take shape in my own home waters?

We would have to oppose the Makah tribe's ambition of reviving their long-deceased culture of whale hunting.

CHAPTER 2

A Harpoon to Slay
One Thousand Whales

They say the sea is cold, but the sea contains the hottest blood
of all, and the wildest, the most urgent.

WHALES WEEP NOT, D. H. LAWRENCE

MAKAH BAY, WASHINGTON STATE
MAY 17, 1999

On May 17, 1999, a three-year-old California gray whale, post-humously given the Makah name Yabis (meaning "beloved") by Makah tribal elder Alberta Thompson, was slain near Point of Arches in Makah Bay. It was the most publicized, possibly the most controversial, and certainly the most expensive killing of a whale in history, and it was the culmination of years of events, conflicts, conspiracies, and cultural clashes involving several governments, the international media, and hundreds of organizations and individuals worldwide.

It was also the first time that the conservation movement came into a head-to-head confrontation with the Indigenous-rights movement, and this clash of politically correct forces created a rift damaging to both sides. It was appropriate that the date was May 17. It was nineteen years since the eve when Mount St. Helens lost her temper. My fear was that the aftershocks of that day in Neah Bay would prove to be more devastating—at least to the whales, and perhaps to the conservation and Indigenous movements.

Looking back after seventeen years of trying to prevent the death of that whale, I could now plainly see that the cultural clash, the shattering of mythical alliances, and the betrayal of the whale was unavoidable. So was the betrayal between so many people. I lost some friends and allies because they were forced to believe that they would have to choose between whales and Indians, between culture and international conservation law, and between our friendship and a politically correct myth.

This was no simple Aboriginal subsistence hunt in a remote American reservation village. It was part of a high-stakes game on an international playing field.

The media tried, as the media is wont to do, to simplify it. The conflict played out in the American press as a cowboy-and-Indian drama. This little Indian village simply wanted to take five whales a year so that they could restore their pride from a time long past, and what was the problem with that?

It did not take long until the media and the public were taking sides in a typically American "if one side is right, the other side must be wrong" attitude, and depending on your point of view, it was a choice between whales and Indians. To some media and some members of the public, a choice of whales over Indians was an automatic confession of racism. The story went from whale conservation versus cultural survival to animal rights versus Native rights to the good guys versus the bad guys, with the definitions of "bad" and "good" being in the eye of the beholder (along with their inclinations and political bent).

Outside the tunnel vision of the provincial American media, a different picture could be seen. The controversy was watched very carefully by Makah supporters in the sushi bars of Yokohama, in the Icelandic, Norwegian, and Faroese Althing (houses of parliament), in the right-wing Wise Use Movement, and the Norwegian High North Alliance offices in the Lofoten Islands. Across the water from Neah Bay in Port Alberni, the newly formed World Council of Whalers, seeded with Japanese and Norwegian money, watched with eager anticipation, and the White House (in particular, the office of the vice president of the United States) followed it all with nervous interest. Equally interested were the whale supporters in the Australian, Mexican, German, British, and French governments; hundreds of conservation, animal welfare, and animal rights organizations from around the globe; and millions of whale lovers the world over.

The five-year debate that ended with the waters of Makah Bay running red with the hot blood of a young whale raged in Iceland, Scotland, Australia, Norway, Monaco, Oman, Hawaii, Canada, Alaska, and Grenada. It was a whale hunt that has had an enormous impact on the conservation politics of countries like Canada, Norway, Japan, Iceland, Denmark, Tonga, Grenada, St. Vincent, the Philippines, Russia, Korea, Peru, and New Zealand. The importance and impact of the hunt provoked controversy outside the bounds of the issue. It was a whale hunt that sent a tribal police chief to prison and helped win an election for a Republican congressman. It was a whale kill that frightened the governor of Washington into mobilizing the National Guard and disrupted a campaign rally for vice president Al Gore. It was an elaborate chess game with the Japanese presiding as reigning grandmaster.

The Makah did not kill just one gray whale on May 17, 1999. The harpoon that left Theron Parker's hand that morning had the potential to extinguish the lives of thousands of whales of all species and may yet be the cause for the extinction of one or more entire species of leviathan.

For me—after so many years of frustrations and elations, victories and defeats—to watch it all unfold in these once-friendly waters was a heartbreaking experience. We (all of us who were there to oppose the hunt) are not ashamed to say that we wept in Makah Bay the morning of May 17. We wept for the death of one whale, and we wept for the loss of trust and the loss of innocence in watching the very symbol of ocean conservation being harpooned by that other traditional symbol of conservation—the American Indian. It seemed to be a betrayal of each side by the other.

I thought of Iron Eyes Cody and recalled the tear that trickled down his cheek in the television ad against pollution and how powerful a statement that had been. And then I laughed to myself when I realized that old Iron Eyes had recently been outed as a fake Indian. He was an Italian, but did that make his statement less powerful?

It was not the Makah harpooner or the heavily armed Wayne Johnson that betrayed us that day with his .50 caliber antitank gun blowing holes in the whale. They never were what we thought they were. We had been betrayed by our own mythology.

It was a devastating revelation, especially for me since I had invested so much trust into a mythical relationship. It was actually agonizing to see it slip away, beneath the dark waters of Makah Bay, oozing away and cooling like hot blood into a frigid sea.

On May 17, 1999, I buried my myth at Makah Bay, and I mourned like an aggrieved parent for a baby whale and for much, much more—so very much more.

NEAH BAY, WASHINGTON STATE, 1995

I would have liked to believe that those Makah who wanted to go whaling did so for spiritual reasons. I really wanted to believe that they honestly desired to revive their ancient traditions. I saw so little evidence that this was so. It certainly was not in the beginning, and it was hard to swallow the costumed posing for the media after we had seen the course of events that had led up to the media circus in the first place.

Dan Greene was no traditionalist but he was a damn successful businessman. He was also a business partner to some very heavyweight Japanese corporate connections in the whaling industry. In 1995, we did not hear any traditional proclamations coming from Danny. Neither Dan nor any of the other young whaler wannabes had bothered to consult with the elders, who still had knowledge of the way of the whalers. Not until much later.

There were some Makah who saw the potential of using the whaling issue to assert treaty rights. Dan Greene told writer Shawn Blore of the Vancouver weekly the *Georgia Straight* in September 1996 that "trying to sustain our treaty rights has been an ongoing battle. The whaling issue is just another one of those issues hanging there."

Tribal councilor Marcy Parker certainly looked upon it as a rights issue. "It's our right," she said to Blore, "like the right to bear arms or the right to free speech. How'd you like it if someone said you couldn't write what you wanted?"

Marcy Parker obviously had little experience with editors.

According to Greene, the Makah had a treaty right to kill whales, seals, and sea lions, and they very much resented the federal laws that had prevented them from killing seals and still prevented them from hunting whales. In short, the Marine Mammal Protection Act and the Endangered Species Act were an affront to their treaty rights, and this had become a stone caught in their craw.

Until the early eighties, the Makah were subject to the same regulations as any other American citizen. If they shot a seal or a sea lion, and if they were caught, they were charged just like any other citizen. According to Greene, federal agents raided a Makah home in 1982 and confiscated a freezer full of seal and sea lion meat. It was that incident that motivated the Makah to threaten a court action against the National Marine Fisheries Service (NMFS). The feds backed down and the NMFS agents simply turned their backs as the Makah openly shot the animals. The law was no longer color-blind.

Then, in 1987, two Makah tribal members approached the tribal council and requested the right to take a whale. It was very suspicious timing. The moratorium against commercial whaling had taken effect in 1986. According to Tadahiko Nakamura of the Japan Whaling Association, the Makah were not unaware of the demand for whale meat in Japan in 1987. In fact, the Japanese had spread the word through their vast global network of fishing corporations that they were in the market for whale meat.

The Makah tribal council demanded their "right" to hunt whales, but this time the US was not about to accept the killing of whales as meekly as they had capitulated over the law protecting seals. They informed the Makah that they would see them in court, if they wished.

It seemed that the Endangered Species Act was more valid than the Marine Mammal Protection Act, possibly because the public perception of one was more reverent than the other. The government knew very well that although the public might tolerate the killing of seals, the killing of whales was clearly in a different league.

The Makah were adamant but didn't want to risk a legal defeat battling the US Endangered Species Act (ESA). Instead, they led a campaign, headed by Dave Sones, the Makah assistant director of fisheries management, to delist the gray whale from the ESA. Sones argued that the population had risen from under one thousand in 1911 to over twenty-two thousand in 1990. It was a success story and, by his account, the gray whale was safe. The Makah never mentioned any plans to go whaling, citing instead the need to delist the gray whale to allow more funding for salmon. In 1994, Sones got his wish. The gray whale was removed from the ESA list but remains on the Convention on International Trade in Endangered Species of Wild Fauna and Flora (CITES).

By the spring of 1995, the Japanese were ready to make their opening gambit. They had been patient for nine years, biding their time in preparation for the unleashing of a well thought out strategy to circumvent the moratorium.

MALMØ, SWEDEN, 1986

Nearly ten years before, in 1986, the International Whaling Commission was meeting in late May in the port of Malmø, Sweden. I was there with my flagship, the *Sea Shepherd II*, in the harbor directly in front of the hotel where the IWC meeting was taking place. American Ben White was the official Sea Shepherd delegate to the IWC, and he was taking quite a bit of flak from the animal welfare and nongovernmental whale conservation groups who thought our presence with the ship was provocative in light of the implementation of the global moratorium on commercial whaling.

"What's the good of a moratorium, Ben, when we don't have enforcement?" I asked him in a meeting in a waterfront café. "The IWC can't enforce anything."

Ben smiled. "You don't need to tell me. Greenpeace and the Humane Society of the United States have asked me to ask you to lay low. They want to let the IWC have a chance to show that this moratorium will work."

"Oh, it will work, all right," I answered. "We'll damn sure make it work."

Later in the day, I received the unexpected pleasure of a visit from IWC secretary Ray Gamble. I gave him a tour of the ship and he was very cordial.

"Dr. Gamble," I said, "do you believe the moratorium will last and will make a difference?"

He looked at me thoughtfully and said, "We can only wait and see."

Before leaving, he told me that he appreciated our involvement.

"That bit of drama with the *Sierra* was a tad excessive, but it did illustrate the problem with pirate whaling," he said with a slight smile.

In 1979, I had hunted down and twice rammed the *Sierra* in the harbor of Leixões in Portugal. The vessel was a pirate ship under a Cypriot flag of convenience, operating completely outside of IWC regulations and selling its whale meat to Japan. It killed anything it could find, without regard to species, size, or sex. After the vessel was repaired, she was mysteriously sunk in Lisbon harbor. The bottom was blown out of her, and she went down and never rose again, her outlaw career permanently brought to an end.

Although we rammed her as she fired upon us and sunk her with a limpet mine, no one was injured or killed. We had, however, established ourselves as the unofficial enforcement agency for the International Whaling Commission.

In April 1980, the Spanish whaling fleet owned by Juan Masso, operating out of Vigo in the north of Spain, had exceeded their quota on fin whales. They continued to kill, ignoring the IWC-imposed quota. Half of Masso's fleet was sunk, sending the *Isba I* and *Isba II* to the mucky bottom of Vigo harbor.

We sat in Malmø harbor in the spring of 1986 as a ship and an organization with a reputation. We relished our unpopularity with the whaling nations, and we were amused by our unpopularity with the more moderate conservation groups. Aside from the visit from Dr. Gamble, we received visits and donations from many local Swedish environmental groups and from some prominent individuals attending the meeting. Dr. Bill Jordan brought the BBC down to the ship to do an interview, and Sir Peter Scott, the son of the Antarctic explorer Robert Falcon Scott, dropped by for dinner and a chat. However, not one of the representatives from any of the anti-whaling groups wanted to be seen anywhere near our vessel for fear of being associated with us. This was fine with me, although I'm mystified how these critics could always be so nice at conferences and meetings. They would constantly bad-mouth us behind our backs and get all flowery when we had cause to meet with them socially. As a result, I tend to joke that the *Sea Shepherd* crew are the "ladies of the night" of the conservation movement. People agree with us in private but don't want to be seen in daylight with us for fear of association.

Now they were patting themselves on the back and announcing victory because the IWC had declared a moratorium. The truth was that they had indeed made a considerable contribution in their efforts to lobby the member nations of the IWC and the moratorium was indeed a great achievement. But victory was premature. A moratorium without enforcement would be meaningless. Already we were hearing that Iceland intended to ignore it and that their commercial whaling operations would continue—business as usual. But not if we could do anything about it. The previous summer, I had taken my ship to Iceland and we had scouted out the harbor and the whaling station at Hvalfjörður. We were prepared for Iceland.

Our press conference for the international media was well attended. The advantage of a ship to an organization is tremendous. It makes a hell of a prop and an anti-whaling ship is a natural backdrop for interviews from a whaling regulatory meeting. After welcoming the media on board, I opened the dialogue by saying, "We are here to receive instructions for actions against the whalers."

"Do you take instructions from the IWC, Captain Watson?" asked one reporter.

"No," I answered. "We observe the decisions of the IWC and act accordingly in response to those decisions."

"What does that mean?"

"It means that once the IWC has outlawed an activity by ruling against it, then we recognize that ruling as our mandate to intervene, interfere, shut down, and permanently close the illicit activity. A moratorium on commercial whaling has been ruled. We intend to see what measures the IWC will take to enforce this ruling. If they do nothing to uphold their own rulings, then we will take it upon ourselves to uphold their rulings for them, whether they [the IWC] like it or not."

"So," said a reporter from the Icelandic newspaper *Dagblad*, "what will you do if Iceland goes whaling against the wishes of the IWC?"

I smiled. "That's simple. If the IWC does not stop Iceland, and if the United States does not sanction Iceland, then we will sink their whaling ships."

Another reporter, a young fellow from Norway, asked, "What gives you the right to take the law into your own hands?"

I looked at the reporter patiently. "You know," I replied calmly, "I have never understood why those who champion peace, life, liberty, and environmental sanity are always asked this question. Why do you never ask this of the whalers, of those who wage war, or of those who ravage the Earth? But I do have an answer to your question. We have the right to intervene given to us by the United Nations World Charter for Nature. It was passed by the United Nations General Assembly in 1982, and it states that individuals and nongovernmental organizations are empowered to uphold international conservation law."

The reporter interrupted. "And who determines what is illegal?"

I raised my voice to emphasize my answer. "I attended the 1972 United Nations Conference on Environment in this country. That conference condemned whaling, and since 1972, every international organization and treaty that has dealt with this issue of whaling has ruled that whaling must stop. Yet all the warnings, all the rulings, all of the studies have been ignored with contempt because the voices of the international community are stifled by the political muscle purchased by that most notorious whaling nation—the renegade whale-killing state of Japan."

A Japanese journalist broke in. "That is a racist statement. Admit it, you are opposed to whaling for the same reason that most anti-whaling nations are opposed to whaling—because it is a way to punish Japan. It is a plot against Asians. You are a racist. You are . . ."

I interrupted him in turn. "That is ridiculous. What a load of cod crap. If I was anti-Asian, I would not have married a Chinese woman and my daughter would not be half Chinese. The Japanese have earned no right to whine about racism. In Japan, if you are not Japanese, you are a second-class citizen. Ask any person of Korean heritage living in Japan. Japanese respect for other Asian nations was well documented at Nanking and Shanghai. I will not accept a charge of racism against me from a representative of the media of one of the most racist nations on Earth. There is no plot against Asians. We do, however, plot against Japan, and Norway, and Iceland, and Russia, and any other nation that flagrantly violates international conservation law and then has the audacity to hide behind the politically correct skirts of racism. Personally, I find it extremely offensive that an issue as important and as serious as racism should be used as a tool to justify illegal whaling."

The Japanese reporter was not about to retreat. "You are just manipulating the facts. There are plenty of whales. You have your own agenda."

"That's correct. I do have my own agenda. It's the agenda of saving lives, saving whales, and I admit it differs radically from your agenda of profits at the expense of life and beauty, your agenda of slaughter. But, if you want to talk about manipulation, perhaps we should ask why the whaling commissioners of St. Lucia, St. Vincent, and Trinidad were replaced by their governments last week in favor of commissioners more sympathetic to Japan. Perhaps you can enlighten the other media here as to what deals were made, promises made, and palms greased to buy the votes of those three nations?"

"I know nothing about this," he answered.

"That's the problem. You know nothing about this issue. Perhaps you should investigate the real issue here—greed."

Meanwhile, Iceland was attempting to prostitute science by requesting an IWC permit to kill over two hundred fin whales for scientific research studies. The reason given was that it would benefit the whales to kill them because it would be the only way to conduct the research necessary to determine what was causing fin whale populations to decline in the North Atlantic.

By the end of the meeting, it became quite obvious that the United States had joined the Caribbean sell-out nations, and the Reaganites were all smiles as they licked Japanese boots. It was evident that the US would not impose sanctions as required by US law. The Reagan administration had decided to discriminate on the application of the law. Conservation organizations, including the Sea Shepherd Conservation Society, filed a legal protest. Both the lower courts ruled that the president was obligated to apply the law without prejudice. The Reagan administration retaliated by appealing to the highest court in the nation. The US Supreme Court voted five to four to reverse the two earlier court rulings that had sided with our demands that the US government exercise sanctions under the Packwood-Magnuson Amendment. This ruling gave the Reagan gang and the Japanese their victory and guaranteed continued illegal whaling. Trade considerations had once again triumphed over conservation law. The Supreme Court had, in effect, knocked the teeth out of any IWC rulings. The moratorium was doomed to failure, and the United States had engineered its defeat.

Canadian author David Day wrote of this decision in his book *The Whale War*. "If the administration had sanctioned Japan—as the American people wished it to do and American legislation had required it to do—Japan's and all other whaling operations would have ceased, and the Whale War would have ended."

After the IWC meeting ended, the *Sea Shepherd II* made a course for the Faroe Islands to oppose the slaughter of pilot whales. We spent a month playing sounds into the water to deflect pilot whale migrations and found ourselves defending our ship from a party of irate Faroese police who attempted to board my ship outside their twelve-mile limit. As the BBC recorded the confrontation, we successfully repelled the boarders with our water cannons, from which we shot drums of chocolate syrup and cream pie filling. Slimed and humiliated, the police retreated, and the BBC aired a one-hour documentary called *Black Harvest* that proved to be very embarrassing to the Faroese government and very educational to the British public. In the documentary, we asked British citizens to boycott Faroese fish products, and there was a positive response.

REYKJAVIK, ICELAND, NOVEMBER 1986

We had not forgotten Iceland. After our ship returned to Bristol, England, two of my crew, Rod Coronado of the US and David Howitt of the UK, made plans to go to Iceland, where they were able to secure jobs in a meat-packing plant as a cover to launch an attack on the pirate whaling operations of Iceland.

After careful observations, these two valiant crew members infiltrated the Icelandic whaling station in the late hours of November 8. They destroyed as much machinery as possible, including all of the refrigeration equipment, before leaving for Reykjavik harbor, where they calmly boarded three whalers. They discovered a sleeping watchman on the outermost ship and cut that ship away from *Hvalur 6* and *Hvalur 7*. It slowly drifted apart from the other two ships as Rod and David descended into the inky blackness of the engine rooms, armed with heavy-duty monkey wrenches.

By dawn, the two whalers were on the bottom of the sea, and Rod and David were on an Icelandic Airlines flight bound for Luxembourg. Back in Vancouver, I was ready with the media releases.

We had enforced the moratorium against Iceland. The damages were estimated at some ten million US dollars. It was a hard blow against the whalers, and we were deeply satisfied at what our courageous young duo had achieved. No one was injured, the targets were whalers not sanctioned by the IWC, and the political gains even outweighed the material damage that we had inflicted.

The resulting news stories ripped away the blanket of false security that the moratorium had cast over a complacent public. Most people believed that whaling was now over. Our sinking of over half of the Icelandic whaling fleet was an international news event that sent a powerful message that the whalers had not given up and the movement to save the whales was still strong and persuasive.

The reaction was amusing. A vigorous surge of indignant disapproval rolled over us. We found ourselves being condemned by politicians, journalists, and other conservation groups—the usual self-righteous gang of whiners. It was all the more frustrating to them that they could do nothing about it.

"Arrest us. Deport us to Iceland," I taunted.

The accusations were there. Iceland labeled the action a terrorist attack. Canadian politicians vowed that I would be brought to justice.

While I was speaking on a talk show on CKNW radio in Vancouver, hosted by Dave Barrett (the twenty-sixth premier of British Columbia), some anonymous nimrod called in a bomb threat to "protest the violence" of the Sea Shepherd Conservation Society. As I stood with Mr. Barrett on the sidewalk outside of the evacuated radio station, a flurry of journalists descended to cover the story of how I was provoking people to violence because they disapproved of my own violence. One excited radio news jockey thrust a microphone toward my face and demanded to know my response to the fact that Greenpeace, my former colleagues, had just issued a media release calling me an ecoterrorist.

I laughed and said, "Oh, what do you expect from the Avon ladies of the environmental movement?" Greenpeace has never forgiven me for that statement, perhaps because I was able to sum up what they are all about—a legion of door-to-door solicitors capitalizing on people's concerns about their environment. Speaking into the microphone, I added, "I don't know what Greenpeace is upset about. An illegal whaling operation has been shut down, whales have been saved, and no one was hurt. What's the problem?"

Rod Coronado was making the media rounds in the United States, and the US authorities had not even questioned him. Obviously, Icelandic accusations of terrorism were not impressing the Americans.

A few days later, I ran into John Frizell, a person who owed his position with Greenpeace to me. I had hired him back in 1975 to work on the seal campaign with me, and now, in 1986, he had advanced to eco-bureaucrat in the Greenpeace International office in England. John gave me a missionary-like look of disapproval when he saw me.

"You know, Watson, all of us in Greenpeace think that what you did in Iceland is despicable, criminal, and unforgivable."

"And your point is what, John?" I asked.

"I thought you should know what we think. Your actions have embarrassed this whole movement, you arrogant bastard."

"So?"

"You really don't care, do you?"

"No, I don't, John. We did not sink those whalers for Greenpeace or for you, or for the movement, or for any human being on this planet, John. We sank them for the whales, John. The whales, not you, and frankly I could not give a damn what you or anyone else thinks. Find me a whale that disagrees with what we have done and maybe I might give your opinion some thought. Until then, keep doing those walkathons and those direct-mail programs. Keep knocking on those doors, John. I hope our saving a few whales has not been overly inconvenient for you."

REYKJAVIK, ICELAND, JANUARY 1988

I did try to answer for our alleged crime. My letters requesting the nature of any charges sent to officials in Reykjavik went unanswered. This was somewhat mystifying. After our November 1986 attack, prime minister Steingrímur Hermannsson had called an emergency cabinet meeting and a debate in the Althing, the Icelandic parliament. Afterward, Hermannsson had delivered an angry speech on Icelandic radio and television.

"The saboteurs are regarded by the Icelandic government as terrorists," said the prime minister. "All efforts will be made to get the people who are responsible for this inhuman act prosecuted."

Attorney general Hallvarður Einarsson had said that he would use all possible channels to have the saboteurs extradited and then prosecuted in Iceland. Despite the obvious posturing for the press, Iceland did not seem to be interested in anything more than name calling. I remember saying on one radio talk show, "If we were terrorists, then by God, we should bloody well be treated like terrorists." No wonder the war on terrorism was going so badly. An honest terrorist could not even turn himself in when he wishes.

In January 1988, a year and two months after the ships were sunk, I grew weary of the continued accusations that we were terrorists, and I hopped on an Icelandic Airlines flight out of Luxembourg bound for Keflavik Airport in Iceland. Sten Borg, our Swedish director, accompanied me to Iceland. This was a move that took the Icelanders completely by surprise. They wanted to promote the idea that I was a terrorist, but they did not want to put me on trial for terrorism.

I had decided to adopt the Brer Rabbit strategy and demand that the Icelanders charge me with terrorism, knowing full well that if they believed that I wanted to be charged, they would most likely not be enthusiastic about charging me.

It was a risky move, but I had little to lose. If they did charge me, they would be putting themselves on trial in the court of international public opinion because I would do everything to publicize their illegal whaling practices. They would probably give me five years at the most. Five years of my freedom for the destruction of the Icelandic whaling fleet sounded like a fair trade to me. If they did not charge me, they would have to put an end to calling me a terrorist.

We were met at the airport by about fifty police officers and a score of reporters. The chief immigration officer approached me. "Captain Watson, how long do you intend to stay in Iceland?"

I smiled. "Well, I don't really know. Five minutes, five days, five months, or five years. I'm afraid that only Iceland can answer that question."

"What are your intentions in coming here?"

"I'm curious to see if your government wishes to charge me for the sinking of the two whaling ships in November 1986."

Looking puzzled, the officer asked, "Are you saying that you are responsible for sinking those ships?"

"Of course we're responsible. Everyone knows we did it, we admitted doing it, we have proof of having done it, and we intend to do it again at the first opportunity."

"I see." He seemed confused but added, "Will you come with us to the police station for questioning?"

"That's what I'm here for."

The police hustled me out a side door and into a waiting car. I was not allowed to speak with the media, although Sten granted them an audience after the police escorted me into Reykjavik for further questioning.

At police headquarters, I was led to a room to speak with a prosecutor. Iceland appointed a lawyer to represent me, and the Canadian consul was called to be present. I was asked if I was claiming responsibility, and, again, I said that yes indeed, the Sea Shepherd Conservation Society and I as its founder and president were responsible for the attack on the Icelandic whaling industry. "I gave the order to sink the ships."

"But," the prosecutor paused before continuing, "you yourself did not actually sink the ships."

"No, of course not. I'm too well known in Iceland, and at the time, I was under an expulsion order, since expired from the Faroese, that would have prevented me from getting into the country, or it would most certainly have red flagged me. It was not possible for me to have participated."

They then informed me that they were not interested in charging me but that they would be interested in charging Rod Coronado and David Howitt. I told them that if they wished to do that, I would arrange to have Rod and David return to Iceland, but only if they agreed to charge me as well.

The prosecutor looked visibly angry, and his face reddened. "It is not your place to decide who and when to bring charges. That is our prerogative. We don't have to respond to your requests simply because you make a request. Our investigations dictate our actions."

I laughed. "What investigations and what actions? The situation is simple. Iceland kills whales illegally. My crew, acting under my instructions, retaliated by sinking two of your ships. We did it, although we will plead not guilty for the benefit of a show trial. It's quite straightforward. What do you need to investigate? A deed was done, the perpetrators admit doing it, and we throw ourselves before you to do with us as you will, and you respond by doing . . . nothing. Frankly, gentlemen, I'm a trifle confused."

They placed me in a cell for the night. The next morning, I was released and turned over to an escort to be taken to the airport without any explanation.

As we exited the police station, I could see a group of journalists jockeying for a position to ask me questions. One reporter yelled out to me, "The police say that you deny any involvement with the sinking of the whaling ships. Is this true?"

I shouted back. "No, it's not true. I told the police that Sea Shepherd is responsible for sinking the ships, and I am responsible for the actions by Sea Shepherd."

Before another question could be asked, I was pushed into a police car to be taken to the airport, where they escorted me on board an Icelandic Airlines flight to New York City. Two police officers flew with me to the US, just to make sure that I didn't hijack the flight and return.

I found out later that the Icelandic attorney general, Hallvarður Einarsson, had given a speech before parliament the morning of my deportation. His speech made a mockery of his earlier position that all efforts be undertaken to make sure we "terrorists" would be brought to justice for our "inhuman act."

Einarsson said, "Who does this man Watson think he is? He comes to our country and demands to be arrested. Well, we are not going to play his game by his rules. We're not going to do it. I move that he be deported and banned from entering any Scandinavian country for five years."

It had been so moved, and I was so deported.

I always thought that to be deported, you had to be charged and given an opportunity to defend yourself. But governments make their own rules, and just as they had chosen to ignore their legal obligations to the IWC, they also had chosen to continue to call me a terrorist without the benefit of a fair trial to pronounce that judgment.

One advantage of my visit, however, was that I was given an opportunity to explain our position to the people of Iceland. The largest Icelandic newspaper, *Dagblad*, was not very happy with the Icelandic government denying them access to interview me. I had previously made arrangements to give a public lecture sponsored by Magnus Skarphedinsson, who had formed a group called Hvalvin-urfelag, which means the "Whale Friends Society." Magnus had given them a copy of my planned speech, and they ran it uncensored under the heading of "An Open Letter to the People of Iceland":

I would like to address the people of Iceland as an ambassador. I do not represent any form of government; I am speaking to you on behalf of the Cetacean Nation.

I am representing whalekind in an effort to reach a state of co-existence with humankind.

My credentials in this regard are simple. I am a human who has swum with, communicated with, studied, and respected the great whales all of my life. I have repeatedly risked my life and freedom to protect and conserve the whales. My love for the whales is such that I would not choose to live upon this planet without them.

> I have touched and I have been touched by the whales. I have been with them when they frolicked freely in the seas, knowing that their mighty hearts were filled with the joy of life.
>
> I have been with them at the moment of their birth, when they have taken their first breath. I have been with them in death. I have felt their hot blood on their skin as the life ebbed slowly away from the horrendous, shattering impact of the grenade harpoon. Once, on the rolling Pacific swells, I comforted a dying child whale, a young sperm killed illegally by a Soviet whaler. I felt its last breath against my face and closed one of its large eyes, but not before seeing my own reflection in the eye of the whale. I knew then, as I know now, that the survival of the whales is the most important objective of my life.

In 1975, Robert Hunter and I were the first people to physically block a harpooner's line of fire when we intercepted a Soviet whaling fleet and placed our bodies between the killers and eight fleeing, frightened sperm whales. We were in a small inflatable boat, speeding before the plunging steel prow of a Russian kill boat. As the whales fled for their lives before us, we could smell the fear in their misty exhalations. We thought we could make a difference with our Gandhi-inspired seagoing stand. Surely these men behind the harpoons would not risk killing a human being to satisfy their lust for whale oil and meat. We were wrong!

The whalers demonstrated their contempt for our nonviolent protests by firing an explosive harpoon over our heads. The harpoon line slashed into the water and we narrowly escaped death. One of the whales was not so lucky. With a dull thud followed by a muffled explosion, the entrails of a female whale were ripped apart by hot steel shrapnel.

The large bull sperm whale in the midst of the pod abruptly rose and dove. Experts had told us that a bull whale in this situation would attack us. We were a smaller target than the whaling ship. Anxiously, we held our breath in anticipation of sixty tons of irate muscle and blood torpedoing from the depths below our frail craft.

The ocean erupted behind us. We turned toward the Soviet ship to see a living juggernaut hurl itself at the Russian bow. The harpooner was ready. He pulled the trigger and sent a second explosive missile into the massive head of the whale. A pitiful scream rang in my ears, a fountain of blood geysered into the air, and the deep blue of the ocean was rapidly befouled with dark-red blood. The whale thrashed and convulsed violently.

Mortally wounded and crazed with pain, the whale rolled, and one great eye made contact with mine. The whale dove, and a trail of bloody bubbles moved laboriously toward us. Slowly, very slowly, a gargantuan head emerged from the water, and the whale rose at an angle over and above our tiny craft. Blood and brine cascaded from the gaping head wound and fell upon us in torrents.

We were helpless. We knew that we would be crushed within seconds as the whale fell upon us. There was little time for fear, only awe. We could not move.

The whale did not fall upon us. He wavered and towered motionless above us. I looked up past the daggered six-inch teeth and into the eye the size of my fist, an eye that reflected back intelligence and spoke wordlessly of compassion and communicated to me the understanding that this was a being that could discriminate and understood what we had tried to do. The mammoth body slowly slid back into the sea.

The massive head of this majestic sperm whale slowly fell back into the sea. He rolled and the water parted, revealing a solitary eye. The gaze of the whale seized control of my soul, and I saw my own image reflected back at me. I was overcome with pity, not for the whale but for ourselves. Waves of shame crashed down upon me and I wept. Overwhelmed with horror at this revelation of the cruel blasphemy of my species, I realized then and there that my allegiance lay with this dying child of the sea and his kind. On that day, I left the comfortable realm of human self-importance to forever embrace the soulful satisfaction of lifelong service to the citizens of the sea.

The gentle giant died with my face seared upon his retina. I will never forget that. It is a memory that haunts and torments me and leaves me with only one course to chart toward redemption for the collective sins of humanity. It is both my burden and my joy to pledge my allegiance to the most intelligent and profoundly sensitive species of beings to have ever inhabited the Earth—the great whales.

Despite the criticisms, the name-calling, and the controversy, one indisputable fact emerged from our raid on Reykjavik: it was successful.

The two whaling ships were razed, although their electronics and mechanical systems had been totally destroyed. Insurance did not cover the losses because the owners had stated that terrorists sank the ships, and apparently they were not insured for terrorism.

Most importantly, from that day of November 8, 1986, to sixteen years later in the year 2002, the Icelanders did not take another whale. What talk, compromise, negotiations, meetings, letters, petitions, and protests had not accomplished, we achieved with a little monkey-wrenching activity in the wee hours of the morning.

Were we terrorists? No, not even criminals, for we were never charged with a crime, even though we made ourselves available for prosecution. We had simply done our duty, and we put an end to an unlawful activity.

The only repercussion was that Iceland moved before the International Whaling Commission in 1987 that the Sea Shepherd Conservation Society be banned from holding observer status at the meetings of the IWC. After this passed, Iceland resigned from the IWC, leaving us with the distinction of being the only organization to enjoy the status of banishment from the IWC.

How ironic, I thought, *to be the only organization banned from the IWC because we were the only organization to have ever enforced an IWC ruling.*

It was not much of a punishment. I had never enjoyed listening to the delegates of the member nations barter whales like they were bushels of wheat or pork bellies. I also never had much use for the posturing of the nongovernmental organizations pretending that they were actually making a difference by attending this annual circus. All that we were interested in were the rulings of the IWC, and we fully intended to continue to enforce those rulings.

I have been asked many times why we consider the IWC rulings important. Why not just oppose all whaling everywhere? The answer is that we do oppose all whaling by everyone everywhere. However, we only actively attack whaling operations that are in violation of international conservation law. The reason for this is simple: We do not presume to be the judges and jury. We simply execute the rulings of the IWC or the Convention on International Trade in Endangered Species of Wild Fauna and Flora or any rulings from international conservation authorities, and we do so in accordance with the definition of intervention as defined by the 1982 United Nations World Charter for Nature, Implementations, Principle 21, Section (e):

> States, and, to the extent they are able, other public authorities, international organizations, individuals, groups, and corporations shall: Safeguard and conserve nature in areas beyond national jurisdiction.

As a seaman, I have a great and abiding respect for the traditions of the law of the sea. To attack without a vested authority would be piracy. Thus, the difference between a privateer like Sir Francis Drake and a pirate like Blackbeard was that the former was in possession of a letter of marque from a sovereign authority and the latter practiced the same trade solely upon his own authority.

I have never considered it my place to judge the illegal activities of others. However, I feel that when there are laws and international treaties, that it is the responsibility of individuals and nongovernmental organizations to strive toward the implementation of these rulings, especially in light of the fact that there is no international body empowered to police these international laws. Nation states intervene when it is advantageous for them to do so, but little enforcement is carried out in the interests of the common good of all citizens of the planet.

It is worth noting that it was not the British or Spanish navies that brought the piracy of the Caribbean under control in the seventeenth century. There were too many conflicts of interest, too much corruption, and too little motivation for any real action to have been taken. The bureaucracies in the British admiralty and the Spanish court did nothing because the very nature of a bureaucracy is the maintenance of the status quo. The achievement of first shutting down piracy on the Spanish Main is attributed to one man—a pirate himself.

Henry Morgan did what two nations chose not to do: he drove the pirates to ground and ended their reign of terror. As a result, the "pirate" was made governor of Jamaica, although history would show that the man was far more effective as a pirate than as a politician. In fact, he was more of a pirate as a politician than he was as an actual pirate.

When Andrew Jackson failed to get the support of the merchants of New Orleans to back his attack on the British, it was a pirate who came to his service in the personage of Jean Lafitte. When the United States successfully endeavored to cast off the yoke of British rule, it was a pirate who achieved the most dramatic and successful naval victory at sea. That person was captain John Paul Jones. Consequently, it is a pirate who was the founder of what is today the world's most powerful navy.

Today, with the pirates of corrupt industry aided by corrupt politicians plundering our oceans for the last of the fish, killing the last of the whales, and polluting the waters, we find that there is very little real resistance to their activities upon the high seas. Once again it is time for some good pirates to rise up in opposition to the bad pirates, and I believe that the Sea Shepherd Conservation Society is just such an organization of good pirates.

When our critics call us pirates, I have no problem with that. In fact, we have taken their criticisms in an aikido-like manner; we have incorporated their accusations into our image. Our ships are sometimes painted a monochromatic black. We have designed our own version of the red bandana, and our black-and-white flag flies from our mast during campaigns. We even carry cannons, with the difference being that our guns fire cream pies and not red-hot balls.

As good pirates, we have evolved to suit the time and culture in which we live, and this being a media-defined culture, our primary weapons are the camera, the video, and the internet. Like modern-day Robin Hoods, we take from the greedy and give back to the sea. We don't profit materially, but we profit tremendously both spiritually and psychologically.

THE LOFOTEN ISLANDS, NORWAY, 1992

Norway was the next nation to flagrantly violate the IWC moratorium. They simply announced a commercial whale hunt in the summer of 1992 and dared the IWC or any member nation to do anything about it. I had attended the United Nations Conference on Environment and Development in Rio de Janeiro, Brazil, in June. The IWC was recognized at the conference as the sole authority to regulate whaling.

I had called a media conference at the Hotel Doria, attended primarily by the Scandinavian media, to announce that the Sea Shepherd Conservation Society would not tolerate any attempt by Norway to ignore the moratorium.

"What will you do if Norway does go whaling?" asked one reporter from Oslo.

"We will begin sinking Norwegian whalers," I answered.

In July, Norwegian whalers went whaling, and the North Sea ran red with the blood of the minke whales. We waited for some retaliation from the United States or any of the IWC member nations. There was not a word. It was time to go hunting for whalers again.

In mid-December 1992, I landed in Stockholm, Sweden, and rented a car. I drove north across the border to Trondheim before heading northward toward Bodø to catch a ferry across to Svolvær on the Lofoten Islands. The other member of the crew was Dwight Worker. He landed in Stockholm on a different flight, journeyed north in Sweden, and crossed the border closer to Narvik before driving on to Andenes. I was looking for whalers, and I located two in Reine. Once they were located, I drove back to Stockholm to catch a train to Amsterdam to prepare a media strategy. Dwight Worker moved into Reine and boarded the whaling boat *Nybræna* on the evening of December 26. He located the saltwater intake valves and proceeded to flood the engine room.

Dwight called the Hotel Doria in Amsterdam on the morning of December 27 to inform me that he had succeeded in scuttling the *Nybræna*. In turn, I informed the police in Svolvær and then proceeded to call the Norwegian and international media.

The publicity was enormous. We had not only dispatched another whaler but also once again focused attention on the reality that illegal whaling continued to be a problem.

The Norwegians were furious. We informed the Norwegian authorities that we would cooperate with their investigations, and in the spring of 1993, I met with Lofoten police inspector Elizabeth Kass in the offices of the Federal Bureau of Investigation in Seattle. We admitted our responsibility and requested that Norway apply for an extradition hearing to send us back to trial in Norway. Inspector Kass asked why they should apply for extradition when we were admitting our responsibility for the attack on the *Nybræna*.

"Because," I answered, "we want to give this issue as much publicity as possible. We would like an extradition hearing in the United States so that we can publicize the issue in this country. Win or lose, we will still return to Norway for the trial, where we will plead not guilty so as to use the trial there to focus attention on illegal Norwegian whaling."

Norway, unfortunately, had other ideas. They held the trial against us without applying for extradition; they simply declared that the trial would be held in absentia. The government selected our lawyers for us; we were not allowed to hire our own lawyers unless we appeared in person.

I agreed to appear if the trial was moved outside of the jurisdiction of the Lofotens, as we had received numerous death threats there. The Norwegians refused. We then informed them that we would come to the Lofotens if the police supplied us with protection. The police refused. Finally, we decided to let the trial proceed, as our attorney in Norway said that afterward we could file an appeal to be heard in Oslo.

At the trial it was ruled that Dwight Worker had acted as a functionary, and despite the fact that he had physically sunk the whaler *Nybræna*, he was acquitted. I was convicted and sentenced to 120 days in prison.

I filed for an appeal on the grounds that I was not allowed a fair trial because I was not in attendance to defend myself due to the refusal by the authorities to guarantee my security. The Norwegian Court of Appeal denied the appeal without giving a reason. As far as I was concerned, we were not given due process, and without being given the right of a defense, I had no intention of simply delivering myself into incarceration—especially not into a hostile Norwegian prison.

I delivered my answer to the Norwegians in January 1994, when one of our agents, Chuck Swift, boarded the Norwegian whaler *Senet* and scuttled it in the harbor. He left a calling card pinned to the engine room door, so there would be no doubt that the scuttling was deliberate. The card that I gave was inscribed with a verse from Edmund Spenser's poem "Colin Clouts Come Home Againe":

> Whom when I asked from what place he came,
> And how he hight, himselfe he did ycleepe,
> The Shepheard of the Ocean by name,
> And said he came from the main-sea deepe.

In the summer of 1994, we purchased a former Norwegian ship in England called the *Skandi Ocean* and renamed her the *Whales Forever*. In July, we set course for the northern coast of Norway to harass the Norwegian whaling fleet. On board we carried an international crew of volunteers and a dozen journalists. Our objective was to use the notoriety we enjoyed in Norway to create an international incident to focus attention on Norway's illegal whaling activities.

The Norwegian navy played right into our hands. As we approached the Lofoten Islands, the warship *Andenes* attempted to snare our prop with a long rope. I was able to outmaneuver the faster vessel, forcing the Norwegian skipper to approach closer in a second attempt. He failed again and miscalculated his third approach, his port side slamming into my bow, ripping away the thick steel in a shower of sparks accented with the screeching tear of metal as our mangled bow retaliated, ripping a long slash along the warship's hull.

I was ordered to stop. I refused.

The Norwegian commander's voice crackled over the radio. "You will stop your ship. I have orders from the highest authority in Norway to do whatever it takes to stop you."

With the reporters standing nearby, I answered, "Really? Whatever it takes? Does that include sinking my ship and killing my crew?"

"Whatever it takes," he replied.

I did not hesitate. "Then whatever it takes will be what you have to do. I will not stop this ship for you. We are in international waters, and you rammed us in international waters. You have no authority over this ship, my crew, or myself."

My first officer, Bjorn Ursford, a former Norwegian naval officer, was at the wheel. He turned a little pale and said, "You can't talk to them like that. No one can."

"Or?" I asked.

"I don't know. I just know that they won't let us go easily."

"Easy or hard, we are going, and the only way they will get this ship is by force, because we will not surrender. You have my word on that."

The Norwegian answer was to fire a shell across our bow. I ignored it. They fired a second shot over our wheelhouse. I ignored that.

The voice on the radio came back. "*Whales Forever*, I advise you to send all your crew to the stern. I will be placing a shot into your bow."

Chuck Swift heard that, and without any orders from me, he quickly assembled the crew to stand along the entire side of our ship. The Norwegian commander furiously barked back that he would hold me personally responsible if his guns killed any of my crew.

"It's your finger on the trigger, sir. Justify it all you want. Pull that trigger and you will be a murderer."

The *Andenes* fell back and we continued on. I had set a course for the Shetland Islands some five hundred miles south, the whole way paralleling the coast of Norway. It would be a long trip, just under two days of running with an increasingly frustrated Norwegian skipper on our stern and no telling what reinforcements he would bring in.

He caught up with us again shortly, but this time he was accompanied by two large, high-speed inflatables crewed by commando units. The first raced in front of us, and I saw a crewman toss a football-sized object into the water directly in front of us.

"What the hell was that?" a reporter asked.

He got his answer a few seconds later when we heard a muffled explosion and the entire ship shook.

Bjorn yelled, "It's an underwater explosive—a depth charge."

A second boat raced before us, followed by a second explosion.

The commander's voice followed with another order to surrender.

"You'll have to bloody well sink us first," I answered.

The pursuit lasted another eight hours, and then the Norwegians dropped away. Later we discovered that the commander claimed I had left him no option but to sink the *Whales Forever*, and he was not prepared to do so.

Our unarmed resolve had beaten back the guns of the Norwegian navy. We sailed into the Shetland Islands knowing we had humiliated the Norwegians and further exposed their illegal whaling operations to the world.

In 1994, I was not anxious to leave the Atlantic. We had plenty of work still to do against the Norwegians, and there was also the continuing pilot whale slaughter in the Faroe Islands that needed our attention. Events were also shaping up in the North Pacific that we felt would be pivotal in the overall game plan of the Japanese whalers and their Norwegian allies. I directed the *Whales Forever* to depart for Key West, Florida, where it would be ready for campaigns in either the Atlantic or the Pacific.

CHAPTER

Idi:gawé:sdi

idi:gawé:sdi: Cherokee singular form translates to "something that one says, thinks, or sings designed to influence actions."

NEAH BAY, SPRING 1995

We had been watching the situation for over a year. Reports first came in from some supporters on the Olympic Peninsula in early 1994. Not that this was a surprise. We had been fighting the Japanese whaling industry since 1974. We were well acquainted with their latest scheme to maneuver around the International Whaling Commission's moratorium on commercial whaling.

We knew that they had been talking with the Tongans, meeting with the Maori, schlepping with the Siberians, gabbing with the Greenlanders, chatting with the governments of a few Caribbean Islands, and getting nice and cozy with the Nuu-chah-nulth on Vancouver Island. We also knew that they had met with the Makah, and we knew what the discussions were all about. Japan was lobbying Indigenous people and Third World communities around the world to get involved in whaling.

Their loophole of scientific research on whaling had its limitations. The numbers they were taking each year were already hundreds beyond what was required for legitimate research.

A solution was to push for Indigenous whaling. If a justification for cultural need could be established, it would not be difficult to argue that no other people had a greater cultural need to whale than the Japanese. But first a foundation for traditional whaling would have to be laid.

The Japanese had pondered the question of where to lay the first stone in their plan toward establishing an Aboriginal kill precedent. The Nuu-chah-nulth were overly eager and had no bones with publicly demanding commercial whaling rights. The Tongans were overly independent, and the Maoris were only semi-serious. But the Makah were ripe for the plucking.

They already had a trade relationship with the Makah over the whiting and sea urchin fisheries. They had a good man in Neah Bay they could rely on—Dan Greene. Finally, they saw the poetry, not to mention the political advantage, of setting their precedent in the one group that had persistently been a thorn in their side for over two decades: the whale-loving public of the United States of America.

It looked like it would be Neah Bay, Washington, as the place where the Japanese would manipulate the first move in their quest. Fortunately, the location was convenient for us. I had been utilizing the Port of Seattle as our Pacific Ocean base since 1981. In 1995, we had our ship the *Sirenian* in Lake Union. We did not anticipate using our larger ship, the *Whales Forever*, but if required, she was in Florida and could be off the West Coast with a month's notice.

The Makah Reservation is situated on the northwestern tip of Washington's lovely, lonely, and very rainy Olympic Peninsula. The reserve has only one town, Neah Bay, and back then it was a small hamlet with two streets squeezed between the beach and the clear-cut slopes. There were three motels, two gas pumps, one general store, and a café called the Makah Maiden, named after an Edward Curtis photograph of a young Makah girl. The houses were peppered with satellite dishes, and a few lawns were adorned with the cannibalized rusty hulks of old Fords and Chevy pickups.

We had already sent in a scout to map out the location and to make inquires while posing as a sports fisherman. We quickly gathered a list of the primary players and those who could be potential allies. After our initial research, we placed the issue on an alert status. Sea Shepherd Pacific Northwest director Michael Kundu would be the regional coordinator.

I understood the strategic importance of Neah Bay but decided I would be most useful once we needed to take a ship to the site. Until then, I had my hands full defending myself from charges in Newfoundland for having chased Cuban and Spanish drag trawlers off the Grand Banks. Although I had not injured anyone, nor had I damaged any property, we had severely embarrassed the Canadian government, and for that I was facing two times life plus ten for charges of conspiracy to save fish and mischief for interfering with illegal fishing activities.

It was a minor but costly inconvenience, both in money and time, although I fully expected to win. Canada was always pulling this crap on me, and it was amusing to see each time that they really thought they could put me away for life for the "crime" of saving whales, seals, or, in this case, cod. My trial was scheduled for September, so there was still time for our initial official visit to Neah Bay sometime in the summer.

In May 1995, Michael Kundu and I could see a tough road ahead of us. The Japanese and the Norwegians were an inflexible, hardheaded bunch, but no one argued with us about their morality. They were wrong for killing whales because killing whales was bad and saving whales was good. That was the moral high ground that we had been enjoying for twenty years. Now we were up against a more politically correct adversary. These were Indians, North American Indians, with treaty rights and an army of white liberal defenders. In fact, it was the same army of self-righteous supporters in the public and the media that we usually could depend on to help us protect the whales.

In this game of global aquatic chess, the Japanese king could be kept out of sight as the Makah pawn was advanced toward the International Whaling Commission's pieces scheduled for assembly in the Catholic diocese of Dublin in late May 1995. The Japanese had chosen their courageous little pawn well.

To this day the Makah themselves are a stubbornly proud people. They have long taken great pride in their whaling traditions. Harpoons have been handed down from generations before and remain the most treasured possession of the whaling families.

As the debate to resume whaling began to blossom, Makah elder Charles "Pug" Claplanhoo reverently held his family's yew wood harpoon, carved more than a century ago. Each of the 131 metal tacks adorning the shaft marked a whale killed by the harpoon he held.

Pug himself had never killed a whale and had no wish to see one killed. Not that he was opposed to whaling; he just felt that the tribe had more important priorities.

"Let's move on, take care of the tribe," he said.

"Our needs are different today," added Makah elder Dottie Chamblin. "We don't need to whale to keep our tribal identity. We know who we are."

On May 5, 1995, the Makah tribal council announced their intention to kill the whales. They stated that they would be prepared to kill a whale in the spring of 1996.

The Sea Shepherd Conservation Society replied the same day with the message that we would oppose the Makah proposal every step of the way. We warned that a Makah precedent would encourage whaling by other Aboriginal communities on Vancouver Island and would give encouragement to the major whaling nations. In addition, a Makah whale hunt would seriously undermine the conservation position of the United States and would weaken the International Whaling Commission.

The Makah acknowledged our concerns. Speaking for the tribe in a July 1995 interview with Kim Murphy of the *Los Angeles Times*, Denise Dailey stated that the possibility of inspiring others to resume whaling was certainly real.

"We're hearing rumblings that some of the tribes up in Alaska will want to start whaling too. We know there are three in Washington that would like to. There are thirteen in Canada. We kind of figure there will be a domino effect. Everybody's looking at us and saying, 'See what you've caused?' But as Makah, we always feel like we're in the front of a lot of issues, especially when it comes to treaty rights."

The first prediction was answered within the month when, on May 26, 1995, thirteen British Columbia Native bands announced their support for the proposal by the Makah to kill whales. Our fears concerning the Vancouver Island Nuu-chah-nulth nations were becoming reality. The Makah were themselves Nuu-chah-nulth. Where the Makah would lead, the other tribes would surely follow, especially if there was a profit to be made.

"Whale hunting is on the Nuu-chah-nulth's treaty negotiation list," said George Watts, the acting chief of the Tseshaht Band. "Our whole culture is centered around whale hunting," said Watts. "We can't talk about our issues without talking about whaling."

The British Columbian government was forthcoming with their position. The provincial minister for aboriginal affairs, John Cashore, a former minister for the environment, said that he "takes a very dim view of this prospect."

"There is a great deal of respect toward the Nuu-chah-nulth people and their tradition of whaling," Cashore said. "There is no question that it is a very strong and ancient tradition. But I believe there is a global ethic here having to do with conservation, and conservation has to override every other concern."

Even the leader of the opposition BC Liberal Party agreed with Cashore.

"The laws of all of us should be the same. The hunting of whales is something that has been frowned upon by Canadians and the international community and will continue to be," stated Gordon Campbell.

The provincial minister for the environment, Elizabeth Cull, followed Cashore's remarks with a letter to the US consul general in Vancouver in which she asserted, "The government of British Columbia is strongly opposed to any harvest of gray whales in Canadian or international waters." Cull urged the US government to give priority to conservation concerns.

The federal government released a statement through spokesperson Diane Lake stating that if the Makah attempted to take a whale in Canadian waters, they would be subjected to the same penalties as any foreign fishing vessel. Greenpeace spokesperson Catherine Stewart informed Toronto's *Globe and Mail* that Greenpeace was opposed to reopening the hunt because of the potential it had for promoting a commercial trade in whale meat. Greenpeace International reversed that decision a few days later and announced that they would not oppose the Makah hunt.

I was not surprised. Greenpeace was terrified of appearing politically incorrect. They had withdrawn opposition to the fur trade a decade before, after protests from Native American trappers, and had even made a public apology for opposing the Canadian seal hunt. That hunt did not involve Aboriginal people, but the Canadian government had put out misinformation that the seal hunt had hurt Canadian Native communities, and that was sufficient to scare Greenpeace away for fear of being accused as anti-Native.

The opinion of Greenpeace was irrelevant. Whaling was the province of the International Whaling Commission. The decision to allow the Makah to kill whales could not come from the Makah tribal council or from the US government. Only the member nations of the IWC could rule on this, and it seemed to us in 1995 that such a ruling would be all but impossible due to the very clear criteria for recognizing Aboriginal whaling claims. The Makah would have to prove an unbroken tradition. And they would also have to prove a subsistence need.

It had been nine years since we had sent anyone to the IWC. Although we were prohibited from attending, it was important that we place someone in a position to observe who was meeting with whom and to gauge the attitude of the member nations regarding the idea of reintroducing whaling in North America. As it turned out, one of my former deck officers, now living in Honolulu, contacted me to say that she would be interested in using her trip home to her native Dublin to represent us at the IWC.

DUBLIN, IRELAND, 1995
45TH ANNUAL MEETING OF THE INTERNATIONAL WHALING COMMISSION

The forty-fifth annual meeting of the International Whaling Commission was preparing to meet in Dublin, Ireland, from May 29 to June 2. It was a sure bet that the Makah issue would be one of the controversial topics of discussion, even though the US would not be officially petitioning the commission for a quota for the Makah tribe. Not this year.

Instead, US whaling commissioner Mike Tillman notified the IWC in Dublin that the United States was considering submitting a formal proposal for a Makah whale hunt in 1996 at the annual IWC meeting to be held in Aberdeen, Scotland. We now had to place the Makah hunt into an active status for Sea Shepherd. We would have to escalate our opposition to it, and we had to prepare for a possible intervention. If the IWC gave its approval for the next year, the hunt could take place as early as the autumn of 1997. In response to this, the Sea Shepherd board of directors decided to keep our ship the *Sirenian* on permanent standby in Seattle until the issue was resolved.

I could not see how the IWC would be able to justify giving approval to the Makah. The criteria were clear, but I had enough experience with IWC politics to understand that anything was possible. If the United States decided to throw its weight around, well, the rules could change under the kind of economic persuasion the White House was capable of. After all, it was because of Japanese economic muscle that this entire ongoing controversy had not been resolved years ago.

A week before the IWC meeting was to convene, former Sea Shepherd first officer Angela Moore and her baby boy caught a plane in Honolulu to return to her family home in Dublin. This enabled us to have an official *unofficial* representative at the IWC for 1996.

Although we had been banned from attending since 1987, we always managed to have someone from another organization to report back to us. We had to respect the ban bestowed on us because you actually have to do something to piss off the whalers to get yourself banned, and we were the only organization ever to have received this "honor." Plus, being banned saved us the expense of having to pay an observer fee to the IWC. On top of that, although banned, we could still speak to the media in attendance and, by virtue of our status, we were always sought after for a comment.

Angela delivered a letter from me to IWC secretary Ray Gamble after she spoke with him. The secretary informed her that Sea Shepherd was welcome to apply for reinstatement of our observer status.

Although I knew that the chance of our reinstatement was practically nonexistent, and we actually enjoyed the notoriety of our status, I wrote a letter of request nonetheless because it would put our ongoing opposition to illegal whaling on the IWC record. In my letter I wrote the following:

> It seems only fair that we be represented here, as countries that routinely violate the regulations of the IWC are welcomed and allowed to have their opinions heard at these meetings. As an organization that has attempted to enforce IWC regulations and thus made an effort to carry out the ostensible will of the IWC, we feel it is important to have all parties to this issue represented, including those whose views and actions are unpopular with the pro-whaling members of the IWC.

Dr. Gamble read the statement to the delegates, and, as expected, the Sea Shepherd Conservation Society continued to be the only organization officially excluded from the meeting. The following is Angela Moore's official report to the Sea Shepherd Conservation Society from the IWC meeting in Dublin:

The Norwegians were killing whales in defiance of the moratorium on commercial whaling at the same time the meeting was taking place. The IWC's scientific committee's reevaluation of the methodology and data used by the Norwegians categorically rejected any basis for Norway's continued whaling.

The IWC passed the following resolution on northeastern Atlantic minke whales:

The Commission:

NOTES that the Scientific Committee has unanimously agreed that there is currently no valid abundance estimate for minke whales in the northeastern Atlantic.

AFFIRMS its view that, notwithstanding the objections that have been entered, commercial whaling should not be taking place while the moratorium remains in force.

Accordingly, CALLS ON the government of Norway, in the exercise of its sovereign right, to reconsider its objection to the moratorium and to immediately halt all whaling activities under its jurisdiction.

Anticipating the position of the IWC, Norway had applied to the Convention on International Trade in Endangered Species to reopen international trade in minke whale meat. The 125-member-nation treaty organization rejected Norway's attempt to down list the minke whale from Appendix I to Appendix II. Norway's arguments were destroyed when CITES delegates were informed that the IWC had found major flaws in Norway's whale population estimates. The CITES signatories stated that the IWC was the competent body to make decisions regarding whales and whaling. CITES informed Norway that the Norwegian ploy was a backdoor attempt to undermine the IWC's moratorium on all commercial whaling.

On May 31, the Netherlands delegation presented a motion to call on Norway to recall its whaling boats. The motion passed twenty-one to six. The nations supporting Norway were predictably Japan, Denmark, South Korea, and the Japanese puppet delegates from Dominica and the Solomon Islands. Norway refused to recall its vessels.

It was revealed that, on May 23, the Tongan government rejected a request by a Japanese whaling company to allow massive commercial whaling operations in Tongan waters. The scheme was devised by MACA Pacific, backed by Tasi Afeaki, a Tongan living in Japan. The proposal called for the killing of fifty humpback whales, two hundred sperm whales, and one hundred minke whales annually and was to involve large catcher boats and processing facilities. The Tongan government came under heavy lobbying pressure, but in the end, Tonga rejected the proposal.

Among the reasons for the rejection was Tonga's emerging whale-watching industry. Government spokeswoman Susan Fotu said that the Tongan moratorium on whaling would stand and that "whaling and whale watching do not go hand in hand." (Sea Shepherd sent a letter to the king of Tonga expressing our deep appreciation for their decision.)

The United States continued to sit on the fence, refusing to condone or condemn illegal whaling. Two years before, the Clinton administration had filed a formal certification against Norway under the Pelly Amendment after Norway began commercial whaling in defiance of the IWC ban. The president, empowered by federal law to embargo any and all products from Norway, failed to uphold the law by refusing to embargo Norway. The president's excuse was that the United States would give Norway the benefit of the doubt until an assessment could be made on the validity of Norway's scientific claims.

With the complete rejection of Norway's scientific position, the USA no longer had any excuse for continuing to refuse to uphold US law against illegal Norwegian whaling. Vice president Al Gore, who bent over backwards to accommodate his close friend Gro Harlem Brundtland, could no longer defend Norwegian whaling as "sound science."

The US demonstrated its leadership in wildlife conservation in 1994 when it imposed the Pelly Amendment sanctions against Taiwan for that nation's flagrant violation of the CITES bans on trafficking in endangered tiger and rhino products. Taiwanese exports of wildlife products, ranging from leather and shells to tropical fish, worth tens of millions of dollars annually, were embargoed. The economic repercussions from that penalty and the international humiliation compelled Taiwan to crack down on the illegal wildlife trade.

For the Norwegians, the consideration was a US embargo of fish products. Exports of salmon, sardines, and prawns to the US realized more than $100 million in annual sales. Under the Pelly Amendment, the US would also have been empowered to embargo marine electronics and fishing gear.

Norway appeared to have more influence in Washington, DC, than Taiwan. Despite Norway's continued escalation of illegal whaling, the White House had remained embarrassingly silent. Perhaps it had something to do with the fact that Norway hired the most influential law firm in Washington for the purpose of subverting the strong US policy against whaling. More than $600,000 had been paid to the firm of Akin Gump Strauss Hauer & Feld LLP, whose senior partners were Robert Strauss and Vernon Jordan, two Democratic political cronies of president Bill Clinton and vice president Al Gore. In addition, Prime Minister Brundtland had personally lobbied her close friend Al Gore to support her on the pro-whaling issue.

Japan requested permission to kill fifty minke whales in the Sea of Okhotsk. Its request was defeated by a vote of fourteen to ten, with nine abstentions. The countries that voted in favor of Japan and against the whales were China, Monaco, Dominica, Grenada, Norway, St. Lucia, St. Vincent, and the Solomon Islands. The countries sitting on the fence were Sweden, Ireland, Mexico, Russia, South Africa, Korea, and Switzerland. The member nations defending the whales from the Japanese were Argentina, Australia, Brazil, Finland, France, Germany, India, Netherlands, New Zealand, Oman, Spain, the UK, and the US.

Japan continued to thumb its nose at the Antarctic whale sanctuary by taking 350 minke whales in 1995 and stating their intention to escalate that number in 1996. (According to some delegates that Angela Moore spoke with, the whaling nations were no longer fearful of sanctions from the United States, and they were becoming bolder.)

The senior Norwegian government scientist to the IWC, Lars Walløe, stated that "whales are no more or no less than large wild mammals, and whaling is simply the hunting of them."

Law professor Patricia Birnie of the UK delegation responded to Dr. Walløe by explaining that legally whales are not like any other animals. She reminded delegates that in the United Nations Convention on the Law of the Sea and in Agenda 21 from the 1992 Earth Summit, marine mammals are special animals and that cetaceans are special marine mammals—and that the IWC is a special organization put in charge of their protection.

Angela Moore finished up her report with a summary of violations for the year:

A host of violations were reported in 1995 to the IWC, all of which went unpunished. Violations included reports of whale meat being sold in Korean fish markets, wasted kills of pilot whales in the Faroe Islands, DNA proof of endangered and threatened whales being sold in Japanese markets, smuggling of minke whale meat from Norway to Japan, and, of course, wholesale illegal slaughter by Norway and Japan.

The only punishment handed out at the forty-fifth annual meeting of the IWC was a renewal of the 1987 ban against the Sea Shepherd Conservation Society attending as an NGO observer. It was good to know that the world's only regulatory agency for whaling had its priorities straight.

Relevant to the Makah, Angela Moore reported some interesting meetings. She observed Dan Greene of the Makah delegation having dinner with representatives of the Norwegian, Icelandic, and Japanese whaling associations. She observed him having conversations with Georg Blichfeldt of the Norwegian High North Alliance.

We were watching the Makah closely. We knew then that the Makah were being encouraged by the whaling nations in their pursuit of the goal of resurrecting whaling. It was important to impress upon the IWC members the dire consequences of a Makah whale hunt. Toward this end, Angela Moore was able to slip an information leaflet into each delegate's box, thanks to her contacts with the Irish delegation. The leaflet simply listed the consequences should the Makah be allowed to whale: "It would undermine the position of the United States within the IWC."

Thirteen Vancouver Island tribal bands had said they wanted to exercise the same rights as the Makah, which threatened to escalate unregulated whaling and could have seriously affected gray whale populations. The Makah wanted to land five whales a year, meaning that more whales would be struck, not landed, and would die from wounds. Five whales landed could have meant ten to fifteen killed.

Killing whales would affect the already established whale-watching industry, forcing the whales farther offshore and making them both nervous and defensive. In addition, Indian communities that profited from whale watching could be affected. The resident gray whale populations near the Makah reservation would have certainly been extirpated.

We were hoping to plant seeds of doubt among the delegates in preparation for the plans by the US Whaling Commission to petition the IWC in 1996 at the forty-sixth annual meeting slated to convene in Aberdeen, Scotland.

On the same day that the IWC meeting began in Dublin, the following petition was published in the *Peninsula Daily News* and signed by seven Makah elders:

We are elders of the Makah Indian Nation, Ko-ditch-ee-ot, which means "People of the Cape." We oppose this whale hunt our tribe is going to do.

The opposition is directly against our leaders, the Makah tribal council, tribal staff, and the Bureau of Indian Affairs, which is an arm of the United States government.

The Makah tribal council has been functioning without a quorum; two councilmen are on sick leave for very serious reasons—cancer.

How can any decision be legal when our by-laws state that the treasurer shall be present at every meeting? The vice chairman is the other man out.

The whale hunt and other important issues were never brought to the people for a vote or simple notification.

The whale hunt issue has never been brought to the people to inform them, and there is no spiritual training going on. We believe they, the council, will just shoot the whale, and we think the word "subsistence" is the wrong thing to say when our people haven't used or had whale meat/blubber since the early 1900s.

For these reasons, we believe the hunt is only for the money. They can't say "traditional, spiritual, and for subsistence" in the same breath when no training is going on, just talk.

Whale watching is an alternative we support.

Isabell Ides, age 96	Viola Johnson, age 88
Harry Claplanhoo, age 78	Alberta Thompson, age 72
Margaret Irving, age 80	Lena McGee, age 92
Ruth Claplanhoo, age 94	

Greene also was not in the mood to listen to critics from among his own people. He called the elders who had signed the petition against whaling "traitors."

NEAH BAY, SUMMER 1995

We were put at a disadvantage at the beginning of the campaign by an article written by Paul Shukovsky of the *Seattle Post-Intelligencer*. In it, he wrote: "'We will directly intervene to protect the whales,' said Paul Watson of the Sea Shepherd Conservation

Society." While this was an accurate quote, it was preceded by the following paragraph:

> The Makah's declaration prompted one conservation activist to announce that he would sink Makah boats if they ignored International Whaling Commission rules. The threat cannot be taken lightly coming from a man who has scuttled several commercial whaling vessels.

I had never said any such thing to Shukovsky, and I'm sure that if I had, he would have put my words in quotations marks. I thought Shukovsky was simply trying to dramatize the story and provoke a little controversy in the interest of sensationalism. He claimed that he had picked up a quote from me to this effect from a story by Neal Hall of the *Vancouver Sun* that had been published on May 25 with the headline "Indian Whaling Ships 'Will Be Sunk.'" I had informed Shukovsky before he published his article that I had not said any such thing to Hall and that the *Vancouver Sun* did not quote me as saying this and did not mention any such threat in the story. It was just a sensational headline.

Shukovsky ignored my protest, and a June 8 editorial in the *Seattle Post-Intelligencer* stated: "Conservationist Paul Watson of the Sea Shepherd Society, meanwhile, has promised to sink Makah whaling boats if they ignore IWC rules. If he does, he should be prosecuted."

According to the newspaper, I not only said that I would sink the canoes but also *promised* to sink them. Shukovsky was not going to let a few facts get in the way of sensationalizing his story.

The Shukovsky story began the disinformation campaign in Washington State. It eventually escalated to the point at which a Lummi spokesperson, speaking at a meeting of the National Marine Fisheries Service, stated that he had heard that "Watson intends to kill two Makah for every whale killed."

I called Shukovsky after the story ran to complain and to correct his use of the term "animal rights activist" to describe me, pointing out that I was a conservationist and that this was a conservation issue. In response, he made a point of deliberately labeling me an "animal rights activist" in every story he wrote about me over the next five years. Right from the beginning it was clear that this issue would be fought with the disadvantage of a hostile local media.

Normally, we would enjoy the support of the liberal press. After all, saving whales had been as American as apple pie for three decades. But that was because we were fighting Russian, Japanese, and Norwegian whalers. Now, for the first time, we were taking on American Indians, and this flew straight into the face of the politically correct media's stance of the day. Whales rated higher than Russians and Japanese, but, as we were to discover, they fell well below Indian whalers in the minds of the guilt-polluted consciousness of white, middle-class journalists.

The Makah had the advantage from the beginning with the media. We knew in the summer of 1995 that this would prove to be one of our toughest media battles. In our favor, the Makah did not have the benefit of a government-subsidized public relations agency in 1995, and, as a result, they were more inclined to speak the truth in their own words.

In another article written by Paul Shukovsky, Makah fisheries manager Dave Sones was quoted as saying: "The value of the Asian market is huge." Sones added that they did not intend to go into commercial harvest "at this time."

In the same article, Makah tribal general manager Andrea Alexander was quoted as saying: "It would be nice if it could be a commercial endeavor. But I think we are a long way from that." Alexander was not ruling it out for the future.

Jerry Lucas, a member of the Makah tribal council, stated in an interview with the *Christian Science Monitor* that he could not see commercial whaling happening while he was on the council, but "I'm not going to say what may happen in the future."

It was also clear from Shukovsky in the *Post-Intelligencer* article that he was not interested in conveying the real reason for our opposition. Barely a word was mentioned about the impact a Makah hunt would have on international whaling politics, despite the fact that this was our primary argument.

Fred Felleman, who described himself as a whale biologist, told Shukovsky that the "Makah's cultural authority to take whales is indisputable." Felleman further stated, "The population of gray whales can withstand this level of take."

As a "whale biologist," he did not seem to have much knowledge of IWC regulations or of the concern we were trying to express for the precedent that the Makah would be setting. Felleman was indebted to the Makah for their support of his efforts to establish the Olympic Coast National Marine Sanctuary. Now that he had his sanctuary, he did not seem to see the hypocrisy of allowing whales to be slaughtered within its boundaries.

Steve Swartz, a senior scientist for the National Marine Fisheries Service, was also unable to see the threat to all whales posed by this proposed hunt. Swartz was quoted as saying, "From a population biologist's point of view, I don't think it would have a negative impact." He later added, "The US has always maintained that subsistence is a legitimate use of whales and marine mammals."

In point of fact, the Makah had not demonstrated subsistence need to take whales. Thus, this was an inaccurate reflection of the US government's position on the proposed hunt.

On June 10, 1995, I was able to respond to Shukovsky's article and his editorial on the proposed hunt in a letter to the editor of the *Seattle Post-Intelligencer*:

Your editorial ("The Makah's Case for Whale Hunting") contains a few factual errors. I have never said that the Sea Shepherd Conservation Society would sink Makah whaling boats. Sinking illegal whaling ships is something we have a great deal of experience with. We have sunk seven pirate whalers since 1979. However, I have not said that we would, nor is it our intention to, sink Makah whaling vessels.

We will, however, intervene. We will physically protect the whales from Makah harpoons by stationing a patrol vessel between the Makah and the migrating whales. We have the speed and the experience to protect whales from the Makah without the need to sink or damage their vessels.

Your editorial claims that the Makah have a legal right to kill the whales. They do not. They have a treaty with the United States. The United States, however, does not own the whales and neither do the Makah. Whaling comes under the authority of the International Whaling Commission, and without authorization of the IWC, the taking of California gray whales is illegal under international conservation regulations.

The treaty with the Makah was signed a century ago. We live in a different reality now. The world is overpopulated and we are losing an average of a hundred species of plants or animals each week. For that reason, it is the responsibility of all nations, including the Makah Nation, to adhere to international conservation law.

The killing of whales by the Makah will motivate thirteen Vancouver Island bands to resume whaling. Whaling in US waters will undermine the credibility of the country before the IWC and will effectively weaken the international whale conservation movement to the benefit of Japan, Norway, and Iceland—countries that seek to escalate commercial whaling activities.

In the same issue of the *Post-Intelligencer*, five additional letters were printed about Makah whaling, all of which were opposed to the hunt.

Dan Greene returned home from Dublin frustrated at the discussions by the International Whaling Commission. Some of the delegates had already questioned the merit of the Makah proposal; it did not meet the criteria for Aboriginal whaling. The Makah did not need the whales for subsistence, and they had not killed a whale in seventy years. Thus, there was not an ongoing tradition to authorize a quota.

Greene was furious. He protested that no government body or international group had any authority over the Makah's right to kill a whale. He was not going to wait. A whale could be taken by "accident." If he could deliver a whale, it would make the idea of eating whale meat a reality. This would help greatly in soliciting support within the tribe.

As it happened, Greene was the tribe's fisheries director. He was also the only Makah tribal member in the practice of utilizing a marine salmon-fishing drift net.

Several Makah tribal members reported to the *Peninsula Daily News* that Greene was very much aware of the location and movements of the gray whales when he deliberately set the net in their path. On July 22, Dan Greene netted a young whale that reportedly drowned when it became entangled with the mesh and was dragged down by the heavy weights attached to it. It was reported that the weights were much heavier than what Dan usually used to net salmon. Tribal general manager, Andrea Alexander, said the timing was "about as bad as it could get."

"Understanding how fanatical Dan is about reasserting our right to hunt whales, I know this is not a deliberate attempt to catch a whale. Incidental takes of marine mammals is authorized, and there have been incidental takes up and down the coast," she said. Alexander expressed her concern that it was the timing of the take, right on the heels of the IWC meeting, that gave a false impression that the kill was deliberate.

It was interesting to see, however, that the Makah were ready with the tools to butcher the whale, and Dan was able to see his whale distributed to tribal members. But none of the Makah had any idea about how to actually butcher the whale, so Greene recruited an Inuit woman as a knowledgeable butcher.

According to Alberta Thompson and other elders that I spoke with, a great deal of the distributed whale meat was disposed of at the Makah dump site. I sent a Sea Shepherd observer to the site, and he took photographs of the discarded whale meat.

Our complaint to the National Marine Fisheries Service was met with the excuse that, since the take was accidental, there was nothing wrong with the meat being dumped. They were not interested in responding to our question: "If the Makah are not ready to eat whale meat, why should they be allowed to kill whales?"

Dan Greene wasted no time putting this "accident" into service to further his cause. "There are some elders who said this was our answer for whaling, that it's time to go whaling again. This one gave itself up to let us see how much everybody wanted to do it."

4

CHAPTER

The High Road
to Scotland

ABERDEEN, SCOTLAND, 1996
46TH ANNUAL MEETING OF THE INTERNATIONAL
WHALING COMMISSION

ith the meeting of the IWC in Aberdeen, the possibility of the Makah actually going whaling hit home in the international conservation community. Demonstrators appeared before the hotel where the meeting was convening to denounce the Makah's plans. Progressive Animal Welfare Society (PAWS) activist Will Anderson had come to Aberdeen with Makah elders Alberta "Binki" Thompson and Dottie Chamblin. Sea Shepherd sent down a protest delegation from our group in the Shetland Islands led by Dave Jennings, who had been a volunteer engineer on the *Whales Forever*.

As the IWC met, both sides went into high gear to denounce the position of the other. Representing the whalers and sitting at the table with the US Whaling Commission was Dan Greene and Makah council member Marcy Parker. Representing the whales and barred from entry or access to the US delegation were Thompson and Chamblin.

Back on the media home front, the Makah drafted Lawrence Watters, a teacher of coastal resources at Lewis and Clark College in Portland, Oregon, to defend the hunt. "You shouldn't underestimate the spiritual and cultural significance of whaling to this tribe,"

Watters said. "It's a basic identity, like baseball or the right to drive cars in America."

Makah elder Alberta Thompson countered Watters in the press with a statement from Scotland. "There is no spiritual training going on . . . we believe they will just shoot the whale. There is nothing spiritual about shooting hundreds of bullets into a defenseless whale."

Back in the US, Sea Shepherd's Pacific Northwest director, Michael Kundu, had been working with US congressional representative Jack Metcalf to have the House Natural Resources Committee oppose the hunt. A prepared statement by the House Natural Resources Committee opposing US support for the hunt was relayed to US whaling commissioner James Baker in Aberdeen. Metcalf told the *Seattle Times*, "They [Makah] say they want to kill only five whales a year, but the question is, where would it stop once it starts?"

Five factors came into play to prevent the IWC from granting permission to the Makah at Aberdeen in 1996:

1. The Mexican delegation led the fight to oppose the hunt, citing the fact that the Makah did not meet the required criteria of subsistence necessity and unbroken tradition. Mexico also expressed concern that the hunt would impact the growing whale-watching industry in Baja and had fears that wounded whales might make it to Baja, where they could attack tourists.

2. The participation of Makah elders Alberta Thompson and Dottie Chamblin, and the presented statement of opposition by other Makah elders, demonstrated that the Makah were not united in their desire to kill whales.

3. Some three hundred international conservation and environmental groups opposed the proposed hunt.

4. Congressman Jack Metcalf had a letter delivered to the US delegation in Aberdeen notifying them that the House Natural Resources Committee was in unanimous opposition to having the United States government support the Makah proposal.

5. The last and most important factor was the response of the US delegation to the message from the House Natural Resources Committee. They notified the Makah that they could not support the proposal. This forced the Makah to withdraw their request, and the issue was deferred until 1997.

Alberta Thompson had made quite an impression on the IWC delegates. She was able to convince them that the Makah had commercial objectives. She informed them that traditional whaling required more than a year of physical and spiritual preparation.

"Our young people are like young people on the outside," said Alberta. "How many want to take one year of training, of abstinence, of prayer and fasting, of cleansing their life by swearing off drugs, and booze, and sex? And if they don't do that, then why do it at all?"

Although the Metcalf initiative was the death blow to the US delegation's support for whaling, the opposition had been softened up considerably by the presence of the two Makah elders defending the whales. Kate O'Connell, speaking for Whale and Dolphin Conservation, said the appearance of Dotty Chamblin and Alberta Thompson was vital to those who opposed the hunts:

> We could have talked until we were blue in the face, and the commission probably would have granted permission to kill whales. By telling commissioners and everyone here that the tribe is not united in resuming the whale hunt, those two women changed the course of this conference. They were full of spirit and were a breath of fresh air. People listened to them. They were like two pebbles dropped in a pond. They made waves everywhere and touched a lot of people. Who would have thought that two elderly women would capture the attention of the world in their simple request not to kill whales?

Binki was very humble about her contribution. I called her at her hotel room in Aberdeen to thank her for helping the whales. She insisted on thanking us for persuading Congressman Metcalf to have the House Natural Resources Committee condemn the US government's support for the hunt. She said, "That letter is what did it. Baker and his pro-whaling delegation would not give us the time of day. Because of Metcalf, it did not even get to the table. I do not agree with Metcalf and his position on our treaty rights, but I'm glad he is a friend to the whales, and I would like you to thank him for what he did."

I assured her that I would convey her message and acknowledged her humility in downplaying her role, but I told her that without her and Dottie, the whales would have been at a disadvantage. "We thank you both for your wisdom and your energy in coming to Scotland. You both really made a difference," I said before putting down the receiver.

James Baker was furious at being outmaneuvered by the congressman and the two Makah elders. In a message to the media, Baker stated, "The United States and the Makahs will continue to work together on the request, which we fully expect will be accepted by the commission next year."

Binki and Dottie were greeted with some hostility when they returned to Neah Bay from Aberdeen. Whaling supporter Helma Ward told the media that the tribal council was considering a vote to strip both women and all their descendants of the prestigious right to call themselves whaling families.

Said Ward, "There is a road out of town, and they can take it." Ward added that the elders who had signed the petition should also be stripped of their family heritage.

The meeting at Aberdeen had been a victory for the whales. We knew, however, that it was only a short-term victory. This issue was not going to die peacefully. Fortunately, we were beginning to see more and more media support across the United States. An editorial in the *Pocono Record* of Stroudsburg, Pennsylvania, June 29, 1996, was representative of the opinions of many Americans across the country:

Whale Hunt: A Fish Story

Some traditions are better off ended. Such is the case with a request by the Makah Tribe of Neah Bay, Wa., to be allowed to kill five gray whales in the seas off Washington next year. Protection of the species is more important than what the tribe claims as a ritual. The request even had the backing of the US delegation to the IWC until recently, when the Sea Shepherd Conservation Society brought the issue to Congress.

The Makah had presented the hunt as a tribal ritual, lending it an air of ancient sanctity, although there are suspicions that business is its main interest. Either way, it shouldn't come off. Helping to kill off an endangered species can't be justified by tradition or ritual, lest we allow traditions—religious, social, or political—to justify something even worse.

There are already too many crimes chalked up to ancient beliefs or disputes. They're all traditions that ought to come to an end.

LORINO, SIBERIA, SOVIET UNION, 1981

It has been decades since I landed on the beach at Lorino on the Chukchi Peninsula of Siberia to document illegal whaling by the Soviets. We traveled to this remote corner of the world in August 1981 to investigate an IWC violation. We had good reason to believe that the Soviets were not acting within the regulations, specifically clause 13B of the IWC regulations governing Aboriginal whaling. By international agreement, the Russians were authorized to "take" (a modern euphemism for "kill") 179 California gray whales for the subsistence of the Aboriginal people along the Siberian coast. Aside from the fact that 179 whales would provide an excessive quantity of poor-tasting meat for a Native population of fewer than three thousand, there was also the historical fact that prior to 1957 the average number of whales utilized annually by the Siberian Natives was forty-one. In 1957, they quite suddenly needed nearly two hundred whales a year to survive.

It had smelled somewhat fishy to me, and I suspected that back in the mid-1950s, some enterprising, upwardly mobile young communist had set up a mink, sable, or fox farm collective and needed a cheap source of meat to feed Russia's manufactured need and desire for fur coats. Some members of the IWC's scientific committee had similar suspicions, but they were unable to obtain confirmation for the simple reason that the Soviet Union would not allow any official observers into the area. At the annual meetings of the IWC, the Russians maintained that the hunt was Aboriginal. Each year they refused permission to observe, and each year they requested and received the quota they desired.

So, I thought, *if the Russians won't allow observers in, then we will simply go to Siberia uninvited.*

The Makah were not the first Aboriginal community that we had confronted. Here on the bleak shores of Siberia, way back in 1981, lay a community that the Soviet government claimed needed whales for subsistence. We proved otherwise. Three of us (engineer Bob Osborne, United Press International photographer Eric Swartz, and me) landed on the beach below the cliffs, upon which rested the town of Lorino.

As we approached the shore, we saw and photographed two Soviet soldiers patrolling the beach. They did not seem overly concerned. Looking back toward the *Sea Shepherd* a mile offshore, we realized that she actually could pass as a Russian ship. Her red ensign could pass for the red Soviet flag, and her trawler design made her appear like a fishing boat. I realized that no one had invaded the Soviet Union since World War II, and there was no reason for the Soviets to believe that we were anything other than Russians ourselves.

From the beach, we took pictures of the structures on the hill and the building on the beach. We noticed a conveyor belt that ran from the beach up the slope. It was not very difficult to recognize what was going on. On the top of the bluffs were thousands of wooden cages set in long rows. On the beach was a whale-meat flensing station. The conveyor belt took the meat from the station directly to the cages. Inside the cages were thousands of animals. We could smell them and hear them, but we could not determine if they were fox, mink, or sable. Because of the armed guards on the beach, I was inclined to believe the animals were sable, since the Soviet Union had a monopoly on sable and the penalty for smuggling sable out of the Soviet Union was a death sentence.

Great. I had just read the novel *Gorky Park*. I had not anticipated that we might find ourselves charged with attempting to steal sable.

The Soviet soldiers were walking toward us from down the beach. The crunching of their boots on the shell-strewn beach became louder. They were of Mongolian descent. The shorter one wore a peaked cap with a red star badge. The other wore a wool Cossack hat, also adorned with a red star. Their uniforms were dark green.

Some children had come down to the beach to gawk at us. By the whale-flensing station, I could see a small group of women who had stopped work to stare at us. I quietly motioned for the other two to get back into the boat with me.

We had pushed out a few feet when the first soldier shouted, "Sto eta?" He was pointing at our inflatable.

I had taken a year of Russian at university but I was not very confident about passing myself off as a Russian. Nonetheless, I answered his query, "Eta Zodiac."

"Nyet," he yelled. "Eta Mercury, eta Amerikan!"

He began to unsling his rifle.

"What's wrong?" Osborne whispered.

"I think our Mercury outboard has given us away," I whispered, as I smiled at the soldier.

The soldier stepped hurriedly backward, fumbling for his rifle. It was easy to read their minds. Lights had gone on and bells were ringing inside their heads as they realized that standing before them was . . . The Enemy.

The two slack-jawed Russians backed up behind the nearest beached boat. Instinctively, they were seeking cover. One of the soldiers yelled at me. I couldn't understand him. I smiled and pointed to my ship. He yelled again. I was nervous but I fought not to show it. Stepping into the boat, I pulled the throttle up slowly, answering him but allowing the roar of the outboard to drown out my reply.

I turned my back to the soldier and slowly began to motor away. "What is he doing?" I asked.

Eric looked a little pale. "He's bringing up his rifle, and the other soldier is unslinging his."

"Smile and wave to them," I said.

It was difficult to resist the urge to turn and look at the shore. I was gambling on the soldiers being unwilling to shoot me in the back, and that Bob's and Eric's smiling and waving would serve to confuse them.

Despite our behavior, they had to have some doubts. It would not have been a good move career-wise to shoot what may have been a Soviet research party.

The risk paid off. Bob told me that they had brought down their rifles and were now running up the slopes to the town.

We returned to the ship elated with the evidence that we had captured. This whale kill was commercial, and we had the proof we needed to present to the IWC. But first we had to make it back home with the evidence.

The two soldiers had apparently run into town for help, and help was not long in arriving. We saw a large vessel approaching from the southwest at a very high speed, and it did not take long to catch up with us.

The ship was big and she carried one very big gun on her foredeck. Smaller guns stuck out on the sides. Her name was the *Iceberg*, and the number 024 was emblazoned in big white letters on her gray hull. A landing platform for helicopters was raised off her stern. She pulled up alongside us, fifty meters off our starboard side.

We could plainly see the Soviet sailors, some of whom carried AK-47 rifles. Her captain looked down on us from her four-story-high bridge. The Russians raised some signal flags, ordering us to stop.

Marc Busch, my second officer, asked, "What do we do now?"

"How far are we from US waters?" I replied.

"Just over eleven miles."

"Ignore them. Keep the present course and speed."

For ten minutes the Russians chased us as we ignored their flags and Aldis lamp signals to stop. Two helicopter gunships circled above us, firing flares across our bow. I could see one crewman perched behind a .50 caliber gun in the side door of the chopper.

Suddenly, the VHF radio erupted with a deep voice speaking badly broken English. "*Sea Shepherd, Sea Shepherd*, stopa your engines. Immediate!"

I picked up the mic and said, "Stop killing whales!"

There was a slight pause on the other end, but then the voice replied, "*Sea Shepherd*, stop your engines. Prepare to be boarded by the Soviet Union."

I answered with a nervous chuckle. "Sorry, we do not have room for the Soviet Union."

The Soviet captain responded, sounding a little irritated. "Stop your engines now. You are in violation of the laws of the Soviet Union. You are under arrest! This is an order!"

Marc looked at me and said, "Well, mate, that's that, isn't it. We have to stop now."

"Marc, the one absolute thing we are not going to do is to stop our engines."

Marc looked alarmed. "But what if he threatens to fire?"

"Then we call his bluff."

"Then what do we do if they do fire?"

"Then they will have an international incident on their hands, and that will publicize this illegal whale kill. They won't fire. I'm pretty sure about that."

The Russian's voice interrupted us. "*Sea Shepherd*, you are under arrest."

I answered the Russian captain. "You are in violation of the regulations of the International Whaling Commission. Your nation is involved in illegal whaling operations. We have already radioed this information to the United States. I do not intend to stop this ship, nor will I allow your men to board us. We do not recognize the authority of a pirate whaling nation."

The Russians tried to stop us by trailing a hawser behind their ship as they crossed our bow, hoping to foul our prop. This did not work because my prop was encased in a Kort nozzle, and we steamed harmlessly over it. They tried to make me stop by placing their ship in my path, but it was a game of chicken that I had no intention of losing. They surged out of our way at the last moment to avoid colliding with us.

The Russian captain was becoming more and more frustrated and clearly more angry as we approached closer and closer to the boundary line. He pulled up close beside us, and we could see the sailors pulling the tarps off the .50 caliber machine guns mounted on the midship's main deck. This was the moment of reckoning. I ordered most of the crew below. It looked to me as if the Soviets were preparing to rake my deck with those lethal shells and then board us. I could see other sailors preparing two launches. The silence over the radio was ominous. There was no more talking.

If there hadn't been so many witnesses, I wouldn't dare to report this. I'd be in the position of somebody who had just seen a flying saucer. Who would believe me? But this is what happened. There was a sudden cheer from the deck. It seemed senseless. I thought at first my crew was flipping out. But it wasn't just my crew. The Russians had stopped their attack preparations and they were pointing wildly at the water.

Suddenly, without warning, the narrow space between the two ships erupted in a shower of water. It obscured our view of the Russian ship for a moment, and then the mist dispersed into rainbow-tinted droplets. My crew continued to cheer wildly and the Soviet sailors gaped openly in surprise.

A large California gray whale had surfaced between the two ships and spouted. It remained for a few moments, its huge backside looking like a steppingstone between the two ships, then dove beneath the surface. The Soviets swung their wheel to starboard, and Marc instinctively swung to port as the space between the two ships widened.

A whale! A glorious, beloved, wonderful whale! Like the hand of Poseidon coming up from the sea between us and the Russians. I shuddered. Damn! Nobody who experienced this moment could help but feel that something mystical had taken place, something beyond the pale of anything we had a rational hope of expecting.

Years before, a man who knew more about whales than I ever will told me that if I could get my act together enough to get out to sea and aid the whales, I could depend on the whales for help.

"The whales will come to you when you need them," Dr. Paul Spong had promised. "You can trust them to be there."

I had put the thought aside, preferring to depend on the realpolitik and real economics of making the sea a no-man's land for whalers. I would depend on pistons and willpower and ask nothing of nature that Mother Gaia could not easily grant. Oh, but by a miracle, here was a whale, a lone California gray whale coming up out of the water between the warship and us! Just as I had put my body between harpooners and cetaceans, Leviathan now had placed its body between mine and the naval vessel that would have destroyed us. We could not have been more astonished, more awed, if an angel had intervened.

Eric raced up to the bridge. "Christ, did you see that? It was incredible."

I didn't answer.

The Russians were falling behind. One of the helicopters suddenly turned around, and a few seconds later it was followed by the second. It was a relief not to have the thudding roar of their jet engines above us.

I ran into the chart room and made a few quick calculations before returning to the bridge.

"Ladies and gentlemen," I announced, "we are safely back in American waters."

We who would shepherd the whales had been shepherded by a whale through the valley of the shadow of death.

SIBERIA, SEPTEMBER 1997

We had presented our evidence to the IWC infractions committee at the IWC meeting in 1982. The Soviets simply stated that our activities in gathering the documentation was a violation of their sovereignty and dismissed the complaint. They requested a further quota of whales for 1983 and it was granted. So much for trying to cooperate with the authorities. But we did what we could, and, like it or not, the so-called Aboriginal hunt in Siberia was exposed for the fraud it was.

The Greenpeace Foundation duplicated our campaign, and a few of their crew were arrested by the Soviets in 1983 in Lorino. This campaign, once again, focused international attention on the illegality of the Siberian "Aboriginal" hunt. No official action was taken.

It was not until September 1997 that we were able to launch another investigative probe into Siberia. The timing was perfect. It was a month before the scheduled meeting of the IWC in Monaco, and we knew that the Makah request would be on the table again, this time with a more determined US government effort to push it through.

We sent our Pacific Northwest coordinator, Michael Kundu, to Siberia. He joined a three-person TV crew from Parador Television Productions out of Salt Lake City, Utah. The goal of the team was to photo-document a gray whale hunt, gather evidence related to commercial whaling and the cruelty inherent in the hunt, and get the evidence to Monaco, where they would join up with our ship in time for the IWC meeting.

The following is Michael Kundu's report from Siberia:

Starting in Nome, Alaska, with a team producing new material for the Fox/Sky TV program called *Earth Undercover*, we met a woman named Dazé—a US citizen who had settled in Russia and had married a prominent local official, whom I suspected was well connected with unofficial forces in Provideniya and who might be of help at a later date.

I hope you guys are not with Greenpeace or something like that, Dazé said, because I've had people from England and two newspapers call and ask me about you.

Concerned about her comment, I assured her otherwise and started thinking that we might be facing some serious problems in Provideniya. "I don't want to talk anymore about this. But as far as your plans are concerned, I hope you've got the right permits, or you may find yourself in a brick room for the rest of your tour," she added.

When we landed at Provideniya, we met our guide, Vladimir Bychkov, who we later discovered was a Russian government employee. He was most curious about our intentions, and we told him the purpose of the trip was to film a documentary on the Chukchi people. Bychkov, clearly unsettled, responded by saying, "We will see . . ."

I knew I had to get Bychkov to take us to the fox farms at Novoye Chaplino, a few miles north of Provideniya, while also trying to convince him to get us to Lorino, the village Sea Shepherd had visited in 1981 and the current known center of commercial whaling and fox farming.

"We can go to New Chaplino," he said, somewhat concerned, "but you will find little of interest there. The fox farms are all empty."

We left for New Chaplino the next morning. The stench of petroleum, animal oil, and smoke was sickening when we reached the edge of town. Large platforms with raised gray cages stood out against the tundra, each containing movement. Vladimir informed us that he was unaware that the foxes were still alive, but he had recently learned that they were scheduled for slaughter in early October.

I left the crew and headed in the direction of the fox farm. On the way I found the fox food-preparation area and slaughter yard, along with a still-smoking "soup" caldron. Bones were scattered around the cauldron. The smell was absolutely assaulting. Whale vertebra, walrus ribs, fox skulls, and walrus jaws surrounded the steaming pot. I opened the lid and saw an oily black soup of flesh and gristle, mostly unidentifiable, but some of it clearly textured, pitted walrus flesh.

Repulsed, I moved away and started toward the fox pens. Behind me, the film crew was meeting with a local resident who sold them a fox pelt and showed them the fox-skinning operation. I waited for their arrival under the first pen, where the sound of screaming and fighting foxes echoed like an air raid siren.

I counted eight hundred cages, each containing a single, pacing, and clearly insane blue fox, held in a three-foot by two-foot wire enclosure. I climbed the ladder, slipping on gore as I approached the pens for a better look at the animals. The crew had climbed another pen, but our guide was getting agitated, telling us we needed to come down and leave. A screaming Russian woman started toward us, shouting in rage and waving her hands.

"We must go," said Vladimir. "She says you will contaminate the fox with disease."

We were told that there were no longer foxes in New Chaplino, but now they were concerned for the welfare of foxes they would be slaughtering in two weeks. With adequate documentation in hand, I headed for the beach, where I found the remains of three gray whales and dozens of walruses. With our guide unsettled and increasingly curious, we left New Chaplino.

Vladimir approached us. "You know the Russian government is concerned about groups attacking us on the issue of whaling, and I hope you are not with these groups, but I am concerned about what you are doing."

I explained again that we were working on a documentary, so we needed to see all facets of the Chukchi Natives' livelihood. He said it would only be possible to go to Lorino by sea, and then only if the weather complied.

The next day, Vladimir informed us that we would be traveling to a place called Hunting Base, where we would meet with Chukchi Eskimos who would take us as far as we could go toward a walrus-hunting village called Yanrakinot. After a three-hour ride, we pulled up to a small bay that was covered in skeletal remains and bundles of flesh, meat, and body parts. Walrus meat was the most abundant, slabs of which were covered in canvas while others were exposed, clearly awaiting transfer to nearby New Chaplino. Near a pile of seal carcasses, a newly butchered gray whale skeleton lay intact, slime coated and gore covered, its yellow bones suggesting it had been killed less than three weeks earlier.

"This whale was attacked by orcas," explained Vladimir. "The Eskimos waited for it to die, then they brought it to shore and butchered it."

"Where is the meat?" I asked.

"It has been taken to the local villages," he responded. New Chaplino was the only village nearby. I thought about the cauldron filled with walrus and other unidentifiable types of flesh.

The arrival of two aluminum boats containing our Native guides, led by Chukchi Eskimo Ivan Tanke, signaled our departure. After packing our equipment, we headed out into the narrows, northward. Clearing into the sea basin, we encountered a large wooden boat containing four Chukchi hunters.

"This is a whaling boat," Vladimir informed us.

The craft was about six meters in length and contained two wells penetrating the hull underneath for two separate 55 HP Evinrude motors. I noticed two hunters in the bow; each had semiautomatic rifles propped against the sides of the boat. One was an old Chinese-made SKS rifle, which fires a NATO 7.62 (.308) caliber bullet. But the second rifle was a new semiautomatic with a stainless steel barrel, a graphite stock, and a ten-shot magazine.

Vladimir said, "These hunters are not after whale. They are hunting walrus."

It seemed odd that the hunters were so close to the area the grays were traveling and so far away from the outside of Ostrov Yttygran, the walrus rookery where Yanrakinot Natives routinely hunted.

The weather changed dramatically, and our guides refused to continue. We turned in to a small hunting camp on the east side of the bay.

The crew set up tents in the stark wind, but the Eskimos clustered into the small wooden cabin. The weather grew strikingly worse, and we spent three nights in our tents, the last day of which a devastating sleet storm set in, keeping the entire crew contained in the cabin.

Utterly frustrated, I donned my cold-weather gear and went out. Seven kilometers from camp, I found a headless walrus carcass, clearly killed for the sake of its ivory. At that point, the weather took a fearsome turn for the worse, and I was forced to find a small crevasse in the shoreline, where I remained until the storm waned.

After the weather cleared, we made the crossing to Yanrakinot, a town of some four hundred primarily Chukchi Natives. It was rather archaic. While the fox farms appeared to be abandoned, their legacy was evident all along the eastern shoreline.

The first evening, I stood on a bluff overlooking the dilapidated fox-farm pens across the bay from an industrial wasteland of rusting oil barrels interspersed with a whale boneyard. Moving across the spit to a field of white skeletal death, I stopped counting at 120 gray whale skulls, poignantly augmented by at least three bowhead whale skulls.

I did an interview with Leonit, the hunter from my boat. Vladimir translated for me. During the course of the discussion, we had the following important points confirmed by the hunters:

1. It takes between twenty-five and forty bullets, four harpoons, and two hours from the first hit to kill a walrus.

2. It takes five hundred plus bullets, eight harpoons, and four to five hours from the first hit to kill a whale.

3. The animals do suffer visibly during the hunt.

4. Animals are frequently lost and sink to the bottom; they may or may not be reported.

5. The region reports about 100 gray whales are killed a year, but they are allowed to kill up to 140 animals. Unofficially, the kill is around 300, according to Leonit.

Gray whale and walrus meat are fed to foxes, and some is eaten by villagers. The gray whale meat is considered to taste bad, and because it seems to be a laxative, the Chukchi word for the gray whale meat is the "meat that makes you shit."

The foxes are owned by the bankrupt government-run "Collective Farms," which receives the profit and supplies the Natives with minimal, barely adequate goods and bullets for hunting whales and walrus. The Russian government is increasingly concerned about the controversy of using whale meat for fox farms, and there is a movement among the regional Eskimos to close all the fox farm operations. The Chukchi people feel that the fox farms and the government-run Collective Farm industry have stolen their heritage and the true culture of subsistence living.

Vladimir was clearly displeased about having to relay this information, but since we had videotaped both Leonit's response and the translation, Vladimir knew he had to translate accurately. Since it was growing increasingly unlikely that we would get to Lorino and film a gray whale hunt, my concern was that we might not be capable of getting this controversial videotape out of Russia. When the weather became somewhat less dangerous, we pushed Vladimir to ask the Chukchi guides to return us to Provideniya.

The return trip to a bay outside of New Chaplino was completed in high seas conditions. The correspondent and soundman were huddled in survival suits, while the cameraman and I tried to plan what we would do first when the boat eventually capsized. Somehow, we arrived in the dark and faced a difficult landing in high surf. After a two-hour truck ride, we arrived in Provideniya. His obligation to us completed, Vladimir departed, successful in his efforts to keep us away from Lorino.

Our primary purpose was still uncompleted. We needed to film a whale hunt, and the required guides were making that all but impossible.

We made contact with an individual who could help us. I decided to leave at this point to get the twenty beta tapes we had taken safely back on the flight to Nome. We could not risk taking the tapes on the trip to Lorino, where they could possibly be seized.

Our new contact (whose name we must guard) said that he would take the film crew to Lorino. They could go overland in a turretless tank that he could arrange for a price. I contacted Dazé and asked whether she had any suggestions about how to get through Russian customs discreetly.

"Wait there," Dazé said. "My husband and I will take you to the airport."

Dazé had contacted the necessary person to open the border for me since I was the only person flying in or out of Provideniya that afternoon. After our chartered pilot was given permission to land, Dazé's husband unexpectedly ushered me into a small room to "meet" the border guards. Not knowing what she had in mind, I accepted tea and distributed a few packs of Marlboros among the guards. It seemed to be a good strategy, and Dazé called me to see the customs officer almost immediately afterward.

The Russian customs official started questioning me about where the crew was. I responded by telling them something about a "disagreement" and that I had decided to leave them and had no idea where they were. He pointed to my backpack, gesturing me to open it. I moved slowly, only to watch a border guard approach the customs officer, whisper something, and then walk toward my pack. He picked it up and gestured for me to follow, leading me past customs and directly to the visa checkpoint. While I remained to finish processing the exit visa, the border guard carried my pack to the waiting charter plane.

"Dasvidaniya." He nodded.

"Spasiba," I responded.

Within a few minutes I was airborne, heading across the Bering Strait.

The film crew traveled by tank to Sireniki, where the Russian remnants of the Soviet KGB and the military police detained and questioned them regarding the whereabouts of the footage they had taken up to that point. The police were unaware that I had left the country, and they meticulously examined all of the crew's equipment and what little video they had. After a few more days, they were permitted to continue to Sireniki, where they met with the director of the regional fur farm. At that point, our new contact informed the crew that due to the weather and other obstacles, reaching Lorino would be unlikely.

In what would prove to be a worthwhile investment, the crew left a digital video camera with the contact and instructed him to use the camera when he did get to Lorino. The crew then returned to Provideniya under heavy scrutiny from the regional military and local officials. At the end of October, they returned to Nome, Alaska, without further incident.

In November, our contact returned the digital camera to us, via Moscow, complete with utterly horrific footage of gray whales that had been killed that autumn. Our material was circulated widely by Fox television and received international exposure through APTV and CNN broadcasts.

Michael Kundu was able to fly to Nice, France, in late October to meet the *Sea Shepherd III* and to attend the IWC meeting in Monaco.

5

CHAPTER

A Whale of a Crapshoot in Monte Carlo

THE VOYAGE TO MAKAH BAY BEGINS
EDINBURGH, SCOTLAND, 1996

n August 1996, I found a ship in Edinburgh called the *Skandi Ocean*. She was perfect for us. The 50-meter vessel was built in 1960 as a fisheries research ship for the Norwegian government. Her original name was the *Johan Jhort*. She required a great deal of work to get into shape, and my volunteer crew, under the direction of bosun Chuck Swift, worked alongside the contracted workers of the Firth of Forth shipyard to bring her back from retirement. Finally, after eight months of volunteer labor and shipyard repairs, in late March 1997, the *Sea Shepherd III* was ready to put to sea on her first test run.

It was a difficult crossing. Fortunately, the weather was fair and rare for the North Sea at that time of year. But only thirty miles out of the Firth of Forth, the Vulkan coupling on the main engine crapped out, and although the engine was running, it was no longer turning the screw. I did not wish to return to Scotland and decided to risk that our forward azimuth bow thruster could get us across. It did, but at a greatly decreased speed of four knots. The maiden voyage demonstrated that there was still much to do to make her ready for a trans-Atlantic crossing.

Our arrival in Bremerhaven was a welcoming home. During our 1994 visit to this port on the Weser River, we had been received as heroes after our confrontation with the Norwegian whalers and Coast Guard. We were hoping that we could recruit their goodwill again to outfit us for a voyage to the Mediterranean.

Unfortunately, we had not been tied up more than an hour when about twenty German policemen arrived. One of the officers approached and politely informed me that he regretted to do so, but he had no choice but to place me under arrest.

Apparently fearing that our new ship would be heading for the coast of Norway that summer, the Norwegian authorities decided to post an Interpol warrant for my arrest, with a demand for extradition to serve four months in prison for the attack on the *Nybræna* in 1992. It came as a complete surprise. I had been in Scotland for months, and the British had not notified me of any such demand for my arrest by Interpol.

The chief prosecutor for Bremen was not buying the Norwegian warrant. It contained contradictory information. At the same time that it acknowledged I was in Amsterdam at the time of the sinking, it stated that I was the person who boarded the *Nybræna* and scuttled her in Reine in the Lofoten Islands on the same day.

I was released the next day by order of the Bremen prosecutor. I walked out of the jail to the cheers of my crew, accompanied by a local German Bavarian-style band. However, although I was free in Germany, the Norwegians still had the warrant on the computer throughout the rest of Europe. How would I be able to travel to the South of France and Monaco in October to attend the IWC meeting without getting arrested again? The answer would be to get rearrested in another European country and hopefully the Norwegians would see the futility of attempting to extradite me.

Chuck Swift and I enlisted the help of two local supporters in Bremerhaven to drive me to the Dutch border, where I boarded a train to Schiphol airport for a flight back to the United States.

LELYSTAD PRISON, THE NETHERLANDS
SPRING 1997

As I walked through passport control, the officer ran my credentials through the computer and told me to step aside. I was then taken into a side office and notified that there was a warrant out for my arrest. I answered that I was aware of this but that the German prosecutor had released me after seeing the contradictions in the warrant.

The Dutch, however, were being more bureaucratically correct than the Germans, and I found myself being escorted off to the jail in Haarlem to await an appearance before a magistrate.

We contacted the best damned extradition attorney in the Netherlands. His name was Victor Koppe, and he assured me that there was no way that the anti-whaling nation of the Netherlands was going to extradite me to the illegal whaling nation of Norway.

We then turned the arrest and imprisonment into an international campaign to protest Norwegian whaling. I received thousands of letters to my cell at Lelystad prison, where I would spend the next eighty days awaiting an extradition hearing. The Sea Shepherd name and my name became household words in the Netherlands because of the publicity that was generated. I was described by the Dutch magazine *Nieuwe Revu* as "Holland's only political prisoner."

Protests were held at Dutch embassies and consulates in Toronto, Sydney, Tel Aviv, New York, San Francisco, Rio de Janeiro, and throughout Europe. Dutch actor Rutger Hauer came to visit me in prison, and John Paul DeJoria, the CEO of John Paul Mitchell Systems, held a media conference at the House of Blues in Hollywood, where he assembled a large group of celebrities, including Pierce Brosnan, David Carradine, Cher, Jane Seymour, Linda Blair, Steven Seagal, and many others to voice their support. Mick Jagger issued a notice calling for my release. It was rapidly turning into a public relations nightmare for Norway.

I spent the time in my cell writing letters, and the prison allowed me to hold a press conference once a week in the warden's office, where he supplied coffee and cookies. Ivor Verbon and Viola Klepper read about my arrest came to visit me in prison, where they asked if they could organize a campaign to free me. I welcomed them, and they proceeded to turn my case into a Dutch cause célèbre.

A clear message was sent to the whalers on April 30: just because I was in prison, they were still not safe. The pirate whaler *Senet*, the very same ship we had scuttled in 1994, was fire bombed in Slevik-kilen and extensively damaged.

Dr. Roger Payne, having been knighted by the Dutch queen, used his position to request that Prince Bernhard speak out on my behalf. He did so.

Even in Norway, I was getting support. The chairwoman of the Norwegian SPCA announced that she was campaigning to prevent my extradition to her country. I also received the support of NOAH, the Norwegian progressive animals rights society.

It was shaping up so that even if the judges ruled against me, the minister of justice could be called to prevent an extradition from proceeding.

The only sour note was when Greenpeace issued a press release accusing me of being a criminal and calling for my extradition back to Norway. They even stated that I was not a Greenpeace cofounder.

"Watson deserves to go to prison," Norwegian Greenpeace director Kalle Hessvedt told the media. Hessvedt vowed to work with Norwegian police to bring me to "justice."

In Amsterdam, a Greenpeace spokesperson told the media that I was a "ruthless pirate." This prompted former Greenpeace president Bob Hunter, who flew from Toronto to Amsterdam to interview me for Citytv, to speak to the Dutch media to tell them that I was indeed a Greenpeace cofounder and that he was ashamed Greenpeace would betray me to the whalers. Bob wrote the following piece for Toronto's *Eye Weekly*:

Here in the tiny, ancient country liberated by Canadian troops during the Second World War, the only political prisoner is a Canadian.

When I visited him in the brand-new, high-tech, maximum-security prison in the village of Lelystad, a twenty-minute train ride from Amsterdam, Paul Watson looked slimmer than I had seen him in years. Instead of appearing broken or cowed by fifty-two days locked in an 8 x 10-foot cell for twenty-three hours a day, he radiated energy, confidence, and power.

This was despite a pending hearing in which a Dutch judge was to decide whether to turn him over to the tender mercies of the Norwegians, who have been threatening for years to cut off his feet, break his legs, and "blow his fucking head off" the moment they get him in prison and the guards are looking the other way.

The good news is that days after our meeting in Lelystad, the Dutch judges dropped two of the charges against Watson. And just last Monday (June 9), the final decision: Watson will remain in a Dutch prison until June 20. Then having served two-thirds of the 120-day sentence Watson faced in Norway, he will be a free man again.

Watson was busted in Amsterdam on April 2 on the basis of an Interpol warrant issued at the request of Norway, after he was tried in absentia for a 1992 incident in the Lofoten Islands district of northern Norway, where a whaling ship, the *Nybræna*, was scuttled at dockside by agents of Watson's Sea Shepherd Conservation Society.

Following his arrest and imprisonment, Watson had two additional charges laid against him by Norway for "ramming" the Norwegian Coast Guard vessel *Andenes*, despite the fact that there were fifteen journalists with a dozen cameras on board Watson's ship *Whales Forever* who testified otherwise.

I have seen the videotapes. There is absolutely no doubt that the *Andenes* did the ramming. A clumsily edited video version of the incident, shot from a helicopter by the Norwegians, serves to prove only that the Norwegian propaganda ministry employs some of the most incompetent video editors in the world.

But apart from demonstrating one more time that the first casualty of media war is raw tape, the issue of who-rammed-who or who-sunk-what is entirely beside the point. Commercial whaling has been illegal since 1986. Although, like Japan and Iceland, Norway uses loopholes in the International Whaling Commission's regulations to get away with killing whales for "scientific" purposes, the purpose of whaling in Norway is blatantly commercial, as it is in those other countries. This makes the whalers (and their governments) pirates, pure and simple. When Watson goes after them, he is operating in the tradition of British warships that broke the slave trade from Africa by stopping slave ships.

His arrest in Holland was likewise purely and simply a political event. There is an election going on in Norway, and the incumbent prime minister, Thorbjørn Jagland, needs the support of the High North Alliance (the Norwegian whalers association), and the way to do that is to drag Watson into a Lofoten jail in chains.

So why was it, faced with this prospect and trapped in a cage, that Watson looked and sounded so good? Part of it, of course, was Watson's indomitable spirit, which I have seen in action so many times.

The other part was Watson's shrewd calculation that his imprisonment in itself has turned into a powerful campaign against Norway's pirate whale killers. Two weeks ago, about three hundred supporters from Germany, France, the US, Israel, and Canada converged on Amsterdam for a demonstration outside the courthouse where Watson's extradition hearings were held. A brilliant series of full-page newspaper ads and public-service TV spots (narrated by actor Martin Sheen) jolted Dutch public opinion from the coffee shops to the royal palace, where Queen Beatrix herself made her "interest" in Watson's case known.

The Dutch were highly sensitive to the fact that the Germans spurned a similar request from Norway to hold Watson for them. There was Holland, with a proud record of opposing the modern barbarity of whaling, now playing the role of eco-Judas, betraying the world's leading anti-whaling crusader and delivering him into the hands of his worst enemies.

Watson is still in Lelystad prison, and only because he dared to try to enforce the New Age's civilized laws against the slaughter of an endangered species.

—Robert Hunter, *Eye Weekly*, June 12, 1997

My court appearance was a major media event in the Netherlands. Protestors filled the streets outside. Many had traveled from Germany, and some had come from the United States. The courtroom was packed. The judges ruled that I would not be sent to Norway, and to ensure that I would not be arrested in another European country, they ordered me to remain in Lelystad prison for another ten days, by which time the sentence that I would have been obliged to serve in Norway would be completed.

Finally, on June 20, I walked out of prison with the freedom to continue my anti-whaling activities without further fear of arrest from the Norwegians. Upon my release, I held a press conference and issued a statement to the media:

The ruling by the Haarlem court to not grant Norway's demand for extradition is a significant decision. By releasing me, the Dutch court is sending a clear message to Norway that the Netherlands will not be politically manipulated into granting credibility to illegal Norwegian whaling activities.

The Netherlands is one of the world's great defenders of the whales, of conservation, and the environment. By contrast, Norway is one of the world's ecological criminals, blatantly in contempt of the global moratorium on commercial whaling. The Dutch did not side with me against Norway. The court simply upheld the environmental integrity of the Netherlands.

The decision tells the Norwegians that they cannot have it both ways. They demand that their extradition treaty be upheld, yet Norwegians deliberately voted to refuse European Union membership so that they could continue to ignore the marine conservation ethics and the laws of the European community.

Thanks to this decision, I am a free man, and I harbor no grievance against the Netherlands. I am free to continue Sea Shepherd campaigns to protect whales from unlawful whaling. I am free to take my ship and return to the high seas to continue our protection of the whales. The Netherlands deprived me of my freedom for ten weeks at the request of Norway. In return, I would like to respectfully request that the Dutch government actively uphold the international moratorium protecting whales by demanding that Norway stop unlawfully slaughtering the gentle giants of our oceans—the whales.

My release from prison in Lelystad could not have been better timed. The eighty days inside had given us the opportunity to build a solid base of support in Northern Europe. I returned to Bremerhaven to ready my ship for sea.

Before I left, the mayor of the city presented me with a plaque bearing the coat of arms of Bremerhaven and told us that we would always be welcomed back and to consider Bremerhaven our home port in Northern Europe.

However, it was with a great sigh of relief that I watched the river buoy of the Weser disappear to our stern as the *Sea Shepherd III* pointed her bow into the choppy dark blue waters of the North Sea, headed toward the English Channel. Finally, after months of delays, we were heading out to sea again.

We passed through the English Channel and crossed the Bay of Biscay to stop briefly at Gibraltar before entering the Mediterranean on a course toward the French Riviera.

SAINT-JEAN-CAP-FERRAT, FRANCE
SEPTEMBER 1997

The *Sea Shepherd III* and her crew were warmly received with our arrival at Saint-Jean-Cap-Ferrat. Mayor René Vestri motored out to our anchorage with an entourage of local reporters. He requested permission to board, and I piped him and his party onto our main deck. He welcomed me as a returning honorary citizen of Saint-Jean-Cap-Ferrat and informed us that the resources of his office were at our disposal.

"You have this anchorage for as long as you require it," he said. "The town of Saint-Jean-Cap-Ferrat stands for the whales, and we stand with you for defending the whales."

Mayor Vestri presented us with the flag of Saint-Jean-Cap-Ferrat. We ran it up the foremast lanyard.

French photojournalist Bernard Sidler and his girlfriend, Sophie Valentine, accompanied the mayor on board. Bernard was a photojournalist for *Figaro* magazine when I had first met him a few years before. He had originally introduced me to the mayor. Bernard this time introduced me also to Clotilde Taillefer. She was very well connected in Monaco and had volunteered to help us coordinate activities there.

The next day, the mayor returned and we took him on a short voyage to the harbor entrance of Monaco, where we raised and lowered the flag of Monaco in salute before returning to our anchorage at Cap-Ferrat.

With only a few days left before the International Whaling Commission meeting would begin, we concentrated on organizing all the details for our visit to Monaco.

In Cap-Ferrat we were joined by some distinguished guests. The first to arrive was my friend Simon Dick, known by his Kwakiutl name, Tanis, accompanied by Jesse Ides, an elder of the Makah Nation. A few hours later, Chris Strow and Lew Moore boarded. Lew was chief of staff for congressman Jack Metcalf and Chris was his media officer. Both of the men from the congressman's staff were assigned berths on the ship and would stay with us as our guests during the meeting of the IWC.

Hearing that Congressman Metcalf would be arriving in a few hours, mayor René Vestri sent his police chief to personally welcome him to France at the airport and to drive him to his hotel in Monaco.

It was good to see Tanis again. He and I had been in the Amazon together to support the Kayapo in their struggle against a major dam project on the Xingu River, a tributary of the Amazon. Tanis was a spirit dancer for the Kwakiutl Nation and a master carver.

He presented me with a mask that he had recently designed and carved especially for our efforts at protecting the whales. It was the mask of Queneesh, the spirit of the whale.

Michael Kundu arrived to join us, straight from doing his investigation into Aboriginal whaling in Siberia. That evening, the mayor hosted a dinner for us in Saint-Jean-Cap-Ferrat. Congressman Metcalf and his staff joined us, and we had also invited Makah elders Alberta Thompson and Mabel Smith and picked them up from their hotel in Monaco. They had been brought over by another organization to speak for the whales. They were both very happy to see us, and especially to see Jesse Ides.

MONACO, OCTOBER 1997
47TH ANNUAL MEETING OF THE INTERNATIONAL WHALING COMMISSION

We entered Port Hercule in Monte Carlo on October 19, and much to the astonishment of the other nongovernmental organizations, the berth we were given made it look like the *Sea Shepherd III* was the centerpiece for the IWC meeting.

We docked at the Quai des Etats Unis, right below the area where the IWC was meeting. As the most visible presence in town, we were quite impossible to miss. We commandeered the media and held the highest pro-whale profile throughout the week.

We came to Monaco with the blessings of Prince Rainier III and Prince Albert, both ardent advocates of marine conservation. The berth fees in the very expensive harbor of Monte Carlo were waived, and the principality supplied us with a police guard during our stay.

Jack Metcalf arrived and we gave him a tour of the ship. I was impressed with the congressman when he posed for a picture with me on our bow. Chris Strow, his media officer, pointed out that perhaps it would not be wise to have his photograph taken with the *Sea Shepherd*'s Jolly Roger flag directly behind him.

"Nonsense," replied Jack. "I like it. Take the picture."

After the photo session we had a press conference, and I stood with the congressman along with Makah elders Alberta Thompson and Jesse Ides to voice our opposition to the proposal to allow Makah whaling. Jesse Ides wore traditional attire and looked very regal, especially to Europeans, who generally have a fascination with Native American culture.

Congressman Metcalf announced that he was delivering a letter to the United States delegation to the IWC with the names of fifty congressional representatives in opposition to the Clinton/Gore initiative to support the return of whaling in the United States. Tanis did a dance for the whales by the side of our ship.

At the same time, Wayne Johnson and Micah McCarty protested our press conference by holding up pro-whaling signs and distributing literature denouncing those in opposition to the hunt as racists. When some members of the European media questioned how the two Makah elders could be called racist for opposing the proposed hunt, Johnson derisively muttered that they were traitors to the people.

Michael Kundu accompanied me in joining Congressman Metcalf and his aides en route to the hearings on Aboriginal whaling being held that day at the Oceanographic Institute. Both Michael and I refrained from actually attempting to enter the meeting, as we did not want our status of being personae non gratae to interfere with Mr. Metcalf's attendance. But we did enter the building.

IWC secretary Ray Gamble was visibly stunned to see me in the corridor. He walked over and said, "Paul, I never thought I would see you here again. You must know that you are not permitted to be here."

"Nice to see you again also, Ray, but I don't think you can toss me out of Monaco. Besides, I am accredited to attend as a media representative. I write a column for *Ocean Realm*," I responded.

"I don't care if you're writing for *National Geographic*, we will not allow you to attend in any capacity. You are prohibited under all circumstances."

Gamble reminded me that the IWC's members had considered the Iceland action back in 1986 to be in poor form.

I reminded Dr. Gamble that we had upheld his regulations against Iceland's whaling fleet, which was whaling in violation of the global IWC-established moratorium, on which his organization had spent millions drafting volumes of rules and regulations, and we had been the only organization that had bothered to enforce them. Iceland, a pirate whaling nation, demanded that we be expelled, and not one delegate had the guts to remind everyone that it was Iceland that was breaking the law and should have been banned. Besides, unable to get their way, the Icelanders quit the IWC a few years later and now attended as observers only.

Reporters were beginning to cluster. Gamble said nervously, "The decision was made by the delegates, and there can be no further discussion," and walked away.

The International Whaling Commission conference officially opened on Monday, October 20. Monaco allowed us to conduct a demonstration. It was, in truth, the most bizarre demonstration that I had ever participated in. It was completely choreographed from beginning to end.

First of all, demonstrations were not allowed in Monaco, and a few demonstrators had already been arrested and forced to remove their banners. The police had been very polite but firm. The principality was obviously pro-whale, but demonstrations were banned generally and there could be no exceptions.

Except ours. Clotilde had arranged everything. She had gone through the proper channels and coordinated our demonstration directly with the chief of police of Monte Carlo. She told him what we wanted to do and when we would like to do it. He gave us a routing plan, with the place and time to appear to meet IWC secretary Ray Gamble.

"He won't meet with me," I said to Clotilde.

"Oh yes he will. Don't worry. It is all arranged," she answered.

So my crew and I left the boat to walk up to and behind the conference center, where we assembled in a small park next to the Sporting d'Hiver building to await our cue to march up to the front door of the building. Jesse Ides wore his traditional regalia, complete with beaded blanket and headdress. Tanis also wore his traditional dress and carried a drum. I carried the carved mask. A dozen crew members accompanied us, wearing their black-and-white crew shirts.

As I set foot on the sidewalk behind the meeting place of the IWC, the twine holding up the back of the mask broke and it dropped to the concrete, breaking one of its cowry shell teeth. I was quite embarrassed and looked sheepishly at Tanis for damaging his creation.

Tanis looked back at me very seriously. "Queneesh does not like this place. This is not a good place for the whales."

"It was an accident," I answered.

"No," said Tanis, "this was not an accident. When your foot touched this sidewalk, the mask fell. You did not drop it. The twine parted. Queneesh is not happy with this place, and this is not a good omen for the whales."

I held the mask tightly as we proceeded around to the side of the building, where two policemen were waiting. They told us to wait there and to come around to the front of the building when they signaled us. Apparently we were to wait until Prince Rainier gave his opening remarks to the International Whaling Commission. The prince would then leave the building, and we could approach after he had left. It was a protocol measure to ensure that there would be no protest outside the building while the prince was inside.

We waited for about ten minutes, and when we saw the signal from the police officers, we walked around to the front of the building, where photographers and reporters stood at the steps. Behind a police line, there were members of the public, including representatives of the other organizations.

Clotilde had brilliantly choreographed the event. She had the media primed. To take advantage of the outside light, she had actually convinced Ray Gamble to come out of the building to meet us. She told him this would be best in order to avoid a disturbance inside the building.

Suddenly I saw the door to the conference building open, and out came Ray Gamble. He walked down the steps and straight over to us, looking a little nervous about the cameras. I immediately held out my hand and he shook it, more out of habit than as a voluntary gesture.

Before he realized what he had done, a dozen cameras clicked and captured the secretary of the International Whaling Commission shaking hands with what some of the media called the "world's most notorious anti-whaler." Before Dr. Gamble could say anything, I laid into him verbally. He was expecting me to plead my case to allow Sea Shepherd to attend the meeting. Instead, I came at him from an unexpected angle.

"I would like to request permission for Jesse Ides to attend as a spokesperson for the Makah Nation. Only those Makah that favor whaling are being allowed to speak at this meeting, and I would like to ask that Jesse be allowed to speak for the whales on behalf of the Makah."

Gamble responded, "You know, Paul, that you cannot attend. It is the United States that decides who speaks for the Makah, and only those whom they have selected may attend."

I replied that we were speaking on behalf of the majority of the people of the United States, who opposed whaling, and pointed out that president Bill Clinton and vice president Al Gore did not represent the will of the people of the United States nor of the majority of the Makah. If the Clinton/Gore administration wished to betray the whales and to allow whaling in the waters of the United States, such a decision would have been undemocratic and in opposition to the traditions and beliefs of the American people.

Gamble shrugged. "I cannot speak for the United States."

Jesse then spoke up. "We all do not want the whales to die. Many of my people want to see the whales protected. We should be their guardians, not their killers."

"I am sorry, Paul," said Gamble. "It is out of my hands."

Gamble turned and walked away, but we had made our point, and the media did get the message that there were Makah who opposed this hunt.

The two points that I most wanted to convey were that it was the Clinton/Gore administration that was responsible for America's new pro-whaling stance and that the Makah elders who opposed whaling were being denied a voice.

After the protest, the photographer for the *Nice-Matin* newspaper asked if Jesse Ides and I would pose for a picture at Monaco's famous Oceanographic Museum. He wanted us to pose before the massive whale skeleton inside the museum. Unfortunately, the curator of the museum, professor François Doumenge, was also Monaco's commissioner to the IWC. He was informed that I was in the building and intervened to tell the photographer that we would not be allowed to pose in the building. The photographer was shocked. He told us that he took pictures of people here all the time.

The photographer went to the curator's office as Jesse and I waited outside the door. The discussion was getting quite heated in a Gaelic sort of way. The photographer called his boss at the *Nice-Matin* and handed his cell phone over to the curator.

The editor was angry. He told the curator that the paper did many things for the museum, this was not much to ask, and they had never been refused before. The curator answered that he was refusing this time because, in his words, "Paul Watson and the Sea Shepherd Society have gotten enough publicity already."

"You think so?" answered the publisher. "We'll see that he gets more. Don't ask us for any favors in the future."

So, Jesse and I posed back at the dock in front of the *Sea Shepherd III*. The next morning, one of the NGO delegates saw me walking down the gangway and asked us how we had managed the media coup. I walked over and bought a copy of the *Nice-Matin*. There was a front-page photograph of Jesse and me taking up half the page. The back had another half-page color photo of me looking out of the *Sea Shepherd III*'s porthole and showing the large white sperm whale painted on the side of the ship. In addition, there was a news story inside.

On page three, there was the story of the opening of the IWC meeting with a small black-and-white picture of Prince Rainier opening the meeting. It looked like Doumenge had pissed off the editor of the *Nice-Matin* pretty good. His name was not even mentioned.

Later that afternoon, a man came by the ship and asked for me. I went out onto the dock to meet him. He did not give his name but handed me a special invitation to the Principality of Monaco's cocktail reception for the International Whaling Commission's delegates.

Decked out in my dress uniform and accompanied by Michael Kundu, I entered the large reception area of the Hotel Hermitage, where the welcoming party was in progress. I had deliberately arrived late for better effect. The jaws of the Icelandic delegation collectively dropped. Greenpeace delegate David McTaggart glared at me. Ray Gamble saw me. I waved and flashed my invitation and smiled. He turned away in an attempt to ignore me. I could feel the tension rising.

Not one to pussyfoot around, Michael Kundu immediately introduced me to Rune Frovik, the new head of the High North Alliance, the Norwegian whaling association.

"So," I said, "now that Georg Blichfeldt is gone, I guess you're the one who'll be saying nasty things about us."

Suddenly, Frovik turned, as another Norwegian tapped him on the shoulder and gave him a cold look. Frovik spoke with his friend, and, without saying another word, joined the long line of delegates filing their way through the crowd to the door.

The Norwegians had followed the Icelanders who had walked out in protest of my being there. I was flattered, and then I was even more flattered when Tadahiko Nakamura organized the Japanese delegation to depart in protest as well, followed by a few puppet Caribbean nations.

Michael and I both picked up glasses of champagne and made our way into the room, pleased to see that it was becoming less crowded than when we arrived.

Brigitte Sifaoui, the scientific advisor for the French delegation, approached. "I see that you made an impression on our Norwegian and Japanese friends," she said.

I agreed. "When you can actually make a Norwegian whaler walk out on free booze, you know you must be doing something right. So, Brigitte, why is France going to vote for the Makah proposal? I thought France was on the side of the whales."

"It is very frustrating," she answered, "but the answer is simple. Heavy pressure from the United States."

It was amusing to see which delegates had the courage to talk with me. The Brazilian delegation was exceptionally friendly and openly thrilled to have seen the whalers walk out. One delegate from Grenada came over to a Brazilian delegate to speak with him and was introduced to me. He had arrived late and did not realize that his colleagues had walked out. I shook his hand and told him that I had once brought my ship to Grenada to deliver a contribution of supplies from Oxfam.

"Excuse me," he asked. "What is your ship?"

"The *Sea Shepherd*, with the Sea Shepherd Conservation Society."

He actually stepped back and stared at me, and without thinking said, "I cannot talk to you." He turned and almost ran away for fear of being seen with me.

David McTaggart left the reception, which allowed my old comrade John Frizell to approach. I had actually hired Frizell for Greenpeace back in 1976. Since then, he had become an entrenched eco-bureaucrat and a good company man. Some called him "McTaggart's little errand boy."

"Gee, Paul, I never thought I would see you at an IWC meeting again."

"Why not, John?"

"Because," he said, "you know that you're banned from attending these meetings."

"Yes," I replied, "I hear that a lot. That's why I'm here."

It was obvious that John disapproved. "It's not nice to show up at places you're not invited."

"Really, John," I said, "I thought that was why we founded Greenpeace in the first place."

Turning to Michael, I said, "Let's have a drink. This place smells a hell of a lot better than when we arrived."

And we had a fabulous time. We spent some time talking with Alberta Thompson and Mabel Smith. Later, I was speaking with Michael and Ben White when an attractive young lady with a low-cut black dress came toward us. She opened the conversation with what we thought was a rude comment.

"My father does public relations for the Inuit. He took me up to Alaska last year, and I saw where they had just killed a whale. It was the most exciting thing that I have ever seen. It was wonderful."

Michael sneered. "You don't get out much."

She ignored him and went on to tell us how she absolutely loved the whale hunt. "It was so real, so primitive, so in touch with nature."

I said, "You must be sorry you missed the kill, the screams of the whale, the agonizing death throes of a truly sensitive and intelligent creature."

She ignored me and continued. "My father says they are just animals." She answered in a smug all-knowing way. "We have dominion over them, you know."

"Really?" mocked Ben White.

After she rambled on some more, we looked for a polite way to bow out, but she really annoyed me when she said, "Well, you must deep down know that I'm right. After all, you have been listening to me."

Ben was not going to let her get away with that. This girl needed a comeback, and a good one.

"Honey, we three have not been listening to you. We have simply been hanging around because of your pretty face. Too bad you don't have an original thought in your head. Because let me tell you, young lady, any person who can find the brutal killing of a whale to be exciting and wonderful is one sick piece of shit."

We left her there, glass of wine in her hand, looking predictably shocked.

The next day, the nongovernmental organizations hosted their cocktail party for the delegates. Will Anderson had been nominated by the other NGO delegates to see me on board the *Sea Shepherd III*. Will politely informed me that it was requested that I not attend their party, as they desperately wanted the Norwegians and the Japanese to attend, and with me there, they certainly would not show up. I told him that they need not worry. I did not think there would be anything to gain in crashing a cocktail party hosted by an assortment of NGOs that were worried they might offend some whalers.

So, at the end of the day, Michael Kundu and I retired to the Stella Polaris café close to the ship to have a coffee and enjoy the view of our beautiful ship on the quai across the street.

A short time later, Tadahiko Nakamura of the Japanese whaling delegation walked by with other members of his group. They looked like they had been having a good time. Michael invited them over and we bought them beers. They sat down like they were doing something naughty. This was a surprise. Apparently the Japanese did not go to the NGO cocktail party after all. Nor did the Norwegians. Instead, they were having drinks with Sea Shepherd.

"You know," I said, "the United States has voted against every request you have made to the IWC for a quota of whales off the coast of Japan. Now the US wants a coastal quota, and like some puppet nation, you intend to roll over and vote for what they want. Nakamura-san, don't you think that's a little wimpy?"

Nakamura smiled. "The bastards have us over the barrel. We support the Makah quota, but they won't support us."

Hiroshi Yagita, managing director of a Japanese whaling company, spoke up. "Why do you oppose us?"

"Because," I said, "we represent the whales."

I was also able to tell them about my personal experience with a harpooned whale, and they listened very attentively to the story. Dr. Paul Spong walked by and joined us.

"Hey, Paul," I said, "didn't you think the prince's address to the IWC was superb?"

"Yes, incredible."

Nakamura interrupted. "That bastard should be shot."

"Nakamura-san! I am shocked," I said. "You know they have one of the prettiest views from a jail anywhere in the world here, and if you say that any louder, you'll be enjoying the view."

Unfazed and obviously encouraged by drink, Nakamura thundered, "He should be shot for humiliating us like he did."

Dr. Spong quickly changed the subject. "Nakamura-san, why did Oman vote with you on just one issue?"

"They owe us a vote," responded Nakamura.

"But how did you get them to vote against the whales?"

The Japanese delegate laughed and said, "Money, of course."

"But Oman has lots of money."

"Ah, that's not important. The rich always want to get richer. That one vote cost us more than all the other Caribbean votes put together."

"You pay them off?" Spong asked with a look of feigned surprise.

"Of course. And they come cheap."

It is remarkable how alcohol can open up the channels of communication. Yagita was sitting next to Nakamura. I told him I liked his whale tie.

"Ah yes," he said. "It's very expensive."

"I'll bet it is."

I asked Michael to get some Sea Shepherd crew shirts. We gave one to each of the Japanese, who even posed for pictures with them.

Yagita, now feeling obligated to return a gift, reluctantly removed his gold-embroidered silk whale tie and handed it to me. We were getting real chummy now.

After another beer, Nakamura told me he did not think that I was really a terrorist, as the Norwegians had called us, but that Norway had requested they walk out with them in protest the night before, and he had felt compelled to oblige.

I toasted Nakamura and added, "Both you and the Norwegians did us a great honor in walking out. It means you recognize that we mean business. I thank you."

It was a strange sight for some of the NGOs, especially for Greenpeacer John Frizell, to leave the NGO cocktail reception, where the Japanese did not show, and walk past the Stella Polaris, where the Sea Shepherd crew was drinking and talking with the major bad guys from the Japanese delegation. They were wearing our shirts and baseball hats and laughing and joking with us.

We then took the Japanese on a tour of the ship and received invitations to come to Japan, which, of course, I did not take seriously. Nakamura told us that we were worthy opponents.

The next day, Japan voted yes to the US request to kill whales in Washington State. The Japanese commissioner did, however, register the comment that he was sorely tempted to vote against the United States on principle.

Michael Kundu was the official Sea Shepherd observer at the forty-ninth IWC meeting. His report is presented here to illustrate another perspective of the events that transpired in Monaco and serves as a complement to my own observations.

OFFICIAL SEA SHEPHERD REPORT ON THE 49TH INTERNATIONAL WHALING COMMISSION MEETING

by Michael Kundu

As we near the turn of the century, it has been speculated by many groups, and certainly on more than one occasion by Sea Shepherd, that the International Whaling Commission appears to be moving toward its sunset. Chiefly because of its clear inability to enforce against and control violations by member nations, there is also significant and justifiable concern that the IWC has lost its mandate due to its intentional disregard of smaller cetacean species and their conservation.

This year's meeting in Monaco merely added to international skepticism about the world body. There was a clear, emerging pattern of pro-whaling partisanship, with the wealthier Norway and Japan managing to gain support for pro-whaling efforts from the less affluent southern tropical member nations, notably Grenada, Antigua, Barbuda, St. Lucia, St. Vincent, and the Grenadines. The evidence of buyout of these less affluent countries is irrefutable: when quota requests were presented, many of these smaller nations fell in lockstep with the Japanese.

Secondly, there appears to be a climate of overall change looming over the IWC. While it has been legitimately suggested that the mandate of the IWC must reflect the growing global sentiment that whales should not be killed for any reason, leaders of some countries that have historically been anti-whaling appear to be bowing to political pressure applied by Japan and now seem willing to accept some level of compromise.

Yet, what really manifests is that while the anti-whaling countries appear to be moving to the center, the pro-whaling nations are resolutely fastened to the right of the issue—the anti-whalers are giving, while the pro-whalers are merely taking.

In light of this scenario, we have seen steadfast anti-whaling nations, such as the UK, Ireland, and Australia, weaken their stand. Yet the fervent killer nations, such as Japan and Norway, continue to accelerate their illegal killing operations.

Yet, in spite of this increasingly cynical climate, the results of this year's IWC meeting should be considered a draw, since there were notable victories and losses for both sides. Having been banned from attending International Whaling Commission meetings since 1987, the Sea Shepherd Conservation Society has not attended in recent years in any official capacity. This season, as the IWC meetings were held in Monaco, near the South of France, strong regional support for Sea Shepherd allowed us to bring the *Sea Shepherd III* to Monaco harbor to gain a prominent presence among IWC participants.

The *Sea Shepherd III,* her captain, and crew won the majority of publicity and media attention during the seven days of deliberation. The following summarizes some of the salient issues discussed during the seven days in Monaco.

Irish "Global Whaling Sanctuary" Proposal Debated, Deferred

Michael Canny, Ireland's commissioner and last year's vice chair of the IWC, this year discussed the details of an Irish proposal for creating a "global whaling sanctuary"—a misnomer, as the proposal deals with the delineation of areas for the killing of whales rather than global protections for cetacea. Instead of further protection for whales, this proposal of compromise has triggered an avalanche of momentum to adopt the sinister Revised Management Plan (RMP), formerly known as the Revised Management Scheme, an allegedly sustainable quota-based system that facilitates a return to commercial whaling.

Ireland's plan includes establishing a high-seas global whaling "sanctuary" in return for allowing member nations to allocate small-scale coastal whaling quotas within their two-hundred-mile coastal boundaries. The plan was discussed and deferred until May 1998. Many nations, including New Zealand and the United Kingdom, had strong reservations about the compromise. In essence, the Irish proposal suggests that the RMP be adopted, along with the caveat that any permitted whaling must only be for "local consumption." Due to the ambiguity of the term "local"—i.e., whales killed in rural Japan may be sent to larger markets in Tokyo—there is reasonable concern about the Irish proposal.

One need not go far to seek the source of Ireland's sudden concern for Japanese whaling interests. Japanese companies went to Ireland in early 1997 to discuss opening a fishery for bluefin tuna off the southwest coast of Ireland.

Bluefin is the very top end of the world fish market, with each fish potentially worth tens of thousands of dollars at the fish markets in Japan. The Irish fisheries minister is alleged to have granted an exploratory license to a Japanese company to fish inside Irish territorial waters over the opposition of local fishing organizations. Heretofore, Japanese factory vessels have been arrested for violating Irish waters in going after bluefin, with one factory ship recently being apprehended with over one million US dollars' worth of fish on board.

"The bottom line is that the Japanese want to set up a flagship operation, but they do not like talking about flags of convenience," said South and West Fish Producers Organisation chairman Donal O'Driscoll. "They are talking about joint ventures and so on."

While the proposal was eventually deferred, it is the message of the Irish delegation that is the most unsettling element. Ireland, and Commissioner Canny, are ready to compromise. Sea Shepherd ardently opposes any effort to compromise, particularly since a compromise accepts a level of mortality for whales.

The Makah Tribal Gray Whale Hunt—A Possible Loss

The pivotal proposal in front of the IWC this year remained the proposal by the Makah tribe of western Washington State to obtain permission to conduct a "cultural subsistence" hunt for five gray whales annually, as these whales pass the coast of Washington State on their annual migration to and from the Bering Sea.

Sea Shepherd had been leading the effort to defeat this US government sanctioned and supported proposal since 1995, and this year, our efforts included providing a platform for United States congressman Jack Metcalf, who delivered a letter of condemnation that was signed by forty-three other members of the US Congress, including five of the nine members from Washington State. Sea Shepherd has been working very closely with Congressman Metcalf. This effort to develop a bipartisan letter to the IWC was suggested by Sea Shepherd in early 1997.

Speaking at a press conference alongside the *Sea Shepherd III*, Congressman Metcalf delivered copies of the letter to the media and was accompanied by Sea Shepherd representatives Smith, Watson, and Kundu; Makah elders Alberta Thompson, Jesse Ides, and Mabel Smith; and Kwakiutl spirit dancer Tanis, who performed a traditional whale dance for media and public audiences. The media conference received international attention, and the congressional letter became a significant topic of discussion at the IWC, prompting a number of member nations to formally announce their concern about the domestic US opposition to a hunt by the Makah tribe. Lawyers and members of the tribe affiliated with the pro-hunting delegation also attended the Sea Shepherd media conference, clearly concerned about the significance of this letter to both the delegates and international audiences.

Throughout the Makah deliberations, most countries signaled strong messages that if a vote on the matter were to be taken, they would not support the Makah tribe's plans. The Netherlands, Brazil, New Zealand, Germany, Austria, and Argentina, among others, voiced concern that the Makah tribe did not evidence the nutritional nor subsistence need to undertake the hunt. This factor marked a significant moment in the IWC: The US was now compelled to seek other methods to gain the Makah tribe their quota. What the US did next was to set a major negative precedent in IWC protocol.

The Joint Russian/US Whale-Harvesting Proposal

Using obvious subterfuge, the US delegation strategically restructured their proposal to "hide" the Makah's five-whale quota request as part of the Russian quota request for 140 gray whales in the next five years. In exchange for this trade for Russian grays, the US would offer the Russian Inuit five of the US bowhead whales from the new five-year US quota for Alaskan Inuit.

Unfortunately, the US strategy worked. The IWC granted the US and Russian Federation a joint quota of 620 gray whales over a five-year period (140 per year maximum). The Russians will transfer four of these whales to the Makah annually in return for an allocation from the Alaskan Eskimo bowhead quota.

Sea Shepherd was raising alarms over the possible employment of just such a strategy for over a year beforehand. We investigated the possibility that the US would try to use this plan back in June 1997, when IWC chairman Peter Bridgewater stated in a letter to Sea Shepherd that "the IWC allocates quotas based on stocks, not on the basis of countries requesting these stocks. . . . If the US makes such a deal with the Russians, the IWC would have no control over the matter."

On Thursday, October 23, the US managed to reach general "consensus" by all nations that the Russian gray and US bowhead quotas would not impact the remaining populations ("stocks," in their terminology). Underlying this consensus was the hidden trade, which the member nations were cognizant of but not in any position to oppose under this strategy. Many nations spoke out against this strategy in principle, but no official protocol exists to block the effort. In the end, the US was given four gray whales per year, and the Russians received five bowheads in return.

Now our concerns have manifested, and the Makah gray whale hunt may occur. For all intents and purposes, the United States delegation returned to Washington, DC, with a quota for four gray whales per year for the Makah tribe of western Washington.

One Redeeming Argument: The Question of "Need"

Yet one technicality remains that may block the Makah tribe's hunt of gray whales. Australia led the effort to amend the IWC schedule of the convention with the following words: "The only Aboriginal people who are authorized to take gray whales are those whose traditional Aboriginal subsistence and cultural needs have been recognized."

Thereby, the resolution declaring permission for the Russian/US whale quotas technically requires the Makah tribe to provide evidence of "need" prior to any subsistence hunt. While the Makah tribe has survived for seventy-one years without nutrition derived from gray whales, uncertainty lies in who must be convinced of this expressed "need."

That uncertainty was not an accident. Australian activists who saw the amendment in draft form assert that the original amendment to the schedule of the convention read "those whose traditional Aboriginal subsistence and cultural needs have been recognized by the IWC," and that in the final draft, the words "by the IWC" were crossed out under political pressure. Hence, the Makah could theoretically ask the US delegation, which finessed the resolution for them, to "recognize" their subsistence and cultural needs in a rubber-stamp fait accompli.

While we pursue the implications of this potential technicality against the hunt, further clarification on the issue must be released by the IWC in post-conference reports. Pending the acceptance of the Makah tribe's ability to prove "need," the killing of gray whales off the Washington coast is antici-pated to begin in the autumn of 1998.

"Cultural Whaling": The Greater
Ramifications of the Makah Hunt

Sea Shepherd's greatest concern—a concern that has already reared its head—is that the US seemed to have successfully argued quotas on the basis of "cultural" justification. On Monday, October 20, the Japanese probed the

US argument by asking during the IWC plenary session what the difference is between Makah cultural whaling and Japanese cultural whaling.

Now that the US has "won" their quota for the Makah tribe on the "cultural" basis, it is more likely that this argument will be waged by the Japanese, Norwegians, and Icelandics, as well as other pro-whaling nations and Aboriginal groups, for their own coastal whaling requests. The consequences of this US victory may have tremendously negative implications for whale populations in the coming decade.

This, too, was no accident. As Sea Shepherd discovered at this year's IWC meeting, Japan has been running a game on both the US and the Makah. Six members of Japan's IWC delegation, in discussing whaling issues with Captain Paul Watson and his crew at the Stella Polaris café in Monaco on the evening of October 22, revealed the following: "We told the Makah that a gray whale was worth one million dollars on the Japanese market. The truth is that gray whale meat does not taste very good. There is no market for it."

Commissioner Tadahiko Nakamura, when asked why he would tell the Makah that they could sell whale meat for such high prices if they had no intention of purchasing it, replied, "So we can expose the Americans for the hypocrites they are. For years they have voted no to Japanese coastal whaling. Now the US is asking us to vote yes for American coastal whaling. Once those bastards win the right to kill whales in the US for cultural reasons, the IWC will be obligated to recognize Japanese whaling as cultural also. We will have them where we want them."

Japan has successfully manipulated the United States into opening the door to dismantling the commercial moratorium on whaling.

Japan Agrees to Stop Using the Electric Lance

Facing increased pressure to reduce inhumane methods of killing in all allo-cated quotas, the IWC continues to deliberate the tools used to kill whales when killing does in fact occur. One significant victory at this year's IWC was the success of an international effort to eliminate Japan's use of the inhumane "electric lance," a device that is used to deliver an electrical shock to kill whales or to render harpooned whales unconscious before killing.

New Zealand led the argument, providing research that suggested the electric lance was ineffective in rendering whales unconscious and even less effective in killing whales humanely. Japan responded that 50 percent of whales electrocuted died within a few seconds. The UK and Australian delega-tions vocalized the IWC's concern about the inhumanity of the electric lance, and Japan agreed that they would remove the lance as a killing technique prior to the 1998 killing season.

Whale Meat DNA Database Established

Over the past few years, information about the availability of whale meat—in some cases from highly endangered species, such as blue whales and humpback whales—has left international governments concerned about pirate whaling operations worldwide. Japan and Norway have now accepted a tentative proposal by IWC nations to have all whale meat taken during their whaling operations, both commercial and scientific, genetically cataloged using DNA coding. This action will allow better monitoring and tracking of the origins of illegal whale-meat sales, which have been discovered in Japan and Norway.

Norway Condemned Again for
Illegal Commercial Whaling

As in previous years, member nations of the IWC again passed a resolution requesting that Norway cease its commercial whaling operations and adhere to the 1982 global commercial whaling moratorium. In a replay of last and previous years, Norway refused to consider its actions illegal and instead presented a new calculated quota for minke whales, which the country deems "could be killed in the North Atlantic without harming the stock."

Caribbean Nations and Japan
Criticize IWC Whale-Watching Discussions

Fearing that the growing popularity of whale watching may form the basis of a stronger argument against lethal whaling, St. Lucia, St. Vincent, and Japan registered critical comments about the role of the IWC in discussing the merits of whale watching as an alternative to establishing whale-killing quotas. The issue is significant because informal discussions at the IWC demonstrated evidence that in many countries (including Iceland and Australia) revenue from whale watching far exceeds potential and existing revenues from harvesting whales—a fact that the Japanese and their financially supported allies would not like to have made widely known.

Rumors during informal gatherings of this year's IWC suggest that the smaller tropical nations may be allying with the influential Japanese government as a result of receiving "foreign fisheries and development aid" funding from

Japan. This is a significant concern because evidence of this sort of influential bartering would suggest a gross violation of IWC protocols. In fact, discussions occurring during the IWC plenary sessions apparently suggested a "secret ballot" on voting matters so that smaller countries might avoid being influenced by the larger, more wealthy nations.

"Scientific Whaling" in Antarctic Sanctuary Criticized

New Zealand attacked the Japanese government on the issue of "scientific whaling" and criticized that government's continued killing operations in the deceptively named Southern Ocean Whale Sanctuary. A resolution rejecting Japan's ongoing "scientific research" justification was also passed by the IWC. New Zealand, which this year openly expressed its vehement refusal to accept all future commercial whaling initiatives, has become a model country for anti-whaling advocates. Many other nations, including the Netherlands, Brazil, the UK, Monaco, and Germany, supported New Zealand's concerns about whaling in the Antarctic. Japan, however, remained resolute that scientific whaling would continue.

On the counterattack, a paper presented by the Japanese delegation, prepared by University of Washington law professor William Burke, suggested that the basis of the IWC declaring that the Southern Ocean Whale Sanctuary was illegal, under the rules governing the International Convention for the Regulation of Whaling (ICRW). This paper effectively fed the Japanese argument that they should be allowed to kill whales from the sanctuary. The paper was not officially endorsed by the IWC, but it did demonstrate the powers of persuasion and the long reach of the energetic Japan Whaling Association and the Institute of Cetacean Research—the public relations engines behind Japanese whaling—whose primary efforts are directed toward securing international endorsements to create the illusion of support for whaling beyond the offices of a few aged politicos in the Japanese government.

Japanese Coastal Whaling Allocations Criticized, Rejected

Once again, requests to award the Japanese a "relief quota of fifty minke whales" for the coastal villages of Taiji, Wada, Ayukawa, and Abashiri, was rejected by a vote of twelve to sixteen, with four abstentions. The Japanese delegations warned members of the IWC that they would "watch very closely who would vote against the quota request." These villages traditionally killed a number of small and large cetacean species, notably Baird's beaked and minke whales. Recently, the village of Taiji captured ten orca whales, evidently solely for commercial sale to various marine parks and aquariums. Five of these whales were eventually released, two of them died in captivity, and the remaining three are not expected to survive.

IWC Will Meet in Oman in 1998

Ireland's commissioner Michael Canny will take over the chairmanship of the IWC in 1998, which is scheduled to meet again in May 1998 in Oman.

6
CHAPTER

Autumn of the Che-che-wid

All media work us over completely. They are so persuasive in their personal, political, economic, aesthetic, psychological, moral, ethical, and social consequences that they leave no part of us untouched, unaffected, unaltered. The medium is the message. Any understanding of social and cultural change is impossible without a knowledge of the way media works as environments.

—MARSHALL MCLUHAN

I'm not sending two ships and a submarine here to stop five whales from an Aboriginal hunt. My opposition is Oslo, Tokyo, and Reykjavik.

—CAPTAIN PAUL WATSON, *LOS ANGELES TIMES,* AUGUST 27, 1998

NEAH BAY, OCTOBER 1998

The Makah Whaling Commission had announced that starting October 1, 1998, they would begin their whale hunt. We had been preparing for that day for more than a year, ever since the Makah whalers had boasted at Monaco that they would kill a whale in the fall of 1998.

I had brought my flagship, the *Sea Shepherd III*, from Monaco via the Panama Canal to stop briefly in July at Neah Bay before continuing on to Seattle. In Neah Bay we had shown the flag, did some interviews, posed for some pictures, and let the Makah whalers know that we would be waiting for them to go whaling.

The big blue boat got the whole town worked up, although it mostly just sat in the water. Its crew issued no challenge and launched no Zodiacs with aggression. It just floated there beyond the break-water, 173 feet of pretty blue ship, irritating the heck out of the Makah tribe members on shore.

That was the intent.

—The *Seattle Times*, July 24, 1998

We had just been setting the stage.

In August, the Makah tribal council and the federal and Washington State governments expected us to disrupt Makah Days. We never said that we would; we never even hinted that we would. All that I had to do was simply anchor in Neah Bay for a few hours in July to allow the imaginations of the politicians to begin to simmer.

In 1996, we had taken the ship to Makah Days, and we did not disrupt it then. This year, I had no intention of taking the ship to Neah Bay at all.

When reporters asked if we were going to disrupt Makah Days, I answered, "Absolutely not."

Seattle Times correspondent Alex Tizon reported that I had said, "They won't be killing any whales during Makah Days, so there's no reason for us to disrupt it."

Even the FBI called me up and asked if it was our intention to disrupt Makah Days. "Of course not," I replied.

And the truth is that we had absolutely no intention of interfering with a Makah tribal celebration. I knew their annual event was a celebration of their culture, and that was not what we were opposed to. We were opposed to whaling.

But the Makah tribal council was sure we would be there in full force and succeeded in convincing governor Gary Locke to send in the troops. They fabricated a bizarre scenario of some twenty thousand anti-whaling terrorists descending upon Neah Bay. Incredibly, the governor believed them.

Locke called for the mobilization of the National Guard to protect the Makah from rumors of thousands of "militant demonstrators and ecoterrorists." There was some serious overreaction going on, and rumors began to fuel rumors to the point of near hysteria.

Who these thousands of "ecoterrorists" were was a mystery. I would be hard-pressed to name half a dozen people worldwide who could even remotely qualify for the title of ecoterrorist. There was not one shred of evidence suggesting that even one demonstrator would show up, let alone twenty thousand. The media, however, manufactures its own reality.

> The arrogant activists who have vowed to disrupt the Makah tribe's resumption of whaling this fall can be proud of themselves.
>
> With threats of physical obstruction and even murder, some of them have succeeded in scaring a tiny Indian nation, whose sole self-defense consists of trying to revive its ancestral hunt. . . .
>
> So virulent and vicious have been those threats that governor Gary Locke granted the tribal council's plea for National Guard protection during the annual Makah Days celebrations next weekend.
>
> —*Tacoma News Tribune*, editorial, August 23, 1998

On August 26, the *Olympian* newspaper also reported that twenty thousand demonstrators would appear at Neah Bay. And so eight hundred National Guard troops descended on Neah Bay to face a rumored army of anti-whaling protestors.

I was very amused to say the least. I knew for a fact that there would be no demonstrations. We had put the word out for people not to go to Neah Bay weeks prior to any move to deploy soldiers. We did not want to confuse the issue.

The *Olympian* quoted me correctly when I said, "We are not a protest organization. We focus only on intervening against illegal whaling. The state and federal governments could have saved a lot of money if they'd just picked up the phone and called me first."

As it was, the festival, which normally attracted some nine thousand participants over three days, saw its lowest attendance ever as people stayed away to avoid the soldiers. Only about four thousand people attended. Clallam County sheriff Joe Hawe's prediction of twenty-one thousand protestors besieging Neah Bay fell twenty-one thousand short of the mark.

In the end, it cost over one million dollars to send in the National Guard, and Clallam County had to pay $26,000 in overtime for law enforcement. In addition, the FBI and the US marshals were in full force. The troops, officers, and special agents simply stood around smelling barbecued salmon and looking bored. With all the cops around, the party mood was seriously subdued, due to lack of stimulants.

The media tended to be less hysterical outside of Washington State.

> The 1946 International Convention on the Regulation of Whaling still allocates a whaling quota to Indigenous communities whose subsistence or culture depends on it. Russian Inuits can kill 140 gray whales a year. But the British government, along with most other signatories to the ICRW, does not consider the Makah to hold a valid claim.
>
> —*London Times*, September 5, 1998

After Makah Days, Governor Locke took a great deal of flack, despite his spin doctoring to advance the fable that there were no protestors because of the National Guard. Most of the media was not buying that since it had been widely reported that we had said in advance that there would be no protesters at Makah Days.

The *Olympian* reported on August 30 that "Paul Watson, founder and leader of Sea Shepherd, repeatedly promised last week that his group would not disturb Makah Days."

The Makah complained, however, that the media had disrupted Makah Days.

We had outmaneuvered both the governor and the National Guard. We now knew that, when the time came for us to go to Neah Bay, the governor would think twice about sending in the National Guard again. By staying away from Makah Days, we had smoothed the way to return to Neah Bay for the planned hunt.

The only demonstration that did take place was on August 30, 1998, in Port Angeles, by sixty people demonstrating against the one million dollars the governor had spent to deploy the National Guard. In fact, the grassroots leadership in the protest against the whale hunt was taking place in Port Angeles. Chuck and Margaret Owens, Don Munson, and other citizens of the Olympic Peninsula had organized the Peninsula Citizens for the Protection of Whales. They had been lobbying politicians and organizing demonstrations. On September 8, they convinced two Clallam County commissioners—Martha Ireland and Phil Kitchel—to write letters to the Makah tribal council to protest the proposed hunt. Ireland wrote, "In light of the negative public safety and economic impacts, may I take the liberty of requesting that the Makah tribal council reconsider its plans." Kitchel added to Ireland's letter that he supported her statements.

THE MAKAH MANIFESTO

To be fair to the Makah, I would like to include their defense of whaling in this book. On August 23, 1998, Keith Johnson, the president of the Makah Whaling Commission, wrote what he called the "Makah Manifesto" for the *Seattle Times*:

I am a Makah Indian and president of the Makah Whaling Commission, comprised of representatives from twenty-three traditional whaling families of our tribe. For the past three years, we have been reading the attacks made on us by animal rights organizations aimed at stopping our whale hunt. These attacks contain distortions, exaggerations, and outright falsehoods. Reading these things has sickened and angered me, and I feel I must respond.

We plan to conduct a whale hunt this year, sometime in October or November. While we are legally authorized to take up to five whales per year, our management plan limits the number of landed whales over a five-year period to twenty, or an average of four per year. But I want to point out that our whaling commission will issue a permit only if there is an unmet need in the community, so it is possible that as little as one whale per year will be taken if that will meet our needs.

Whaling has been part of our tradition for more than two thousand years. Although we had to stop in the 1920s because of the scarcity of gray whales, their abundance now makes it possible to resume our ancient practice of whale hunting. Many of our tribal members feel that our health problems result from the loss of our traditional seafood and sea-mammal diet. We would like to restore the meat of the whale to that diet. We also believe that the problems that are troubling our young people stem from lack of discipline and pride, and we hope that the restoration of whaling will help to restore that. But we also want to fulfill the legacy of our forefathers and restore a part of our culture that was taken from us.

How Did We Get a Legal Right to Hunt?

Before entering into negotiations with the Makah for cessions of our extensive lands on the Olympic Peninsula in 1855, the United States government was fully aware that our people lived primarily on whale, seal, and fish. They knew that we hunted several species of whales and had a substantial commerce in whale oil that had brought us prosperity.

When US territorial governor Isaac Stevens arrived at Neah Bay in December 1855 to enter into negotiations with our leaders, he was met with strong declarations from them that in exchange for ceding our lands to the US, they demanded guarantees of their rights on the ocean and, specifically, of the right to take whale. The treaty minutes show Governor Stevens saying to the Makahs: "The Great Father knows what whalers you are—how you go far to sea to take a whale."

He went on to promise US assistance in promoting our whaling commerce. He then presented a treaty containing the specific guarantee of the US securing the right of the Makahs to continue whaling. The treaty, accepted by us, is the only treaty ever made by the US that contained such a guarantee. The treaty was ratified by Congress in 1855 and has since been upheld by all the courts, including the US Supreme Court.

To us, it is as powerful and meaningful a document as the US Constitution is to you because it is what our forefathers bequeathed to us. In fact, one of our whalers has said that when he is in the canoe whaling, he will be reaching back in time and holding hands with his great-grandfathers, who wanted us to be able to whale.

Will the Makahs Sell Any of the Whale Meat?

Absolutely not! Yet animal rights groups, such as the Sea Shepherd Conservation Society, continue to insist that we secretly plan to sell whale meat to Japan. That claim has been repeated endlessly by other animal rights groups. It is utterly false.

Although our treaty guaranteed a commercial right, we have agreed to limit ourselves to noncommercial whaling. We have no plans to sell whale meat in the future.

Though it may be difficult for some people to accept, we are acting out of purely cultural motives. In fact, it is costing our tribe an enormous amount of money to carry on the whale-hunting program. It is, if you please, part of our religion, because for us, culture means religion.

Is There Any Conservation Issue?

Absolutely not. The Eastern Pacific or California gray whale has been studied by scientists around the world, and it is established that the gray whale population is currently at an all-time high of around twenty-two thousand. The population continues to increase at 2.5 percent per year, despite an annual harvest, which has gone as high as 165 by Russian aborigines called Chukchi.

The gray whale was removed from the endangered species list in 1994, and the population is now considered to be at its maximum level. In fact, some biologists have raised the question of whether the number of gray whales may be nearing the carrying capacity of their range—that is, the number that can be supported by the food resources. No reputable biologist or whale scientist has suggested that our taking five whales a year will present any conservation threat whatsoever to the gray whale stock.

The fact is no one can legitimately argue that this is a conservation threat. It is one of the main reasons why two of America's leading conservation organizations have refused to join in the attack on our whaling: the Sierra Club and Greenpeace. There are animal rights activists within those organizations who are trying to get them to come out against our whaling, but they have steadfastly refused because they do not see this as a conservation issue.

The Wishes of the Tribe

Our attackers continue to claim that we are disregarding the views of the majority of our members. They repeatedly publicize in the media and elsewhere the views of two women who are members of the tribe and are outspoken opponents of whaling. While we respect the right of all of our members to hold and to express their views on any subject, I must respectfully point out that these two women do not speak for anywhere near the majority of the tribe, and there are other elders who strongly support whaling.

In the last opinion poll we held on this issue, 85 percent of those voting favored whaling. There is a faction within our tribe that is opposed to whaling, but they are a distinct minority. I can say proudly that the Makah tribal council and the Makah Whaling Commission represent the strongly held views of the majority of our members.

We were the premier whalers on the American continent and were able to enjoy a prosperous life because of our whaling trade. Our forefathers bequeathed our right to whale to us in our treaty, and we feel that a treaty right that cannot be exercised is no right. I can tell you that our tribe is not prepared to abandon our treaty right.

How We Plan to Conduct the Hunt

We will hunt the whale from one or two seagoing canoes, each carved from a single cedar log by Indian carvers. Each canoe will be manned by a crew of eight whalers and will include a harpooner and rifleman. Both of these men will be stationed in the bow. The harpooner will use a stainless steel harpoon mounted on a wooden shaft. It will be connected to the canoe by a rope with floats attached. The harpooner will throw the harpoon at the whale. Immediately afterward, or simultaneously, the rifleman will fire a special high-powered rifle using a .50 caliber round.

We are using this specially designed rifle and this ammunition on the specific recommendations of Dr. Allen Ingling, a veterinarian and specialist in arms on the humane killing of animals. This weapon has been tested by Ingling, who has worked with the National Marine Mammal Laboratory of the National Marine Fisheries Service. Ingling has instructed us on the target area to be hit so as to bring about almost instantaneous loss of consciousness and death of the whale.

The use of the special rifle has been attacked by many animal rights groups as brutal and traditional. I believe these attacks are dishonest. In the nineteenth century we didn't use such a weapon; we used harpoons and spears. The whale often died after a prolonged and agonizing time from internal bleeding. That was not humane.

I don't hear any of these animal rights groups attacking us for conducting the hunt with a canoe. The lives of at least eight people will be at risk on the dangerous waters of the Pacific in October and November to hunt the whale. That is our traditional method. If we wanted to abandon all cultural tradition, we would simply use a deck-mounted cannon firing a harpoon into the whale. No, our canoe has been carved by traditional carvers and will be paddled by eight whalers who have sanctified themselves by rituals that are ancient and holy to us. The hunt is being conducted in a manner that is both traditional and modern.

The Dire Prediction

The Sea Shepherd organization has been making sweeping claims that if we hunt a whale, whales will begin attacking humans throughout the waters of the state and devastate the whale-watching industry. This is complete nonsense.

First of all, most of the whale watching is focused on orcas, not gray whales, and takes place in Puget Sound and the eastern area of the Strait of Juan de Fuca. As for gray whales, whale watching on this species is primarily concentrated in Westport, far from any area where we will be hunting whales.

The idea that whales will somehow begin to act aggressively against human boats or change their migratory path to avoid boats is false. The whales passing through the waters of Washington State have come here after being hunted and attacked in the Bering Sea by the Russian Indigenous people called Chukchi. The Chukchi have been hunting the gray whale for more than forty years, and there is no evidence that gray whales have attacked other boats. Nor is there any evidence that whales communicate with each other and spread the message that humans are the enemy, to be attacked or avoided. This is a fantasy promoted by animal rights activists.

What Is Our Cultural Need?

It is hard for us to explain to outsiders our "cultural" attitudes about whaling. Some of us find it repugnant to even have to explain this to anyone else. But let me tell you about my own case.

I have a bachelor's degree in education from Central Washington University, Ellensburg. I was the first Makah teacher in the Neah Bay school system from 1972 through 1976. I received my principal's credentials from Western Washington University, Bellingham, in 1975, and served as vice principal of the Neah Bay schools in 1976 and between 1990 and 1997.

Have I lost my culture? No. I come from a whaling family. My great-grandfather, Andrew Johnson, was a whaler. He landed his last whale in 1907. My grandfather, Sam Johnson, was present when the whale landed and told me he played on the whale's tail. I lived with my grandfather for sixteen years and heard his stories about whaling and the stories of family whaling told by my father, Percy, and my uncle Clifford.

When I was a teenager, I was initiated into Makah whaling rituals by my uncle. While I cannot divulge these sacred rituals, they involve isolation, bathing in icy waters, and other forms of ritual cleansing that are still practiced today. I have been undergoing rituals to prepare me for the whaling this year. Other families are using their own rituals.

I am proud to carry on my family legacy, and my father is overjoyed because he is going to see this in his lifetime.

I can tell you that all of the Makah whalers are deeply stirred by the prospect of whaling. We are undergoing a process of mental and physical toughening now. We are committed to this because it is our connection to our tribal culture and because it is a treaty right—not because we see the prospect of money.

We are willing to risk our lives for no money at all. The only reward we will receive will be the spiritual satisfaction of hunting and dispatching the whale and bringing it back to our people to be distributed as food.

Recently, the Progressive Animal Welfare Society (PAWS) distributed a brochure in which they implied we have lost our cultural need for whaling because we have adapted to modern life. They cite our "lighted tennis courts . . . Federal Express . . . and other amenities."

Well, excuse me! I want to tell PAWS that the two tennis courts on our high school grounds have no lights. How about the fact that Federal Express makes deliveries to our reservation? Does that mean that we have lost our culture?

These attacks on our culture and our status are foolish. No one can seriously question who we are; we are a small Native American tribe whose members were the whalers of the American continent. We retain our whaling traditions today. It resonates through all of our people from the youngest to the oldest, and we don't take kindly to other people trying to tell us what our culture is or should be.

The Domino Effect

Animal rights groups have been scaring each other and pumping up the claim that if we whale, it will mean the collapse of all restrictions against commercial whaling and whaling will be resumed everywhere. This is nonsense. If there are other Indigenous people who have a legitimate whaling culture and whaling tradition, then they should be allowed to whale just as we do. The rest is all hype.

The leader of the pack attacking us is the Sea Shepherd Conservation Society. They have been responsible for a steady stream of propaganda aimed at inflaming the public against us, some of which has been repeated by other anti-whaling groups who have assumed it was factual.

Who is Sea Shepherd? They are a California-based organization that has for years operated on the fringe of mainstream conservation groups. They portray themselves as the swashbucklers of the ocean because they have sunk whaling ships. This action has earned them the label of a terrorist organization, and they have been barred from attending the deliberations of the International Whaling Commission, even as observers, since 1987. They applied for readmission in 1995, and the IWC sanction again denied them admission.

They threatened to sink our boats if we whaled without IWC sanction, smug in the assumption that we would never get approval from the IWC. They have since churned out reams of material attacking us.

We can't hope to keep up with this barrage by Sea Shepherd and others. These groups are well financed. Sea Shepherd operates two oceangoing vessels, a submarine, an airplane, a helicopter, and other waterborne craft. It seems to me that Sea Shepherd is actually in the commercial whaling business and we're their best ticket now.

The Ethical Issue

The arguments and claims by Sea Shepherd and the other anti-whaling groups mask the real aim of these groups: to prevent the killing of a single whale. Some people honestly believe that it is wrong to kill one of these animals. Maybe their minds are made up, but I want to say to them that we Makahs know the whales, probably better than most people. We are out on the waters of the ocean constantly, and we have lived with and among whales for more than two thousand years. We are not cruel people, but we have an understanding of the relationship between people, the mammals of the sea, and land.

We are a part of each other's life. We are all part of the natural world, and predation is also part of life on this planet.

I want to deal with the claims of those who would romanticize the whale and ascribe almost human characteristics to it. To attribute to gray whales near-human intelligence is romantic nonsense, as any professional whale biologist can tell you. The photographs of gray whales surfacing to be petted by people are all taken in the calving lagoons of Baja, California, and Mexico. This behavior is not exhibited by gray whales anywhere else, particularly by migrating whales passing through our waters. The whales we will hunt are migrating whales, and we will not hunt any mother whale with a calf.

Whales have captured the public's fascination. The world has had a similar fascination with our cultures, but whenever we had something you wanted or did something you didn't like, you tried to impose your values on us.

Too often white society has demonstrated this kind of cultural arrogance. To us, the implication that our culture is inferior if we believe in whaling is demeaning and racist. The Makah people have been hurt by these attacks, but nevertheless, we are committed to continuing in what we feel is the right path.

We Makah hope that the general public will try to understand and respect our culture and ignore the attacks of extremists.

I read Keith Johnson's words, and I was at a loss to understand why he considered us to be attacking them with distortions, exaggerations, and falsehoods.

We had evidence of Makah plans to commercialize the hunt, and Makah spokespeople had even said so. Johnson's claim that whale watching did not involve gray whales was ridiculous. The entire West Coast whale-watching industry revolved around the gray whale, and his claim that wounded gray whales attacking people is nonsense simply had no validity. Gray whales historically did attack whalers when wounded. The fact that gray whales are gentle creatures today is because they are not hunted along the American coast. In Siberia, where they are hunted, they have been known to defend themselves. He also said that there is no evidence that whales communicate with each other, and this is not true. The evidence overwhelmingly demonstrates that whales have a highly complex social-communication system.

Johnson went on to say that Sea Shepherd threatened to sink their boats, yet we never made any such statement, nor was it ever our intention to do so.

Johnson claimed that gray whales surface to be petted only in Baja, yet the Makah distributed a film in which Dan Greene and his son were petting a gray whale in Neah Bay.

The manifesto ended with Johnson saying that he hoped the general public would understand and respect Makah culture and that they would ignore the attacks of extremists. But who were the extremists? Those who drove a harpoon into the back of a defenseless whale and blasted it with an antitank gun, or those who sought to avoid this wanton destruction of life?

I cannot accept that saving a life by opposing those who would take that life is an extremist action. Killing is extremism. Inflicting cruelty to a living being is extremism.

But the manifesto gave us an understanding of what the Makah and US government strategy would be. They would seek to portray those who opposed the hunt as ecoterrorists and racists.

Meanwhile in Seattle, we had recruited a crew of volunteers; prepared and stocked the ship for a two-month siege; and loaded our twelve-meter, two-man submarine, *Mirage*, on board. I had my friend, artist George Sumner, come up with his wife, Donna-Lei, to paint the submarine to look like a life-sized orca. The plan was to use the submarine to broadcast orca sounds to frighten gray whales away from the whalers.

As soon as the National Marine Fisheries Service read about our plan in the newspapers, they informed me that I would be charged under the Marine Mammal Protection Act with harassing whales if I played whale sounds near any whales. According to NMFS, it was illegal to protect whales by playing underwater whale sounds to frighten them away from harpoons.

My two ships, the *Sea Shepherd III* and the *Sirenian*, departed from Seattle on September 29. I skippered the smaller and faster *Sirenian*, while Matt Lawson, an Objiway Indian living on Vancouver Island, took command of the *Sea Shepherd III*.

The *Sea Shepherd III* was fully crewed, but the *Sirenian* was understaffed. The crew included Rod Marining, a longtime friend and fellow Greenpeace cofounder. The good news was that we had an excellent engineer in Mike Claw, but the bad news was that he could only stay for a few days.

As we cruised ahead of the *Sea Shepherd III*, we were amused to find a Trident nuclear submarine emerge on our stern and follow us all the way out of Puget Sound.

We pulled into Port Angeles and stopped at the High Tide restaurant, owned by friends of the Peninsula Citizens for the Protection of Whales. Margaret and Chuck Owens greeted us along with quite a few of their supporters, including Marsha and Don Munson. Don, a fisherman and an engineer, volunteered immediately when we mentioned that we were sorely in need of an engineer. He drove home, got his kit bag, and we got underway for Neah Bay at around 5:00 a.m.

The *Sea Shepherd III* had dropped anchor outside the breakwater and was rising and falling with the swells as we came up and tied alongside her.

After years of preparations, we were on the threshold of a long-anticipated showdown. I could not help but wonder about the irony of the situation. I had been a lifelong defender of Native rights and a strong advocate of Native culture and sovereignty, and now here I was leading a maritime force about to besiege a remote Indian village.

I did not enjoy the position that I was in, but I knew that to back down would be not only hypocritical but also racist because the only reason for retreating would be the fact that my lifelong enemies—the whalers—were not Japanese, Russian, Norwegian, or Icelandic this time. They were Native Americans.

I did agonize over the decision to take this stand, but I felt that even this hesitation in itself was racist. I could not discriminate in favor of a whaler simply because that whaler was a Native American.

In the end, my conscience would not allow me to abandon the whales to the whalers. I had sworn so many years before, after watching the light of life extinguished in a sperm whale's eye, that I would serve the whales over and above the interests of my own species. I had no choice but to stand by that commitment—no choice whatsoever.

This hunt had potentially negative consequences for all the world's whales, and I knew that it was an important battle. The Japanese and the Norwegians had manipulated their new recruits very adroitly, and instead of facing them, I was now forced to face their politically correct pawns. So be it.

As the field campaign began to loom closer on the horizon, it appeared that five organizations were preparing active campaigns against the hunt. The Sea Shepherd Conservation Society was the largest group involved, and the only international group opposing the hunt. Our participation was established back in 1995, and our position was rooted in a conservation foundation with a specific concern regarding the illegality of the hunt. We had one primary concern: the hunt did not meet the Aboriginal criteria of the International Whaling Commission, and thus it had not been recognized or approved by the IWC.

The Seattle-based Progressive Animal Welfare Society (PAWS) had appointed Will Anderson to lead its campaign against the proposed hunt. Will was a very dedicated whale lover, and PAWS had very early taken a stand against the plans to promote whaling in Washington State. The PAWS position was from an animal welfare perspective. They were legitimately concerned that the hunt would be cruel.

The third group, and in my opinion the most important one, was the Peninsula Citizens for the Protection of Whales. This was a citizens' group based in Port Angeles, Washington. This group was a godsend. They were local, grassroots, dedicated, and composed of real salt-of-the-earth types like Chuck and Margaret Owens and Don and Marsha Munson. They knew how to give a good protest, and a weekly blockade of the road into Neah Bay certainly got attention. Additionally, Chuck Owens was a giant of a man, and there were few Makah whalers with the nerve to tackle him face-to-face. More importantly, he knew them and they knew him. He had worked with them in the fishing industry. He also gave a damned good interview.

We had been the organization to initiate this campaign, and we would take the higher profile during it. But I knew that, in the end, it would fall to the Peninsula Citizens for the Protection of Whales to carry on the campaign for as long as the Makah expressed any interest in whaling. They were not going anywhere and this was their home, so they were the group to count on to continue the opposition into the future.

The Port Angeles group was opposed to the whale hunt in principle, and they were especially opposed to having whales slaughtered where they lived.

The fourth group was the West Coast Anti-Whaling Society, based across the strait from Port Angeles in Victoria, British Columbia. It had been organized by Anna Hall, who had at her disposal a small fleet of state-of-the-art inflatable boats from the Victoria whale-watching industry. She was the perfect spokesperson for this campaign in Canada. She looked good on television, and even more important, she knew how to talk to the camera and knew what she was talking about. Anna's group was opposed to the hunt on the grounds that it was illegal, unnecessary, and a direct threat to the interests of the whale-watching industry of which she was a part.

The fifth group was an animal rights group led by Jonathan Paul. He named his group Sea Defense Alliance and gave it the acronym SEDNA, the name of the Inuit goddess of the sea. I was worried that the animal rights philosophy of veganism would serve to alienate the general public into thinking that we were all simply people on the fringe who could not be taken seriously. They were, however, entitled to demonstrate their opposition and their participation, especially in the spring of 1999, when they actually prevented the killing of a whale on two Makah attempts. Jonathan Paul arrived with a boat called the *Auk's Revenge*, with crew members Jake Conroy, Josh Harper, and Chris Manes.

There were two other groups actively opposing the hunt that were not on the front lines but were helping to publicize the hunt overseas. There was BREACH in Great Britain and Australians for Animals in Australia. Both groups were promoting a legal suit against the United States government to block the hunt.

A few more small groups formed as the campaign progressed. In the Path of Giants was a group of two: Heidi Tiura and Steph Dutton. They had been working on a documentary film about whales when the October hunt began and decided to try to convince the Makah tribal council to develop a whale-watching industry as an alternative to killing whales. They also offered to help raise the funding to set up this alternative.

A loose cannon named Bill Moss decided to take a break from his construction business to come to Neah Bay. He volunteered for Sea Shepherd but found he didn't like to follow orders, so he decided to form his own group. He called it the World Whale Police and bought himself a run-down old boat and printed up a supply of T-shirts.

Moss was a wing nut of the first order and gave us all a bad name by cruising around Neah Bay broadcasting on the VHF about "drug-taking and alcoholic Indians" and taking personal shots at specific whalers and journalists. He accused Associated Press reporter Peggy Anderson of sleeping with whaler Wayne Johnson and publicly accused others of everything from child molestation to drug smuggling. Moss was the perfect example of how you can choose your enemies but you can't always choose your allies.

Moss was always verbally assaulting his allies, accusing us of cowardice, egotism, hoarding our funds, and not supporting the little guys like him. He even initiated a lawsuit against In the Path of Giants for using the words "world whale police" without his permission.

At times, I was very tempted to ram and sink his decrepit little troublemaking boat, but that would have just given him a forum, and, for the most part, the media did not give him much credibility.

Toward the end of November, another group arrived called People for the Makah and Whales. This group was formed by former Sea Shepherd director Ben White of Friday Harbor and seemed to be an attempt to support both the whales and the whalers with a Rodney King "can't we all just get along" approach.

In Neah Bay, we could see a small army of media arriving. There were at least four satellite-transmission trucks, and they were lined up near the marina.

We assessed the media bias on the first day of October. The *Seattle Post-Intelligencer* was overtly pro Makah whaling. The *Seattle Times* was more impartial but leaning toward the Makah. The Associated Press reporter out of Seattle was very much pro whaling, while the regional Washington State newspapers were divided between pro whale and pro whaler. We focused on the most important one, the *Peninsula Daily News*, which actually was the most impartial of the lot.

The television stations were better than the newspapers and tended to be more concerned about facts, although the reporter for KIRO-TV just did not seem to get it. Outside of Washington State, the media tended to be pro whale.

Our strategy was to keep the *Sea Shepherd III*, painted with life-sized whales, at anchor, to serve as our floating headquarters and as a base to launch small boat patrols off Makah Bay. The *Sirenian* would serve as the main patrol and pursuit boat and would be the supply boat for the flagship.

On board the *Sea Shepherd III*, captain Matt Lawson was responsible for the security of the ship, and the chief engineer maintained the engineering systems. The *Sea Shepherd III* carried a much larger crew, and they came from all over the world, including Australia, Brazil, Canada, France, Germany, Israel, Italy, and the United Kingdom.

On the morning of October 1, we dispatched a patrol to Makah Bay, where we found assistance from a small fleet of high-speed inflatables—technical marvels that Anna Hall and the West Coast anti-whaling movement had provided. On the water were two small boats from SEDNA, a small boat from PAWS, and another small boat named *Sea Dawg* from the filmmaking research team, In the Path of Giants. There was also the whale-watching vessel *Selkirk* from the Tofino whale-watching community across the way on Vancouver Island and a small boat called the *MeAndHer*, crewed by a dedicated young married couple from Oregon, Bret Siler and Cheryl Rorabeck-Siler. I was confident that, with the number of boats we were deploying in Makah Bay, no whale would die on the first day.

At five in the morning, I pulled the *Sirenian* into Neah Bay and, with a small crew, took a small inflatable ashore to conduct an on-the-beach press conference with the television media. I was well aware that the Makah police had orders to arrest me for trespassing if I set foot on the reservation. On August 25, the tribal council had passed an ordinance making it illegal for anyone actively opposed to whaling to land upon the marina floats or the boat ramp. With the interview completed, we walked down the marina dock to our inflatable when the police spotted us and began to run toward us. We kept walking casually, passing the whaling canoe the *Hummingbird* as we made our way toward our boat. We jumped into our inflatable and pushed away from the dock just as Makah tribal police officer Eric Svenson caught up to us to tell us we were under arrest.

"Sorry, Svenson," I said, "we're not in your jurisdiction anymore. Oh, and by the way, you guys should put some security on that whaling canoe over there."

The entire rest of the day was spent doing interviews with media visiting our ships. The sky was dotted with media and Coast Guard helicopters, and the Coast Guard had brought in some muscle in the form of a number of patrol boats, including some specially trained military help.

We predicted a media circus and by God we now had one. This meant that the campaign had already scored a significant victory. This hunt would not be an out-of-sight, out-of-mind event. The whole damned world would be our witness, and there was no way a commercial whaling operation would be established here in Neah Bay.

The first day of October was indeed a media circus. The media was local, national, and international, and they had every motel from Neah Bay back to Port Angeles booked. We spent most of the day doing interviews, and this included receiving television crews from as far away as China, Australia, Norway, Germany, and Italy.

For all intents and purposes, we had won the first battle. It was a media success. I knew that what the media reported, either positively or negatively, was unimportant. What mattered was that they covered the controversy.

Obviously nervous, the National Marine Fisheries Service boys had told the Makah to pick a migrant whale and not to touch a resident whale. At the interviews on the beach in the early morning, I had stated that this fiasco could not be called a hunt. They were obviously targeting a resident because the migration would not even begin to pass this point until late November. To kill a resident would be as sporting as shooting a puppy dog. These guys actually come to the boats to be petted. I also pointed out that there was nothing traditional about hunting whales with antitank guns, speed boats, government subsidies, and the full support of the United States Coast Guard imposing an exclusionary zone to keep anti-whalers away from the harpoons. In addition, I pointed out that this hunt was not about Neah Bay and the Makah.

"This is about sending a message to Tokyo, Oslo, and Reykjavik," I said. "It's about setting a dangerous precedent of allowing a whale hunt that is not recognized by the International Whaling Commission."

At one point, the Makah whalers issued a report that a dead whale was on the beach at Makah Bay. This was quickly proven false, and I thanked the Makah whalers for the drill and for keeping us on our toes.

The first day was a great one for us, and the support we boasted on the water was encouraging. Tensions were so high that Canadian Coast Guard patrol boats were on alert in case the whale entered Canadian waters. The National Guard had small gunboats stationed at Sekiu just down the coast—reportedly on a routine maneuver.

Norwegian filmmaker Terje Nilsen and his crew came on board to do a scheduled interview for a for Norwegian television profile. We picked him up at Neah Bay and dropped him off hours later at Sekiu. Unbeknownst to us, one of the Makah whalers informed the Coast Guard that we had kidnapped a Norwegian film crew. The FBI and the US State Department were informed. They were preparing to storm my ship by force when it was discovered that the "kidnapped" Norwegians were sitting in a bar at Sekiu. No one had bothered to call us on the radio and inquire about the journalists. It was plain to see that the federal and state authorities were viewing us as hostile right off the bat.

I advised the crew on both of our ships to be careful to not break any regulations. "Let's not give them an excuse to harass us," I said.

Greenpeace USA informed *USA Today* reporter Patrick McMahon that they had no objections to the Makah hunt.

"So why do *you?*" McMahon asked me.

"The difference between Greenpeace and us is that we are not fair-weather whale savers like them. They act when it's politically correct and when they can coordinate their actions with a million-piece direct-mail campaign asking for money. There is a big difference between asking for money to save whales and actually saving them," I answered.

> I have to address the issue of Greenpeace and its atrocious cowardice in not opposing either the hunt or the possibility that the Nuu-chah-nulth Nation may resurrect a hunt of its own.
>
> As the former media spokeswoman for Greenpeace Vancouver, I am utterly appalled at the craven reversal of this formally wonderful organization. And it's all for the wimpy excuse of "political correctness."
>
> Let's hope that the provincial government isn't as cowardly as Greenpeace.
>
> —Beverly Pinnegar, letter to the *Vancouver Sun*, October 16, 1998

Ironically, a few of my old shipmates from the first Greenpeace voyage nearly thirty years before joined my crew at Neah Bay. Bob Hunter, Dr. Lyle Thurston, Rod Marining, and I had all sailed together to protest nuclear testing at Amchitka back in 1971.

During that voyage, we were honored in the tribal longhouse of the Nimpkish Band of the Kwakiutl Nation at Alert Bay. We were presented with a Kwakiutl flag and were made honorary members of the Kwakiutl Nation.

One other original Greenpeace crew member, Patrick Moore, jumped into the fray to criticize us. "The environment must be in pretty good shape, if that's all he can dredge up. Indians killing one whale, is that the worst environmental issue on the planet?" he told the *Ottawa Citizen*.

We were not surprised.

"Good old Pat," said Bob Hunter. "He just never seems to get it."

As Pat was a well-paid lobbyist for the British Columbia forest industry, we chuckled that the *Ottawa Citizen* had described him as an "environmentalist."

"If Mr. Clear-cut can be called an environmentalist, that must make the rest of us environmental saints," said Rod Marining.

I called a meeting to tell the crew that the tough thing for the rest of the month would be to keep the media from getting bored.

"We know that they can't take a migrant until late November," I said, "so we must concentrate on protecting residents. The Makah and the government say they won't take a resident. If this is true, then this is all a charade, and all I hear is Keith Johnson saying they are going to take a whale any day and since the only whale they can take is a resident, that will be where we will focus our attention. In the meantime, we must use our imaginations to create angles for the media to report. The trick is to keep them here for as long as there is a threat to the whales."

I continued. "Perhaps the Makah are just hoping to bore the media so they will go away before the migration."

On October 3, tribal chairman Ben Johnson held a press conference to announce that the whale hunt could happen anytime and his people were unconcerned about the protest boats.

"I'm pretty proud of our people," Ben Johnson said. "We don't get pissed off."

A few hours later, Associated Press reporter Peggy Anderson reported that the whalers had gathered at dawn at the marina to practice. It was obvious she was not there to witness the practice since we had the area under surveillance continuously and we didn't see a whaler anywhere near the marina. Her article detailed how the Makah paddled right past our ships and around to Makah Bay.

Interesting, I thought. *Peggy is either working off Makah press releases or she has been hired on as a propagandist. That canoe has not hit the water since we arrived.*

I was surprised that the media continued to hold on, as each day came and went at Neah Bay without a whale being killed. In fact, the Makah were not even attempting to hunt a whale, although every day they held a press conference and promised that a whale "would be taken very soon, any day now, really, just wait and see."

On October 5, the poster boy for the whalers, Micah McCarty, left the whaling team. He said that he had decided to return to school, where, in his words, "I will be able to support my people by getting an education."

It didn't figure. Micah had spent two and a half years advocating for the return of whaling. He was the only member of the whaling crew who had actually trained and had sought spiritual guidance.

Secrets don't stay secret on reservations long, and it did not take much time to discover that Micah had received a scare on a recent practice exercise when the line attached to the harpoon that he had just thrown into a Steller sea lion became entangled around his ankle. The whalers were using the big marine mammals as practice targets to hone their harpoon skills, and this explained why we had encountered a few sea lion corpses floating about in Makah Bay.

Micah had gotten a close taste of just how dangerous whaling could be, and this reality was all that was needed to send him back to school. Apparently, Micah was also upset that he had not been chosen as the captain of the whaling crew. That position had gone to Eric Johnson, the son of tribal councilwoman Marcy Parker.

Micah's departure was a major blow, since he was the designated harpooner.

On the morning of October 6, the Makah whaling crew was scrambling to recruit and train a new harpooner. The departure of Micah revealed that there were tensions broiling beneath the surface. Traditionally, the whaling crews had been family affairs. The Makah had never before in their history conducted a tribal hunt, and this was causing all sorts of problems in what had always been a caste culture.

In Makah culture, the whaling captain had unquestioned authority. He chose his crew, primarily from his own family. Now, everyone was questioning the whaling captain, and even descendants of slave families had a voice. Traditional Makah whaling, it appeared, had now more to fear from democracy than from anti-whalers.

I could see the whalers self-destructing in the near future. I knew that as long as we could continue to focus on opposing the commercial aspirations and international conservation law that traditional whaling desires would never make it.

These Makah were not their great-grandfathers. They were Americans. Democracy-believing, Christian, capitalistic Americans—three things that the whalers of the eighteenth and nineteenth centuries definitely were not. How could a people so different from their forefathers—

politically, spiritually, and economically—ever recapture the spirit of Aboriginal subsistence whaling?

I knew that they could not and would not do so. But I also knew that they wanted to see the blood of a whale.

I felt that we needed to humanize the whales to help endear them to the public. Whales with names attract sympathy and become celebrities. We just had to look at Keiko to see that people care very much about celebrity whales. We named one of the resident whales Buddy, another Neah, and a third Monica, after President Clinton's girlfriend.

> "The ancient Makah hunted not out of 'cultural or traditional impulse,'" said Watson. "They hunted to survive. The primal equation between survival and the arduous and dangerous hunt gave real meaning to the cultural traditions that arose from life-and-death matters of the time.
>
> "Without that equation," said Watson, "the hunt is an act of make-believe, an empty gesture toward a vanished past with only one component that will have a real, immediate meaning: the violent death of a living creature that has every right to be left alone."
>
> —*Bremerton Sun*, October 5, 1998

By October 7, no attempt to kill a whale had taken place, and in a brilliant public relations move, the Makah decided to host a feast for the media. I could see where this was going. Living among the Makah, eating in their diner, shopping at their stores, living in their motels, the journalists were becoming neighbors with the whalers while we were forced to remain offshore as relatively elusive strangers. The Makah were becoming humanized in the eyes of the journalists, and we were at risk of being dehumanized.

The feast was a tactic to bring the journalists even closer, and a few were won over by their hosts. Four of my crew infiltrated the feast posing as journalists and were nauseated by the open adoration of some of the feted reporters. Almost all of the invited guests partook of bread dipped in seal oil, and our people were looked at suspiciously for declining the grisly treat.

The tribe was actually able to make some money out of the feast, despite having invited everyone as guests. Associated Press reporter Peggy Anderson took it upon herself to pass the hat, and she was able to guilt a substantial accumulation of donations from the seal-oiled fingers of the fourth estate.

As the reporters feasted and the Makah presented traditional dancers for their entertainment, we were busy patrolling the waters, fearing that the banquet may have been planned as a cover for the whalers. Our spies at the party had phoned to tell us that they could not see whaling captain Wayne Johnson there.

It was Bret and Cheryl on the *MeAndHer* who found Wayne. He was on his boat with a German film crew, and he was right beside Buddy near Seal Rock. His boat was sitting by the whale without lights. Bret and Cheryl had been assigned to specifically guard Buddy.

The *Sirenian* raced to Seal Rock from the strait, and the *Sea Shepherd III* dispatched two small boats to head out to aid Buddy. As our boats approached Johnson, the German video crew on board aimed a powerful searchlight to blind them, while Wayne started up his engine to move out. Suddenly, the searchlight probed directly toward the wheelhouse of the *Sirenian*, and our crew in an inflatable saw what looked like a rifle in Wayne's hand. My crew intercepted the whaler's course and forced Johnson to veer off.

Wayne Johnson then headed off toward Neah Bay, two miles to the west, at full speed without running lights. In the darkness, he almost ran down one of our approaching boats from the *Sea Shepherd III*.

We reported to the Coast Guard that the Makah boat had been running at high speeds without running lights. The Coast Guard answered that they had no jurisdiction over the Makah.

The next morning, however, the Makah complained to the Coast Guard that Sea Shepherd had harassed them while they were innocently filming a gray whale. The German film team backed up the Makah in this allegation, which was not surprising, as we learned that the Germans were the Makah's official documentation crew and had received funds from the Makah tribal council toward the making of the film.

There ought to be a better way to heal the Makah's social problems than bringing back the vicious killing of gray whales.

Luckily, a few groups will continue doing all they can to stop them. Members of the Sea Shepherd Conservation Society are walking a fine line with dignity. This group of environmentalists is morally opposed to the Makah whale hunt, and they're not about to sit by quietly.

In a manner that all conservationists should admire, Sea Shepherd is not attacking the Makahs. Instead, the protesters are doing everything they can to keep gray whales away from the harpoons. More power to them.

Sea Shepherd understands the importance of Native American history. The group appreciates the value of tribes to the Pacific Northwest culture.

But in this day and age, the life of a gray whale is more paramount than a symbolic hunt. There are other ways to revive their tribe without hurting innocent whales in the process.

—*Peninsula Daily News*, editorial, October 12, 1998

I was at the helm of the *Sirenian* on the afternoon of October 14. We were in pursuit of a Makah whale-spotting boat, and our ship was rolling and heaving on the swelling North Pacific as we sped through the narrow passage between the rocky shore and the treacherous, jagged-rock reef off Tatoosh Island.

The cell phone rang. I struggled to keep my footing on the heaving deck as I answered it, keeping one eye on our quarry as the whalers attempted to shake us off their trail in the fog-shrouded maze of rocky outcroppings lacing the rugged Washington coastline.

Carla Robinson, our administrator, was calling from our office in California. She was calling to tell me that Cleveland Amory had passed away in his sleep during the night. Putting down the receiver, I hit the throttle and swerved around the point of Tatoosh, hot on the stern of the whalers. As the *Sirenian* continued the chase, I found my eyes getting moist and a feeling of overwhelming sadness came over me. Cleveland Amory was like a father to me. More importantly, if it were not for Cleveland, I would not have been at the helm of my ship on the day he died. I would not have had a ship at all, and there would never have been an organization called the Sea Shepherd Conservation Society.

Cleveland's assistant, Marion Probst, had requested that I give the eulogy at the service, which was scheduled for November 9. I agreed to do so knowing that I would have to leave Neah Bay but confident that my crew could handle things when I would be away.

On October 21, Sea Shepherd posted a $2,000 reward to any person who could provide us with advance warning of the hunt. This sent a ripple through the reservation because there were quite a few people among the Makah who opposed the hunt: they thought it was just a gravy train for the Parker and Johnson families.

On October 23, Michael Kundu's request under the Freedom of Information Act finally was delivered, and he rushed the documents to the *Sea Shepherd III*, where we held a press conference to expose the information. Finally, we were able to produce some hard evidence that the original intent of this hunt was commercial. The Makah attorney, John Arum, had stated flatly that the Makah had never met with any Japanese representatives of the whaling industry and there had never been any discussion about commercial operations. The documents—email correspondence between officials of the National Marine Fisheries Service and notes from a meeting of the NMFS Pacific Scientific Review Group in April 1995—specifically linked the Makah with commercial whaling interests in Japan and Norway. The documents demonstrated that when the Makah initially approached the US fisheries officials in 1995 to seek approval to hunt whales, the discussions included commercial whaling.

A memo dated April 27, 1995, to Michael Tillman, the deputy US commissioner to the International Whaling Commission, from a National Marine Fisheries Service staff member, under the heading "Notes from the discussion of treaty rights during the April 1995 Pacific Scientific Review Group," states the following:

> The Makah intend to harvest gray whales, harbor seals, California sea lions, minke whales, small cetaceans such as harbor porpoise and Dall's porpoise, and, potentially in the future, sea otters. The Makah are planning to operate a processing plant so as to sell to markets outside the US. The Makah have started discussions with Japan and Norway about selling their whale products to both countries. The plant could be used to process the catches of other tribes as well.

According to an internal email from the National Oceanic and Atmospheric Administration (NOAA), Makah tribal attorney John Arum met with NOAA's Secretary of Commerce Ronald Brown in March 1995 to inquire about obtaining a whaling permit for the tribe to pursue commercial whaling.

> Maggie informed me that Arum had told her that Japanese interests had approached the Makahs about selling whale meat to them. So I wasn't surprised that he asked me generally about commercial sale.

I was able to tell the media that the documents vindicated what we had been saying all along—that the hunt was initiated for commercial purposes:

> They have been denying that there was any question about commercial whaling. This first hunt may well be that—cultural. But down the

road, it's commercial. The documents even state there were negotiations with the Japanese, and this the Makah have firmly denied and
have accused us of lying when we have mentioned it. I think these
official documents prove that the liars are the whalers, not us.

Attorney John Arum and Denise Dailey, the director of the Makah
Whaling Commission, backpedaled furiously but admitted to the media
that, yes, there were early discussions with the Japanese and there was
some talk about commercial possibilities, but that idea died in 1995.

"This is not a commercial hunt," said Dailey. "But the 1855 treaty
says we have the right to whale commercially, and that means that
commercial whaling is an option for the future."

We had gotten them to admit that they not only had discussed the
commercial possibilities but also were still contemplating them. We
considered the day a major victory for our side and for exposing the
truth behind this hunt.

On October 24, another federal agency decided to take up arms
against Sea Shepherd. We already had a hostile Coast Guard and a suspicious FBI monitoring our every movement. This time when I took the
Sirenian into Port Angeles to refuel, I was ordered to appear at the Port
Angeles customs office.

I had cleared US Customs for Neah Bay from Seattle and had
done everything that was required for reporting. Jerry Slaminski, the
head honcho for customs in Port Angeles, decided to throw his weight
around. Being head of customs in Port Angeles is like being the head
of the border patrol in Tennessee. In other words, you don't see a hell
of a lot of action.

Slaminski wanted to get involved, and so he decided that my two
ships were not actually registered as yachts, despite our registration
papers from Belize and Canada that stated that we were. "No," said
Slaminski. "Yachts are for pleasure, and protesting is not a plea-
surable activity. Thus you are commercial, and as such you will be
required to pay commercial fees to be in our waters. In fact, you will
be required to pay these fees each and every time to come ashore for
supplies or to refuel. That will be $850 for the *Sea Shepherd* and $200
for the *Sirenian*. Cash only. We don't take checks."

I protested that I had been operating my vessels in US waters
since 1979 and not once had I ever heard that we had to pay commercial fees. I asked Slaminski why this had never come up before. He

replied, "I guess any other customs officer you have talked to over the years did not know the law. I, on the other hand, do know the regulations and this is your requirement. You will pay this fee by the end of the day or I will have your ships arrested."

I looked at Slaminski. "You call this whatever you like. I call it harassment. We will meet your demands and we will take this to court."

"You do whatever you think you must, but you will pay this fee today," he said.

As I walked out his door to go to the bank, I said to him, "You know I deal with this shit in Mexico, Kenya, and Brazil, but this is the first time that I've had to deal with this in the United States."

"Just what are you referring to?" responded Slaminski. "Are you accusing me of extorting this money from you, because if you are, I . . ."

"No, not at all," I said, then smiled. "I was just referring to the overwhelming stench of bananas in this room."

I shut the door, went to the bank, and then called the media and accused Slaminski of harassment.

Slaminski wasn't talking to the media. "I think I'd prefer not to comment," was his only answer to reporters' calls.

I referred the matter to our lawyer, and we found out later that Slaminski was not acting within the regulations; he was interpreting them to serve his political views.

I could not help but admire the US Customs Service for allowing Slaminski to rise to the level of his competence and predicted that he would retire before he ever saw promotion to any port of entry more significant than Port Angeles. Just another hurdle in the race to out-maneuver the bureaucrats.

> The Sea Shepherd is out in Neah Bay doing OUR job for US, and we are throwing every loophole known to man at their feet. The last straw was the "reclassification" of their vessels to commercial! What great mind in our customs office thought this one up?
>
> We must support the Sea Shepherd in its efforts to protect these gentle giants of the sea, who grace us with their presence as they migrate.
> —Sandra Tiller, letter to the *Peninsula Daily News*,
> November 3, 1998

On October 30, the US Coast Guard received permission from Belize to conduct a boarding inspection of the *Sea Shepherd III*. They were unable to get permission from Canada to board the *Sirenian*.

No defects or problems were found, but the Coast Guard was researching angles and asked for our manning certificate. I informed them that a Belize-registered yacht did not require a manning certificate. The Coast Guard contacted Belize and came back and stated that they had convinced Belize that a manning certificate was necessary. In response, I contacted Belize and was promptly informed that a manning certificate could be issued for a consideration of $10,000 to the proper officials. When I told the Belize shipping master, Richard Haas, that I had been assured upon registry that a manning certificate was not required, he responded arrogantly by saying, "It is now."

The problem with a manning certificate was that it would have forced me to hire a completely professional crew, and there was no way we could have afforded that. We were promptly informed by the Coast Guard that until the manning certificate was acquired, the *Sea Shepherd III* would not be permitted to move from Neah Bay.

On Halloween day, the people from Port Angeles set up a roadblock at the border to the reservation, and there was a hostile exchange of accusations and name-calling. I brought the *Sirenian* into the marina at the same time as the roadblock, and we played whale songs as we attracted a small crowd of Makah, who screamed obscenities and shouted what I considered to be racist comments at us. One Makah shouted up to us from the dock and asked why we weren't saving the president.

"The president is in trouble for having sex with a whale. Why don't you go help the president."

Turning to one of my crew, I said, "What the hell does that mean?"

He laughed. "The hell if I know."

Another Makah, a teenage girl yelled, "You don't have whales on board. Those aren't real whales. That's a tape-recording."

Dinah Elissat laughed and shouted back at her, "Duh!"

I told my crew to not rise to the bait and to not return insults. That's when a Seattle television reporter pointed his microphone at us and asked one of the most asinine questions of the entire campaign: "Did the whales tell you that they wanted you to be here?"

That I could not ignore, and I turned on the *Sirenian*'s loudspeakers and made one comment. "Just because you were born stupid doesn't give you any right to remain stupid. What the hell do you think?"

In her article in the *Seattle Times* the next day, Lynda Mapes quoted me completely out of context. She had it appear as though

I had made the comment to the Makah. Considering the two really stupid comments from the two Makah, I probably would have been justified in addressing it to them, but the fact was, I addressed the comment to the reporter.

It was inevitable that the rising tensions on both sides would burst the bounds of patience. After a month of whalers and anti-whalers firing shots at each other through the media and glaring at each other across the waters of Neah Bay, something was bound to snap. And snap it did on Sunday, November 1, 1998.

It started out like the four Sundays before it. The different groups would pull their vessels into the marina for a few hours of showing the flag, playing whale sounds and music, and shouting anti-whaling slogans. The *Sea Shepherd III* stayed at anchor as I brought the *Sirenian* into the inner harbor. We were followed in by three Prince of Whales Zodiacs, the SEDNA boat *Bulletproof*, numerous small boats, and a large whale-watching boat from Victoria.

As we had done every weekend, we began to play whale songs. And, as usual, many Makah protestors began to shout insults and obscenities. This time, however, the mood was different. It started with one kid throwing a rock, then another, and then another. When it became obvious that the tribal police had no intention of stopping the rock throwing, it all began to escalate. Slingshots were brought out, more rock throwers began to join, and it did not take long before all hell broke loose.

I radioed the *Sea Shepherd III* and asked Matt to bring her into the harbor with all her water guns on full force. I then pushed the *Sirenian* closer to the shore, and the protestors and issued helmets to my crew along with instructions to not respond to the rock throwers and to ignore them.

Peter Brown and Dinah Elissat were in an inflatable between us and the shore, and Peter was piloting for a reporter and a photographer amid a hail of rocks, all of which miraculously failed to hit him or his passengers. They failed to hit him even after he took to bowing before them and taunting them by turning his back to them and daring them to hit him. From the wheelhouse of the *Sirenian*, I could see the splashes erupt all around his boat as he cruised nonchalantly through the attack.

The *Sea Shepherd III* roused a chorus of cheers from all the whale supporters as she cruised outside the breakwater, radiating rainbows from the mist raised by her numerous spouting water cannons. Into the harbor came Matt Lawson, at the controls of our large inflatable. With him was Lorena Brooks.

I had spotted Alberta Thompson on the ramp above the marina and told Lorena that this would be an opportune time for her to escalate this situation by going ashore to support Alberta. Matt and Lorena, along with Janet Cook as the photographer, moved toward the dock, dodging the rocks.

Lorena stepped onto the dock as Alberta welcomed her and began to walk toward the courageous Makah elder. Suddenly, Dan Greene violently shoved her off the dock and into the water as the crowd of Makahs erupted in laughter and war whoops. Lorena ignored the taunts and walked defiantly up to the shore where tribal policeman Eric Svenson grabbed and handcuffed her. He then pulled her by the hair and pushed her into a tribal police car.

In the confusion, Matt had come too close to the dock, and a Makah grabbed his inflatable and pulled it to the boat ramp as others reached out and violently wrested Janet's camera from her hands, practically strangling her with the camera strap in the process. Both Matt and Janet were physically dragged from the boat by the mob and hauled to the tribal police, who handcuffed them and bullied them into the patrol cars.

Matt Lawson loudly protested to the police as they pushed him into the car. "I didn't willingly come ashore. My boat was pulled."

With the outboard still running, the Makah mob pulled the inflatable from the water and up the boat ramp as the US Coast Guard stood by and refused to intervene. Refused, that is, until Bret Siler, in frustration at the violence against the Sea Shepherd crew, drove his Jet Ski toward the dock and, in a quick turn, sprayed a cascade of water over the Makah on the dock, leaving Dan Greene as soaked as his victim. The Coast Guard quickly ran Siler down and arrested him for reckless operation of a watercraft.

"You'll never see this Jet Ski again, boy," yelled the Coast Guard officer. "You're fucking busted."

Peter Brown, in an attempt to avoid the mob grabbing his boat, gunned his outboard and backed away from the chaos. He was stopped by commander Bob Coster himself, and as rocks fell around both Peter and Coster, Peter was warned that he had exceeded the speed limit for the marina.

"For Christ's sake, man, I was trying to avoid being hit with stones and having my boat seized."

Coster responded with a sneer. "There is never any excuse for exceeding the speed limit in this marina."

As this exchange took place, Wayne Johnson and Don Swan in the background jumped into the captured inflatable and hoisted a Makah Nation flag as the Makah crowd cheered. Tribal member Joe McGimpsey began to sing a Makah victory song through a megaphone.

He shouted out toward us. "You came to war, and we beat you. And you went away in tears."

I responded on the ship's loudspeaker, "You make war on women, attacking them from behind, and you call yourselves warriors. No one is crying here."

"Show respect, white man," yelled McGimpsey.

"We respect the right of the whales to live," I replied. "You should respect the same thing."

On the dock, a young Makah wearing a hood and looking like the Unibomber was giving me a finger and screaming, "Fuck you, white boy."

I couldn't help but recall Ben Johnson's arrogant boast a month before: "I'm proud of my people. They don't get pissed off."

Will Ben still be proud tomorrow? I wondered.

As the rocks continued to strike our ship, I invited reporters on the nearby media boat aboard for a press conference. They assembled on the aft deck, and as I began to address them a round of rocks came in, one of which struck the Associated Press photographer Jacob Henifin on the ankle.

"I don't think there is anything more to be said," I commented. "You can see for yourself that this violence is one-sided."

As the reporters left the boat, Peter Brown returned to the *Sirenian.* "It looks like they are winning the day," he said as he stepped on board.

"So it seems," I answered. "But we're not going to let them think they can take one of our boats without any response from us."

For the last hour, Ken Nichols had been requesting that I send him ashore. Ken was nothing if not a hardcore whale defender, and he was ready to do whatever he could to stop the hunt, including martyring himself.

"OK, Ken, you've got your request," I said. "Go ashore and ask for our property back. We need a dog soldier here."

Ken, wearing his survival suit, eagerly jumped into the inflatable, and Peter ran him right up the boat ramp, where Ken leaped deftly onto the shore.

As Peter backed the inflatable off the ramp in time to avoid it being seized, Ken boldly walked up to Eric Svenson and demanded our boat. Svenson immediately grabbed Ken by the neck and wrestled him to the ground; two additional tribal officers ran up and assisted him. While the crowd cheered and Ken continued to demand our boat, the officers slammed Ken's face against the concrete ramp and split his forehead. When the tribal police grabbed him by the hair and pulled him to his feet, the cameras caught Ken's bleeding, defiant face before he was brutally thrown into the back of a patrol car.

Looking through the binoculars, I was satisfied. "We've got our image. There's tomorrow's front-page photograph, by God, or I don't know the media."

And sure enough, it was Ken's face that led the evening news and adorned the papers in color the next day, not just in Seattle but around the world.

We had lost one inflatable, suffered some minimal rock damage to the *Sirenian*, and had four of our people arrested. In exchange, we won the battle of November 1, 1998, because we took the images and we had demonstrated a courageous but nonviolent stance against violent attackers.

As Peter stepped on board the ship, I smiled. "Hey, brother, this is a wrap. I think it's Miller time. What about you?"

After we withdrew from the marina, I went ashore and picked up our four arrested crew members at the Cost Guard station. They had not been charged. We did, however, request that charges be brought against Eric Svenson for assault and filed the complaint with the Clallam County sheriffs present at the station.

Ken Nichols was all smiles, although he still had blood running down his face. We also saw Alberta Thompson at the Coast Guard station, where she had fled after police chief Lionel Ahdunko had threatened to have her arrested for inciting a riot. She was being supported by half a dozen tribal elders.

"I invited Lorena ashore, and it is my right to do so," she said to reporters. "These people are my friends because they are protecting the whales."

Ironically, after the day of receiving barrage after barrage of rocks, we retired to Sekiu for the evening to assess the damage and to find that Alex Tizon had written a full-page profile of me for the *Seattle Times* that was amusingly titled, "My job is to rock the boat?"

Finally, a reporter had made an attempt to put forth our side of the story and to inject some balance into the controversy:

> Watson's single-minded goal is to protect the whale, using whatever means necessary.
>
> Not surprisingly, Watson is anathema around here (Neah Bay), as popular as smallpox. Some tribe members have publicly called him anti-Indian and the Makah's Custer, a charge that flies in the face of his history.
>
> For two decades, he has been an equal-opportunity activist, going to war against whalers and fishers of all races and nationalities, making a lot of people mad in the process but also saving a few whales and fish.
>
> "I'm not here to win popularity contests," he says. "My job is to say things people don't want to hear and to do things people don't want to do. My job is to rock the boat, sometimes to sink the boat."
>
> A major report released last week by the National Academy of Sciences warning of a collapse of global fish populations was to Watson an affirmation of his twenty-two-year crusade to save marine life. He has been saying this all along. Maybe the most affirming part of the report was its call for "radical changes in attitudes and practice."
>
> For good or bad, radicalness has been a standard part of his MO.

Tizon also addressed my commitment to Native American causes.

> It (the hunt) has also put Watson in an awkward situation. A lifelong advocate of Native American rights, he now finds himself at odds with a tribe whose general objective—cultural renewal—he normally would support.
>
> But on the issue of whaling, he is uncompromising. "It would be racist of me to treat the Makah any differently just because they're Indian," Watson says. "We can't discriminate in our interventions."
>
> Watson insists that the Makah hunt is illegal because it hasn't been officially sanctioned by the International Whaling Commission. The US government has sided with the Makah, and as such, Watson is the underdog in this fight, a role he's not unaccustomed to.
>
> "I don't care what people think of me," he says. "We'll be judged by history. Five hundred years from now, we'll be judged, and they will know who was on the right side."

The *Peninsula Daily News* ran a full-page ad by the Makah tribal council the same day. I was gratified to see that half of the ad was devoted to attacking me personally and calling me a terrorist.

STOP ECOTERRORISM ON THE OLYMPIC PENINSULA!
It's Neah Bay today, Olympic timber towns tomorrow.

I wish, I thought. I had no problem with shutting down timber towns.

The ad came complete with a coupon asking people to send money to support Makah whaling and stated that it was tax deductible.

"Interesting," I said to Allison Lance, one of our crew. "Killing whales is now a tax-deductible charitable activity."

On November 2, tribal chairman Ben Johnson held a press conference to accuse Ken Nichols of deliberately slamming his own face into the boat ramp. This did not wash with the reporters who actually saw Svenson slam Ken's face into the ground. Johnson was sticking to his story and even accused Sea Shepherd of being the cause of the violence.

"It's a sad thing that's happened," Johnson said. "Sea Shepherd has been pushing our buttons. People can only take so much."

The journalistic slant swung back and forth like a pendulum, with articles appearing to place us in a good light immediately followed by articles and reports accentuating the negative.

Two days after Alex Tizon's positive feature, the *Seattle Times* felt compelled to knock me back down with a cynical column by Eric Lacitis in which he called me a stuntman and accused me of staging and manipulating the entire Neah Bay riot.

The *Seattle Weekly* picked up the Lynda Mapes out-of-context quote and ran a column by some left-winger equating saving whales to the rise of Euro-imperialistic racist fascism. Suddenly I found that I supposedly said that all Indians were stupid.

Ah, the media—able to fabricate facts to fit the desired editorial slant. The *Weekly* defended its position by citing the source for the quote as Lynda Mapes, as if it should be automatically assumed that a reporter is infallible and objective.

It was all fine with me, of course. I am well aware that reality is devoured, digested, regurgitated, and defecated by media. The trick is to let the media loose on an issue like a pack of rabid dogs on a bloodied lamb. As they dramatically rip and tear gory sanguine chunks from the defenseless, screaming carcass, all the noise and violence certainly attracts attention. After digestion, all the juicy tidbits of the story eventually become just lumpy piles of smelly manure, to be sniffed and picked over by tabloids and columnists. However, spread out through as much diverse media as possible, the accumulation serves to fertilize the cause.

Lacitis had called me a media manipulator, as if this was a revelation. Of course I'm a media manipulator, although I prefer to think of myself as a farmer spreading media manure to grow ideas and stimulate controversy. What Lacitis called "manipulating," I simply call "media strategy."

I was delighted. All news is good news, and the more column inches the *Seattle Times* provided for the issue was just fine with me. The tone of the content was unimportant as long as the fires of controversy over the issue were continuously stoked.

Unable to pursue charges against my crew or the other protestors, Makah police chief Lionel Ahdunko set his sights on nailing Alberta Thompson. He accused the seventy-four-year-old grandmother of inciting the violence and informed the media that the tribe was considering pressing charges against her. Ahdunko requested that Makah tribal prosecutor Iris Shue investigate the Makah elder and bring formal charges against her.

The tribal council had spent two days discussing what should be done with Alberta Thompson. Talk included options ranging from fining her to restricting her activities and her freedom to express herself to outright banishment from the reservation. The council was unable to come to any agreement. Ben Johnson was actually relieved to have the matter turned over to the tribal prosecutor.

"The matter will now go through our court system," he informed the media. "It's completely out of the council's hands."

Ahdunko boasted to the media that possible charges against Alberta Thompson could include her getting a year in prison and/or a $5,000 fine. "Banishment from the tribe is another option," he added.

In the meantime, Alberta had become the object of a hate campaign among a few lawless juveniles on the reservation. Her car was vandalized, the windows of her house were broken, her grandchildren were ridiculed, and one grandson was beaten up. Tragically, her dog was shot and killed. Alberta fled the reservation and was given temporary sanctuary in California by supporters.

When asked if she would answer to charges by the tribal council, her lawyer, Helga Kahr, replied, "I'm not going to turn a seventy-four-year-old grandmother over to those thugs. I saw what they did."

We had a responsibility to Alberta Thompson to protect her, and it occurred to us that the best strategy would be to go for her attacker and to neutralize him.

"There's something not right about Ahdunko," I said. "Let's see what dirt we can find on him."

It did not take long. We put the word out, and feedback started to come back immediately—from Nevada. Apparently the Makah tribal police chief was not a Makah himself. He was Navajo and had previously been the tribal police chief on the Washoe reservation near Reno, Nevada. The calls we received from Nevada made it clear that Lionel Ahdunko had a very shady past. Accusations ranged from police brutality to theft of tribal and government property to perjury.

Armed with documents obtained from Nevada, we called a joint press conference at Sekiu on November 5 with Republican congressman Jack Metcalf. We revealed that there was an outstanding warrant for Chief Ahdunko for perjury. We also revealed that he had a previous felony conviction for perjury in a murder trial, and we questioned how the Bureau of Indian Affairs could allow a convicted felon to carry a firearm and preside as a chief of police.

With Ahdunko on the defensive, Alberta Thompson was free to return home. Amid the growing Ahdunko scandal, it was clear that the tribe would not pursue charges against Alberta based on the recommendations of a man who was now himself a target of the law.

We also went on the legal offensive by filing charges against Svenson for assaulting Ken Nichols and Lorena Brooks and filing a complaint with the FBI for civil rights violations by the Makah against our four crew who were illegally arrested by the Makah police.

FBI special agent in charge, Charles Mandingo, told the media, "The FBI is looking at all the events that occurred to determine if there is jurisdiction for the FBI to become involved."

Assistant US Attorney Susan Roe, an expert on Indian law, informed the media that tribes did not have criminal jurisdiction over non-Indians. "Tribal police may escort non-Indians to the reservation boundary," said Roe. "They may hold them for a limited time until non-tribal law enforcement arrives."

On November 5, Jean-Michel Cousteau arrived to bring his eco-celebrity status to bear on the controversy. Initially, I was delighted to have his involvement. There was no question that the Cousteau name carried influence.

Unfortunately, Jean-Michel came off as so wishy-washy on the issue that when he left, no one really could figure just what his position was.

"I don't believe that killing is a necessity," Cousteau said to the media. "Their culture can grow bigger by not killing it. But if they decide to go forth with it, so be it. There is nothing we can do. Their rights cannot be questioned."

He hurt us by stating that the Makah's right to hunt whales was "unquestionable," thereby displaying his ignorance of the "questions" posed by the rules of the IWC governing Aboriginal whaling. Of course, their "rights" could be questioned. That was the whole point of us all being in Neah Bay—to question these "rights."

He then suggested that the Makah hold a symbolic hunt, as if this idea was novel. The Makah had repeatedly rejected a ritualized hunt. Prior to coming to Neah Bay, Cousteau had informed us that he would be visiting the *Sea Shepherd III*. He cancelled the visit because he did not wish to have the Makah think he was in league with us and our opposition to the hunt.

Unfortunately for him and his followers, they decided to have dinner that evening in Sekiu. Since The Breakers was the only decent restaurant in town, he walked right into our dinner party with Jack Metcalf and could not courteously refuse to pose for pictures with us and the congressman. We, of course, used these pictures to present the image of Jean-Michel Cousteau as indeed seeming to agree with us.

Our campaign against Ahdunko was paying off. On November 8, just a week after he was strutting his power over Alberta Thompson and us at Neah Bay, Ahdunko informed the media that he would be surrendering himself to US marshals to face two felony charges of lying to a Nevada court to cover up a traffic accident. Ben Johnson responded to the charges by stating that the tribal council would stand behind Ahdunko and admitting that the council had been aware of Ahdunko's activities at Washoe and the serious allegations made against him. Ahdunko protested that the charges were politically motivated by Sea Shepherd.

That same day, I slipped away from Neah Bay and drove to Seattle to catch a plane for New York City, where I gave the eulogy for Cleveland Amory at the Cathedral of St. John the Divine. I left Peter Brown in charge, and he was able to present the illusion that I was still on board for a few days before the Makah finally realized that I had gone. During that time, Peter had arranged to fly Gitxsan hereditary chief Wii Seeks and tribal chairman Gordon Sebastian to Neah Bay to meet with the Makah. Peter carried them ashore in a fishing boat belonging to one of our supporters and into the Neah Bay marina to meet with the tribal council. They were met by Eric Svenson along with four tribal policemen. In the background stood Ahdunko, sucking on a tootsie pop like he was Kojak.

"You people are not allowed to land here at this marina," Svenson said angrily.

"What people are you referring to?" asked Peter.

"You people," Svenson said.

"What people are we, Svenson?" Peter asked again.

"You people."

So we decided to call our crew the "U People tribe." Dinah Elissat even had an Indian design of a whale tattooed on her wrist with the words "U People" beneath it. We had been officially designated the "U People" by a Swede wearing the uniform of a Makah tribal cop.

After a bit of verbal skirmishing and calls to the tribal council, the decision to allow Wii Seeks and Gordon Sebastian to land was made. Peter was told that he could only join them by going twenty miles back by boat to Sekiu, and he would be allowed to drive into the reservation. This he did, and they met with the tribal council so that Wii Seeks and Gordon Sebastian could speak with them. He requested that they not kill the whale and reminded them that I had helped the Gitxsan Nation when I had provided my ship to help intercept the Columbus ships off Puerto Rico in 1991.

"Sea Shepherd is an honorable organization," said Wii Seeks. "Their opposition is not motivated by racism. They are motivated by compassion."

The council received Wii Seeks and Gordon Sebastian with respect but repeated that they intended to kill a whale. After the meeting, Gordon told reporters that he was not convinced that the tribe's interest in whaling was rooted in spirituality.

"There's a lot of evidence about commercial goals in the future," he said.

After the meeting, Peter talked with Makah tribal chair Ben Johnson.

"Perhaps with Watson gone, we will do it tomorrow," said Johnson.

Peter looked at Johnson. "Look, I'm running this boat, and I've got nothing to lose. You don't want to start this fight while Paul is not here. Paul said not to kill a whale. Not on my watch. Paul told me to make sure a whale was not killed, and damn it, I intend to make sure that a whale is not killed. If I were you, I would wait for Paul to return. He's more reasonable than me. I'll run the *Sirenian* right through your canoe if you try to kill a whale."

Ben laughed nervously. "I hope you'll rescue me afterward."

Peter looked at him seriously. "My job is to rescue the whale, not you," he said and then laughed. "Besides, you're not ready to kill a whale anyhow. We all know that."

As the meeting between our Gitxsan friends and the Makah ended, a helicopter descended onto the field in the tribal center compound. Sea Shepherd director Carroll Vogel emerged, followed by Bob Ratliffe, the top aide to billionaire Craig McCaw. They were accompanied by Charles Vinick of the Ocean Futures Society. The meeting was supposed to have been kept quiet at the request of the Makah tribal council.

The reporters did not see who landed in the helicopter, nor did they see who entered the building. Their interest piqued considerably when a council member came outside and announced who was in the meeting. Ratliffe told me later that this made it look like he was the one who wanted to keep things quiet, when what he had been doing was honoring a request by the Makah to keep the meeting secret.

After the not-so-secret meeting was over, Ratliffe addressed the media, saying, "There's the perception that the tribal leaders are intractable, but they also are concerned about their future. They say they need economic gain, but where is the money in hunting whales? The words and music don't seem to go together. We're trying to see if there's any middle ground between two firm positions. And there are two men—McCaw and Jean-Michel Cousteau—who would rather not take the life of a whale. We threw out some ideas, maybe naively but innocently, concerning ecotourism."

After the meeting, chief Wii Seeks and Gordon Sebastian hitched a ride back to Seattle in Craig McCaw's helicopter.

The Makah announced that they were not interested in developing an ecotourism industry. "Our treaty is not for sale," stated tribal chairman Ben Johnson.

Keith Johnson, however, stated that the tribe might agree to "suspend" the hunt for, say, about $350 million dollars. Ben Johnson said that for $350 million dollars, they would do "some serious considering."

When KOMO-TV reporter Tracy Vedder first came to Neah Bay to cover the story, she probably never thought she'd still be there forty-five days later. But she had little choice. The three major networks were all spending hundreds of thousands of dollars waiting for a whale hunt that never seemed to happen but promised to happen, well, like tomorrow. But tomorrow turned into tomorrow until every day was another day to wait for another tomorrow.

One thing was certain: none of the three networks wanted to pull out first. The competition factor was at work, and they were all scheming and manipulating in Neah Bay to be the first to capture the harpoon throw and transform it into national news.

"We're sort of trapped," a Seattle news director said. "It's been way more expensive than it's worth so far. All these false starts are eating up our resources."

AP reporter Peggy Anderson left the reservation only four times in six weeks, and she didn't go far.

"I'm just sure that the minute I leave, it's going to happen."

Every day the Makah held a press briefing, and every day they presented a new excuse for not going whaling. On the days when weather could not be used as an excuse, problems with outboards or problems with batteries surfaced.

One morning, Ben Johnson announced, "Three of the crew have *E. coli* poisoning."

The next morning, he announced, "Wayne Johnson has a court date in Port Angeles."

"They're playing games with us," said Vancouver-based filmmaker George Tumpach.

The truth was they were trying to save face. Feuds were developing over the use of family songs and over some families wielding more power than others. This was the first time there had ever been an attempted tribal hunt, and things were not going smoothly.

One issue was whether hunters from one branch of a family had the right to sing a song that comes from another branch of the family without first getting permission from elder Helma Ward, the Swan family matriarch.

Dr. Ann Renker, a linguistic anthropologist studying the Makah culture, told reporter Paul Shukovsky, "If someone expresses a profound disrespect by crossing the property line and singing another family's song, you wonder whether you can trust them again."

On November 17, the Makah held nominations for the tribal council. Marcy Parker was soundly defeated in her bid for a second term on the council. This was a very telling decision. Marcy had been the strongest advocate for whaling, and her son Eric was the captain of the whaling crew. She drew only 33 votes of a turnout of 185 of the 613 eligible Makah voters.

The reason for this was best explained by tribal member John McCarty. "This started out that the twenty-three families would take the whale," McCarty told reporters. "Then it got sidetracked to one family, Marcy and her family. It's not a tribal hunt—it's Marcy's hunt."

For two months we had been joking that this was not a Makah hunt at all but rather a hunt by the Johnson and Johnson Whaling Company. Many of the Makah tribal members were beginning to agree. Marcy Parker was the mother of Eric Johnson, the whaling captain. Wayne Johnson was the gunner. Keith Johnson was the head of the Makah Whaling Commission, and his father, Bender Johnson, was the tribal chairman.

It did not help when a Seattle television station aired a story about how the tribal council did not believe that dissent from within the tribe was valid because the dissenters came from slave families, and descendants of slaves had no right to condemn the objectives of prominent whaling families. This accusation was a lie. Alberta Thompson and the other elders opposing the hunt were not from slave families, but even if they were, this kind of rhetoric was scary when it came from people intent on reviving traditions of the past. Would the caste system be brought to the fore once again if whaling was revived?

On November 18, I was invited on board a Coast Guard cutter for a meeting with Commander Kaetzel and US attorney Kate Pflaumer. They asked if we would consider pulling our ships out of Neah Bay.

I smiled at Commander Kaetzel. "I don't think I can pull the *Sea Shepherd* out because the Coast Guard is demanding a manning certificate and I don't have one, and until I do, I've been ordered to not leave Neah Bay."

The commander said that he could arrange for us to be given permission to leave.

"I'm sure you can, since you made sure that we couldn't."

Kate Pflaumer explained that the government was concerned about the potential for violence.

"Not from us," I interjected.

"Tensions are rising, the weather is getting rougher. We would like to request that you consider leaving."

By this time, I was convinced that there would not be a whale hunt in 1998. There were rifts within the whaling crew and schisms within the tribe. The time was ripe for us to pull out to allow those internal divisions to evolve without having us available as opposition. We needed a cover to withdraw, and I decided to offer the Makah tribal council a deal they could accept without losing face: agree to meet with us and we would pull our ships from Neah Bay.

I told Kate Pflaumer that we would consent to leave if she could arrange a meeting between the Makah tribal council and us. She said that she could do that.

"Good," I said. "But we will be back in the spring."

The Makah tribal council met us for a lunch hosted by the Coast Guard station at Neah Bay. I did not think much would be accomplished at the meeting. We stated our position, which they already were aware of, and they stated their intention to go whaling. The meeting did serve to demonstrate that we were reasonable and that we were seeking a solution to the conflict.

In truth, I did not wish to waste any more time on a hunt that was not going to happen until the next spring at least. We had already achieved the objective of assuring that a commercial hunt would not develop in Neah Bay. There was little more that we could do until the Makah made some effort to go whaling.

By December, it was looking as though we could not satisfy the relentlessly hostile Seattle media. After two months of editorials telling us to leave Neah Bay, Alex Tizon wrote an article saying that we had given up. He said that I had yawned and had enough. Alex never bothered to call me to verify that statement. He decided to opt for the Peggy Anderson school of journalism and make it up. He was not about to let me spoil his story with facts.

The truth was that we left Neah Bay when we realized without a doubt that no whale would be killed in 1998. In response to his article, I wrote a letter to Tizon in which I told him that he and the other journalists were like compulsive gamblers who could not bear to leave the table without the blood-and-guts story. We, on the other hand, were quite content to leave without a whale dying. I told him that I would guarantee that a whale would not die in December, and we were sorry to spoil the ongoing cowboy-and-Indian drama that the media had concocted, but there simply was no tactical reason for us to remain on station.

The Tizon story was full of the usual pseudo-romantic nonsense. At one point he wrote, "They've lived here a long time. This is home to them in a way that we'll never know. I would guess that a people who've lived in one place for ten thousand years know how to wait for the right time."

Now, the oldest Makah person might have passed the century mark, but I am certain that not a one has ever made it to two centuries, let alone a century of centuries. Besides, if Alex had done his homework, he would have found that the Nootka-speaking Makah had stolen the land after invading it from across the water from Comox (Vancouver Island). They had brought the vice of whaling with them to the peninsula.

Tizon did admit in his article that he did not have the fortitude for research. He wrote:

> In the end of *Moby Dick*, Herman Melville's epic tale of obsession on the high seas, the peg-legged Captain Ahab finally gets his white whale, and in the process, the whale gets him. I know this because I watched the movie. I couldn't get through the book. It was too ponderous for my late twentieth-century sensibility.

Later in the article he posed as the great authority on American literature by comparing the Makah to Ishmael and myself to Captain Ahab. There's no point in studying American literature; apparently modern journalism allows for the writer to just make it up as he or she goes along.

On March 3, 1999, the Clallam County prosecutor's office indicted Makah tribal police officer Eric Svenson on two counts of fourth-degree assault, accusing him of excessive force and overstepping his authority.

CHAPTER

The Death of Yabis

MAKAH BAY, MAY 1999

ll through the winter we kept in close contact with Binki Thompson and many of the other elders. We knew that the desire to kill a whale among the whalers was still strong, and they were more determined than ever to begin the hunt in the spring.

We also knew that there was a great deal of strife and disagreement among the whaling crew, especially between Wayne Johnson and Theron Parker. The tribe had decided to replace Wayne with Theron as captain of the whaling crew. Wayne was reassigned to a support boat. There was a real concern about Wayne due to his anger-management issues.

It was the beginning of the month of May and the pressure was on. The whalers wanted their whale.

Philanthropist Susan Bloom had made a gift to Jonathan Paul for the funds needed to purchase a fast boat to replace the inadequate *Auk's Revenge* from the last season. He found and purchased a jet boat called *Bulletproof*.

I was in Friday Harbor with the *Sirenian*, waiting for word from the elders in Neah Bay. As we left Friday Harbor, the *Bulletproof* was standing guard for the whales at Neah Bay. Jonathan Paul and his crew with SEDNA (Sea Defense Alliance) were ready when the whalers set out in the early morning hours on a practice run. Whaler Wayne Johnson had been left behind at the dock, and he was not happy.

The whaling canoe *Hummingbird* and the whaler support boats came upon a whale, and their crews made the decision to take advantage of the situation and go for it. They had just activated their permit when the whale defenders swept in like angry hornets, buzzing about with the *Bulletproof* and smaller boats.

The crew on the *Bulletproof* consisted of Jonathan Paul as captain and six crew members, including Jake Conroy, Josh Harper, Erin Fitzpatrick, Erin O'Connell, Eli Owens, and Margaret Owens. Jake and Josh accompanied the *Bulletproof* with a nineteen-foot hard-bottomed inflatable boat.

A whale rose slowly in front of the whalers, but before a harpoon could be lifted, the SEDNA crew aggressively moved in. One of the whale defenders sprayed the whalers with a fire extinguisher as their fast boats whipped the water around the canoe into a frenzy. The next hour was chaotic, with the whalers frantically paddling to catch the whale and the whale defenders chasing the hunters doing all that they could to harass and prevent the lethal intent. One of the whalers called the Coast Guard to report that the protesters were armed and threatening them with guns. A Coast Guard patrol boat rushed in, stopped, and boarded the *Bulletproof*. They did not find any guns.

It was a small delay, and the *Bulletproof* returned to the fray just as Theron Parker stood up in the bow of the *Hummingbird*, harpoon in hand. There was a whale directly in front of the canoe. Theron threw the harpoon, the whale dove, and it was a miss. The whaler defenders let out a loud whoop of joy.

Theron tried again, and once again he missed. The Coast Guard seized two of the small boats from the whale defenders and arrested Josh Harper and Jake Conroy, two SEDNA members. They were charged with second-degree felony assault, and their inflatable boat was seized. The first actual day of hunting for the Makah was now over: the whalers had failed to harpoon a whale.

The media began to return to Neah Bay, and I departed Friday Harbor with the *Sirenian* for the hundred-mile trip to Neah Bay. The next morning we were back. The skies were cloudy and gray, and that was a positive sign. In our fight for the whales, bad weather is always a welcome ally. We had another ally that day: a pod of orcas crossed the bay, making the gray whales very wary of danger.

Day two was a success. The whalers did not return on day three. We stayed vigilant on board the *Sirenian*, settling in for another stretch of waiting and hoping that it would not be another two months of playing these games with the whalers. Keith Johnson had departed for the IWC meeting in Grenada with the official US delegation to lobby to kill whales.

Once again, the media was getting bored. A few days later, the whalers paddled out to sea again. They paddled for ten hours in search of a whale, thanks in part to the scare provided by the visiting orcas. They spotted a whale and approached it and, once again, Theron Parker threw his harpoon and, once again, he missed. Once again the whale defenders swooped in to harass the whalers. It was a long day for both sides that ended when the rain began to fall. The whalers returned to shore and dusk arrived without a whale being struck.

Each day the whale defenders lost boats, seized by the Coast Guard for getting too close to the whalers. I held the *Sirenian* back, outside the Coast Guard–enforced boundaries set by the court. On the day that it rained, four protest boats were lost.

On Sunday, May 16, I decided to return to Friday Harbor to pick up some additional small boats. We did so and departed around midnight to return to Neah Bay. Jonathan Paul, having lost the *Bulletproof*, joined us on board the *Sirenian*.

We were in Sekiu getting supplies for the *Sirenian* when we received word that the whaling boats had been put to sea. As we got underway, Cheryl Rorabeck-Siler sped far ahead of us on her Jet Ski. She was the first to reach the scene in Makah Bay, although Brian Calvert and Dinah Elissat were above her in Brian's plane, the *Sky Shepherd II*.

The *Sirenian* reached the area about twenty minutes after Cheryl arrived, and I dispatched a Zodiac piloted by Allison Lance and crewed by Lorena Brooks. Because Cheryl was the only observer of the events of the first twenty minutes, I am including her account here:

I woke up early on the morning of May 15, anxious to get out on the water. I had just finished filling up the gas tank on the Jet Ski when I was told that the Makah had been spotted coming offshore near Makah Bay. Immediately the protesters began to scramble to prepare the boats. I was ready and headed out, knowing that I had a twenty-mile commute to get to the area where the Makah had launched. Time was critical and it was on the Makah's side. They had the jump on us. I was alone, with no way of communicating with the other protesters. We had all admitted that we didn't know for sure what actions we would take when it came down to it. We had experienced numerous false alarms and placebo acts by the Makah. Was this the real thing? The miles stretched out while my adrenaline increased. What was I going to do? Will the Coast Guard be out there on the water? Oh, how I longed for a radio. The urge to want to talk to the other protesters and reassure myself that they were right behind me was enormous. I tried to remind myself to stay calm, think clearly, and have confidence in myself that I would know what to do when the time came—which was soon. I felt like I was off to the battle—off to battle without a weapon and knowing that the enemy was well stocked with a number of rifles and harpoons.

I had a difficult time concentrating on positioning the Jet Ski through the conflicting swells at Tatoosh Island. My mind kept racing ahead, wondering if I was already too late to stop the kill. As soon as I entered the ocean, my goal was to locate the "hunting" party as quickly as possible. But when you are sitting on a small Jet Ski in the Pacific Ocean with significant swells and saltwater stinging your eyes, seeing into the distance can be difficult. Then I glimpsed a helicopter in the far distance. I guessed that this was a media helicopter and knew that they would be hovering over the canoe.

When I arrived at the scene, the canoe was being towed with the National Marine Fisheries Service boat close at hand. I immediately went right in close to let them know I was there and that I wasn't going to just sit by and watch. I kept talking to myself to keep up my confidence, to keep myself "psyched." I didn't want to let my fellow protestors down; I had to make sure they didn't kill a whale. The thought never occurred to me that they knew what was going on, as they were on the long trip around the point. I didn't realize that *Sky Shepherd II* was close by, relaying what was taking place. I probably would have felt better, not so alone, if I had known this.

As I followed the canoe in tow, my heart thumped against my chest, pounding so hard I felt as though I could hear it over the noise of the

Jet Ski. I felt like I was back on the starting grid, crouched down over the tank of a motorcycle, waiting for the starting flag to drop.

As I was attempting to keep myself feeling aggressive and determined, one of the Makah support boats pulled up right alongside me. We stared at each other in the eyes, and I didn't budge on my position. No way in hell was I going to let them intimidate me! They then motored up just between the canoe and me, and they pulled in line. At the time, they were progressing through a group of rocks heading south, all in line, one right after the other. I found myself sandwiched between the support boat and the National Marine Fisheries Service boat, which was right behind me. I fought the swells and wakes for a bit, determined to not let them think they could bully me out of there. Then I pulled out of line and sped up to a position parallel with the canoe. They were no threat to the whales as long as they were being towed. Shortly, the tow vessel was halted and the canoe was released. They began to paddle. I went up alongside, close enough to converse with the paddlers. My anger was rising with every stroke they made. I wanted to say something but I wasn't sure what. But comments such as, "You guys are looking tired. Isn't it time to get towed again?" and "You're paddling in circles," and "Could I give you a tow to Japan?" are what came out.

They were paddling in a circle and constantly kept looking back over their shoulders at their support vessels. It wasn't long before a whale surfaced right in front of the canoe. I didn't have to think twice before I accelerated to make a pass between the canoe and the whale. The whaler in the bow of the canoe reached for the harpoon but didn't have time to get it into position for a throw.

I wanted to make sure that I would be in the path of the harpoon. I yelled at them that they "would not kill a whale as long as I'm here!" My adrenaline was flowing. I kept thinking, *How much longer before the other protesters arrive?*

The next whale surfaced right in front of one of the support groups. Immediately, a large harpoon (bigger than the one carried on the canoe) was raised at the same time as the big rifle. It caught me a bit off guard because we were immediately in front of the media boat, and I didn't think the Makah would want them to see a whale killed from one of their motorized boats. I quickly went over to get between the surfacing whale and the raised rifle.

I was scared because I knew I was coming in quickly from the side, and the gunman was sighting down the barrel. Trying to prevent the death of a whale was more important to me than my own safety. Not many people understand this, but those who do have probably had a close encounter with a whale at some time in their lives.

The support boat with the harpoon and the .50 caliber rifle aboard began to move northward as whales kept surfacing. In a panic, I tried to make a decision. There is only one of me and three Makah boats. Who do I stay with? I had to make a choice in a matter of seconds, for whales kept surfacing in front of the red Makah support boat. Each time one surfaced, the boat would quickly motor up to the unexpected whale, and the two men would lean out over the bow, harpoon and rifle aimed. I sped into position quickly a number of times to get between the arsenal and the whale.

The media had insisted that the harpoon would be thrown from the canoe. I did not think the Makah would stick with the program. I believed that after a tiring and unsuccessful day of hunting the previous Monday, they had decided to take a whale any way they could, canoe or motorboat.

I tried to keep my eye on the canoe as the support boat continued northward. Each time a whale surfaced, it was farther north, and each time the men would attempt to get to the position to take aim. My husband, Bret, and I had recently discussed possible scenarios. We came to the conclusion that the harpoon could be deadly to the whale, but it was essential to prevent the rifle shot. I felt like I had made the right decision to stay with the support vessel, but in the back of my mind I was wondering if I should leave to go back to the canoe. At this time, I was too far away to see what was happening with the canoe. I concentrated on blocking the rifleman. Every time I convinced myself that I should go check on the canoe, a whale would surface nearby and the support boat would pursue. I couldn't be in two places once. I needed help!

The media maintained their position right near the canoe; helicopters hovered overhead. Nobody seemed to care what was going on with the red support boat that continued to make attempts to kill a whale. I was feeling so alone! How much longer before help arrived? Were the whalers in the canoe also making attempts to kill a whale? Every once in awhile I had the opportunity to scan the waters north, looking for the approaching help. Finally, the *Bulletproof* arrived, with the *Sirenian* right behind it.

I quickly left the Makah boat to tell Jonathan Paul that we should divide up the protest boats and try to cover both areas. He immediately sped off toward the canoe.

I felt a little bit better. My teammates had arrived. We could win this war. The sinister-looking black *Sirenian* approaching was a relief. Its presence alone was enough to scare the Makah. However, the Makah had the United States Coast Guard as their bodyguards. As soon as the protest boats appeared around Tatoosh Island, the Coast Guard sent their troops out in a number of small vessels. My spirit and fortitude took a sharp fall as I saw the Coast Guard vessels approaching. The Makah had called for backup—the US govern-ment! My recent experiences with them had taught me that if I didn't respond to their directions, I would be removed from the water, permanently. I was there to help the whales, and my goal was to stay out there and deter the hunt as long as possible. I bit my tongue as they ordered me to keep a distance of forty feet from the Makah boat. I came alongside an inflatable containing Allison and Lorena and relayed the Coast Guard warning to them.

As we talked, another whale surfaced, and we headed over to upset the killing attempt. I saw the whale surface again right ahead of me and go under just before I reached the area. I hoped that all the commotion immediately above would convince him to dive deep. Again, the Coast Guard ordered me over to their vessel. They used a megaphone to belch out their order. This time I was told that I had violated the Marine Mammal Protection Act! A law that was formed to prevent harassment of whales was being used to remove me from the water!

In other words, I was harassing the whale because I was too close to it when it had surfaced, but the Coast Guard accepts the Makah killing them in a marine sanctuary. What kind of asinine law is that? I was ordered to "stand down, we are boarding your vessel."

As they seized my Jet Ski, I told them, "This is wrong, and you know it."

I was brought onto a cutter and taken to Neah Bay. A small glim-mer of hope remained as I was being towed back to Neah Bay. Sea Shepherd was still out there and the Makah hadn't killed a whale.

The *Sirenian* and the *Bulletproof* arrived in time to relieve Cheryl. She had lost her Jet Ski but she had bought the whale some time. Allison raced her boat into position to block the Makah harpoon and was able to prevent two attempts to harpoon the whale.

I stayed outside the exclusion zone, but I began to make high-speed circles around the Makah whaling canoe. I set the radar alarm on the canoe to ensure there would be no violation. Picking up the mic, I called the Coast Guard.

"United States Coast Guard, this is the *Sirenian*. Please advise me. Is this a no-wake zone out here in Makah Bay?"

The Coast Guard responded, "Of course not. This is the open sea. Why would you think this would be a no-wake zone?"

I chuckled. "Just wanting to make sure. I don't want you guys surprising me with a citation. You may have declared the bay a no-wake zone in the last five minutes, for all I know. This exclusion zone appears unconstitutional to me. Anti-abortion protestors have to stay only ten feet away from women seeking abortions near clinics, but we need to stay a thousand feet away. I bet some of those harassed women would love the kind of protection you're giving these whale killers. Please advise me if you pass a regulation in the next few minutes extending the exclusion zone or making it unlawful for me to produce a wake."

With each circle, the waves I sent inward increased and began to collide with waves that I sent from the other side, creating a very choppy sea that began to bounce the whaling canoe about, making it impossible to stand in the bow with a harpoon.

The Coast Guard radioed me: "*Sirenian*, you could be cited if your wake causes an injury to anyone in the canoe."

"United States Coast Guard, this is the *Sirenian*. I repeat, is this a no-wake zone?"

"No, sir, it is not," the Coast Guard replied, "but it is unlawful to operate your vessel in a reckless manner, sir."

"United States Coast Guard, this is the *Sirenian*. I don't believe I am operating the vessel in a reckless manner. I am remaining outside of the exclusion zone, and I am circling the canoe for the purpose of documenting their unlawful whaling operation. These guys should not be out here if their boat is not suitable for rough seas. This is the Pacific Ocean, sir. It's not some mill pond. Please advise me if I am in violation of any regulation, and I will cooperate with any request you have to stand down. Am I in violation of any regulation, sir?"

"This is the United States Coast Guard. No, sir, you are not in violation of any regulations, but if someone is hurt, you *will* be in violation."

"United States Coast Guard, this is the *Sirenian*. I am either in violation of a regulation or I am not. How can I be held responsible if a Makah whaler can't keep his footing in his canoe? Am I operating this vessel in a reckless manner? Please advise me if I am and I will stand down."

There was a short pause and then he answered again. "This is the United States Coast Guard. I would advise you to be cautious, sir."

"This is the *Sirenian*. Thank you for your advice. We will, of course, exercise extreme caution in our maneuvers."

That day, Saturday, May 15, the Coast Guard seized the SEDNA boat *Bulletproof* for getting too close to a gray whale. Captain Jonathan Paul was arrested. I lost one of our small boats, and two of my crew were arrested for getting too close to a whale.

A reporter contacted me for a response and asked if I intended to continue to break the law with the *Sirenian* like the *Bulletproof* was accused of doing.

"What kind of a crazy farm is this?" I replied. "These guys want to blow a whale apart with a .50 caliber gun, and everybody is concerned that we might get too close to a whale. The fact is that they want to kill this intelligent, beautiful animal, to blow it apart with an antitank gun, and everybody is focusing on, 'Oh, Sea Shepherd might be too close to a whale.' I think it's ludicrous."

On Sunday, May 16, I decided to return to Friday Harbor to pick up some additional small boats. We did so and departed around midnight to return to Neah Bay. Jonathan Paul, having lost the *Bulletproof*, joined us on board the *Sirenian*.

We were only a few hours from Neah Bay when we got word that the whalers had departed with their canoe around five o'clock in the morning. I increased the speed. The skies were cloudy and it was beginning to rain, but, unfortunately, the seas were relatively calm.

We were the last boat remaining, thanks to the US Coast Guard, and the whalers were taking advantage of our having to return to Friday Harbor. As we sped westward, the whalers were paddling out to Makah Bay, intent upon murdering a whale. We felt helpless with the realization that we would most likely be too late. The killers now had the advantage. We were being bested by the US Coast Guard and our lack of boats.

Out at sea, Theron Parker stood up, harpoon in hand. As the canoe rode up behind the unsuspecting and defenseless whale, he did not need to throw it. He simply pushed the steel-tipped lance into the whale's yielding body. He pushed it in deep with the weight of his body. The whale, a juvenile, rolled hard to the right. The harpoon shaft rose out of the water and the whale surged forward, towing the canoe.

At this point, the weather turned and the seas got rougher as Dan Greene, in his red support boat, moved into place carrying the shooter. The shooter had chosen to remain anonymous. We were not even sure he was a Makah. He had not departed with the whaling group but had been picked up at a dock by Dan Greene in his support boat.

The shooter stood up and aimed his big gun, but before he could fire, a media boat crossed the path of the support boat. The shooter waved off the media boat as the whale dove beneath the surface. It had been quite a few moments since Parker had penetrated the whale's body with his harpoon. Later, the whalers would argue that the whale did not suffer, that the kill was quick and humane. That was a lie.

The exhausted whale broke the surface, and once again the shooter took aim. A thunderous blast shook the air. Eric Johnson, who was assisting the shooter, covered his ears. The shooter missed.

Another whaler, Donnie Swan, was preparing a second harpoon. He quickly stood up and threw the harpoon, striking the whale a second time. The powerful tail rose out of the water and slapped like a clap of thunder on the surface of the sea. Donnie boasted that he could feel the pain of the whale, and it felt good.

On the support boat, the shooter was not ready. They were looking for bullets. Wayne Johnson frantically searched around the deck until the shooter realized that there was still a bullet in the rifle. He pulled the trigger a second time, hitting the whale in the head. The whale rolled in visible agony on the surface, as steaming hot blood spread out in a scarlet stain all around its dying body.

We heard the shot as the *Sirenian* moved quickly toward the whalers, but by the time we arrived, the whale was dead. Ignoring the warnings of the Coast Guard, I moved in alongside the whaling boats.

We were angry. We blasted our air horn to overwhelm the cheers of the whalers.

As we watched, the whale began to sink. They had to call in one of the large Makah commercial fishing vessels to winch the carcass up to enable them to tow it back to Neah Bay. Powerboats, hydraulic winches, an antitank gun, two-way radios, and wet suits. I really could not see the tradition in this vicious circus.

We followed the fishing boat *Heidi* with the whale in tow into the harbor and watched as a tractor pulled it in shallows near the beach. A biologist determined the whale was a three-year-old juvenile and then made the unbelievable announcement that the whale had died instantly and the kill was humane. The mysterious shooter was nowhere in sight, and an Alaskan Native was preparing to butcher the whale. Teenagers were climbing onto the whale and doing backflips. I failed to see any sign of reverence or respect, and I was disgusted.

The butchery continued into the night under the glare of klieg lights. The Alaskan Native tried to convince some of the Makah to save the intestines but no one was interested.

The next morning, with the dogs sniffing at the remains, I was asked for a comment by the media. I said, "Yesterday, with speedboats, military weaponry, and the draconian assistance of the US government stifling all dissent, American whalers managed to blast a whale out of existence in American waters on the pretext of cultural privilege."

In an interview with Toronto's *Globe and Mail* the day after the whale was killed, seventy-year-old Charles Claplanhoo told Margaret Wente, "I don't see the point of it. I don't see no use for the meat, you know. Anyway, deer and elk taste much better."

Charlie continued. "All this talk about restoring the whale hunt is ridiculous. Those 'brave whalers' are mostly a bunch of teenagers. They claim to be descendants of the great whalers, but that's long gone. They should have left it alone."

The whalers told Charlie that his share of the whale was forty-five kilograms. "I'm not interested," he said. "I don't even know how to cook it."

It's not that Charles Claplanhoo was sentimental about whales or even interested in the arguments of the anti-whalers. He told the *Globe* that he was not even concerned that the whalers were not practicing traditional rituals or using traditional weapons. His objections were simply pragmatic: "The whale hunt has been terrible for business. People are boycotting Makah art. I used to do a lot of carving—little miniature canoes, paddles, masks. We used to have a pretty good market in Port Angeles and Seattle. Now I can't get rid of any of that stuff."

When asked specifically about the Makah whalers' claim that a powerful mystical connection had been restored with their traditional whaling culture, Charlie chuckled and answered that they "certainly made a powerful connection with government money and were doing some interesting foreign travel." He was referring to the all-expenses-paid trips to Dublin, Aberdeen, Monaco, Oman, and Grenada made by Marcy Parker and her boys.

While the Makah whalers were cheering the death of the whale, others were lamenting the needless death of the young cetacean. Binki Thompson cried and bestowed the name of Yabis (the Makah word for "beloved") upon the whale.

Margaret Owens laid a wreath by the desecrated body of the whale on the May 19. She was threatened by some tribal members and chased away. Her wreath was torn apart. She then painted a memorial to the whale on a rock outside the reservation. That same evening, the rock was splashed with gasoline and the memorial burned and defiled. A Clallam County sheriff stopped a car speeding from the scene. Inside were two Makah and a member of the Coast Guard base from Neah Bay. The sheriff said he had no evidence to hold them.

On the evening of May 21, the Sakya Monastery of Tibetan Buddhism held a memorial at Alki Beach in Seattle. Small pieces of wood inscribed with prayers were burned. The monastery's official statement was: "This is a peaceful gathering and not meant to be a political statement or in any way reflective of the culture of the tribes involved. It is held to pay homage in Tibetan Buddhism to honor the passing of a sentient being."

On the reservation, the atmosphere was jubilant. A military surplus truck towed the whaling canoe through the streets, leading a parade of a dozen makeshift floats and the triumphant whaling crew. A banner declared, "Whale to live. Live to whale."

And Bob Coster no longer was pretending to be neutral. "It's a great day," he said as he relaxed with his family watching the parade. "It was a good hunt."

As the parade made its way through the streets, my ship *Sirenian* remained in the harbor, her sirens wailing in mourning for the young whale.

Demonstrators rallied at the entrance of the reservation, prohibited from entry by the tribal police. The Associated Press reported that the anti-whalers carried signs that read, "Save a whale, harpoon a Makah."

This report caused a flurry of ferocious accusations of racism from Makah supporters and would become the keel upon which the whalers would build their defense that opposition to the hunt was inspired by racism.

The report was false. Chuck and Margaret Owens had banned any anti-Makah signs, and in all the photographs taken of the demonstration that day, not one depicted the alleged offensive sign. "Just more Peggy Anderson bullshit," said Chuck Owens.

It did not take long for our predictions to begin to materialize. On May 20, a Victoria *Times Colonist* headline proclaimed: "BC Natives Claim Whaling Rights."

Attending the Makah banquet that evening was chief Tom Mexis Happynook of the Nuu-chah-nulth of Vancouver Island. Happynook reported on his experience in his newsletter for the World Council of Whalers:

> The celebration lasted well into the night and into the dawn of the following day. Throughout the proceedings, respect was paid to the spirit of the whale, which had so willingly given itself to the hunter.

Happynook also could not resist taking a swipe at us:

> I couldn't help but feel sorry for the lonely boat of the protestors sitting at anchor as we passed. In contrast to the joy and pride of a community united, this black boat seemed so alone; its blackness, meant to intimidate, invoked instead something approaching pity. They were a defeated people on that boat, desperately grasping for esteem in the face of failure. For all their clever words and bold declarations, in the end they turned out to be no match for the power of tradition.

As I read those words, I could not help but feel sorry for just how deeply Happynook had deluded himself. We were not defeated by those whalers. We had stopped them from killing whales in 1998, and although they killed the one in 1999, it was the violence and might of the United States government, Coast Guard, and police that had intervened to ensure the success of the whale hunt. There are, after all, limits to what can be accomplished nonviolently, especially against the most powerful government on Earth. Most importantly, we had shot down the Makah plans to make their "tradition" into a profitable enterprise. The attention we brought to bear would keep the Makah under public scrutiny for some time.

As for our crew being sad, we were indeed. As the whalers celebrated death, we mourned the passing of the whale and felt pity for her killers. They could delude themselves that the whale gave itself to them, but we had seen the hunt and so had millions of people, and what they saw was a young, defenseless, sentient creature dispatched with an antitank gun. If that whale gave itself willingly to the whalers, then I guess it could be said that the Indians gave themselves willingly to European domination or that the Jews gave themselves willingly to the Nazi ovens. All people, regardless of race, seem to have an infinite capacity to justify their cruelty.

On that day, the *Sirenian*'s black hull was the color of mourning for Yabis, the beloved child of the seas that had been murdered not for food, not for necessity, but simply to appease human pride.

MAY 24–28, 1999, ST. GEORGE'S, GRENADA
51ST ANNUAL MEETING OF THE INTERNATIONAL WHALING COMMISSION

The timing of the kill could not have been better for the Japanese and the Norwegians. On May 24, the High North Alliance, representing the Norwegian whaling industry, presented its address to the 51st Meeting of the International Whaling Commission. It began as follows:

> The High North Alliance wishes to take this opportunity to congratulate the USA on the successful gray whale hunt by the Makah tribe last week.

The remainder of the address demonstrated just how involved the commercial whalers were with the ploy to use Aboriginal whaling to push open the door to full-scale commercial whaling.

The IWC has become an anachronism, a show organization that pretends to manage whaling while actually doing no management at all. As a management regime, the IWC has been stone-cold dead for many years, but as the world's leading hypocritical, double-standard forum, it is still jetting around.

The IWC died from dysfunctionality. It had become a global organization that not only failed to fulfill the objectives for which it was established, but also actually took every opportunity to undermine those objectives. The time has come to replace it with regional regimes that are genuinely interested in carrying out the management tasks that the IWC so utterly failed to perform and to bring down the curtain on yet another dark chapter in the history of Anglo-Saxon cultural imperialism.

The sole purpose that the IWC can possibly be said to serve today is as an example of how international cooperation should not be conducted. The whaling ban is maintained, despite the advice of IWC's Scientific Committee that harvests could be conducted sustainably. The anti-whaling lobby is fighting tooth and nail to ensure the whaling ban is never lifted, regardless of the status of stocks. And with no conservation arguments left to support their position, they now resort to tenuous ethical arguments for exempting whales from any consumptive use.

Faced with environmental challenges and yet respectful of cultural differences, the world community has thankfully embraced the principle of sustainable use as embodied in Agenda 21. We have agreed that the use of renewable natural resources is acceptable provided rates of usage are within the resources capacity for renewal.

Yet the West's cultural imperialism would have whales exempted from the sustainable-use principle—an exemption that would, quite simply, place them above and apart from the animal kingdom to which they obviously belong.

True environmentalists, committed to the principle of sustainable development, are concerned not with appearances but with practicing the principles that they preach. In so doing, they have either reached the conclusion, or are getting there, that whaling should not only be continued but should even be increased to provide more people with a healthy and nutritious source of protein in a way that is much more environment-friendly than eating junk food.

I was amused that they had the audacity to say that real environmentalists wanted to see more whales killed. It was also interesting that they cited Agenda 21 as promoting the principle of sustainable use, yet ignored the fact that the same United Nations conference in Brazil in 1992 also gave recognition to the IWC as the sole regulatory body for whales and whaling.

What I found most interesting was the Norwegian accusation of cultural imperialism against anti-whalers. The Norwegian whalers were claiming Indigenous Aboriginal rights like the Makah did, just as we had warned that they would.

The whalers' long-term objective of destroying the IWC's authority was given a terrific boost by the Makah kill, bringing the United States into the camp of the whalers. The US entered reluctantly, but they were now compromised by hypocrisy and could only mutter a few protests as the Japanese and the Norwegians stoked the fires of their discontent. Revelations that would have brought anger from the US a few years before now did not even ruffle the feathers of the emasculated eagle.

For example, scientists from the University of Auckland, New Zealand, revealed that they had tested 120 pieces of meat, blubber, and skin purchased in 1998 and 1999 from Japanese retail shops and fish markets. The tests uncovered products from three protected species: fin, sei, and sperm whales. "The survey revealed a surprisingly high number of protected whales on sale in the Japanese markets," said Vassili Papastavrou, a whale biologist employed by the International Fund for Animal Welfare (IFAW), the organization that funded the DNA investigation. "There is a loophole in international regulations that allows the Japanese to undertake so-called 'scientific' whaling, and that hunt has acted as cover for this illegal trade in protected whales. Pro-conservation countries now need to get serious and act to stop this 'scientific' whaling charade." But the US said nothing.

Naoko Funahashi, the anti-whaling campaign director for the IFAW in Japan, reported to the IWC that "the Japanese whaling industry, with the support of our government, is killing more and more whales, but they don't take any serious measures to control the outlawed whaling and trade. They are themselves proving that commercial whaling can never be managed properly."

The survey also revealed that eight Baird's beaked whales, three Risso's dolphins, and eight pilot whales were on sale in Japanese markets. The investigative team also found two samples labeled as whale meat (that was actually horse meat) with a luxury price tag of $600 per kilo.

The Japanese- and Norwegian-financed World Council of Whalers delivered a paper to the IWC calling for quotas and assistance in encouraging Indigenous whaling in the Caribbean, despite the fact that the people wanting to kill whales were of African descent. The paper argued that the people of the Caribbean had a cultural right to kill whales.

We were now seeing the seeds that the Japanese had so adroitly planted coming to fruition. Commercial whaling could simply continue as a cultural necessity. Of course, trade in whale products was also a cultural necessity, as the Makah had argued and the World Council of Whalers was promoting.

This was not a surprise, since the Caribbean member nations had long been in the pocket of the Japanese whaling interests. In Grenada, they even walked out of the discussion along with the Japanese delegation when the IWC attempted to bring up the matter of unregulated slaughter of Dall's porpoise.

Japan was quick to defend her Caribbean ward of St. Vincent and the Grenadines when that country was accused of capturing a humpback calf to lure the mother to slaughter. The calf was also killed, and the Japanese claimed that the whale hunt was conducted in accordance with traditional methods.

Japan and her Caribbean puppets loudly objected to the vote by the IWC to allocate $125,000 for high-priority scientific research into the effects of pollutants on whales. This was not the business of the IWC, they protested.

Finally, the most controversial issue was Japan's request for a coastal quota of fifty minke whales for a traditional hunt by four Japanese villages. The quota was needed to help maintain the cultural traditions of whaling, they argued. The request was defeated, with fifteen countries voting no and twelve countries voting in favor.

The US delegation stated, "We are sympathetic to the needs of the communities, but because there would be commercial elements in this whale hunt, it would be contrary to the IWC's moratorium on commercial whaling, and the USA could not support it."

Japan retaliated and accused the United States of hypocrisy in allowing the Makah tribe to hunt whales while opposing whaling by other countries. "It's a double standard," said the Japanese delegate Masayuki Komatsu. "I mean, our tribes were whaling right up until the moratorium. The Makahs hadn't killed a whale in seventy years."

As for the Makah, we were expecting that a kill of a whale by an unrecognized hunt would provoke some heated discussion in Grenada. It did not even provoke a whisper. The IWC members dealt with it by not dealing with it at all. Surprisingly, the only voices of criticism were coming from Japan, and that was only to bemoan the double standard the US was promoting and receiving.

When the Aboriginal Subsistence Whaling infractions committee met in Grenada, the kill was not even mentioned. As one Japanese delegate said with a sneer, "Why was it not discussed? Ha! The answer is simple. Infractions of IWC rules do not apply to the USA."

Who was in bed with whom in Grenada was very evident. A group calling itself the Caribbean Broadcasting Union held what they billed as the "International Whaling Commission Media Symposium" at the Spice Island Beach Resort. This was actually a public relations event hosted by the whalers, and it featured three keynote speakers. The first was "wise use" propagandist Eugene Lapointe. The second was Japan's hired publicist in the US, Alan Macnow. And the third was chief Tom Mexis Happynook, president of the World Council of Whalers.

BBC Caribbean correspondent Mattias Peltier attended the media event. He caught on rather quickly that this was a public relations gimmick posing as an impartial media symposium and began to ask some pointed questions. Alan Macnow interrupted him and publicly accused Peltier of being an agent provocateur for the whale lovers and demanded that he leave. Jamaican journalist John Maxwell announced that if Peltier had to leave, he would join him. They both left and were escorted from the room by Antigua whaling commissioner Daven Joseph. Outside the conference room, Joseph saw Henry Shillingford of the Dominica Conservation Association.

Reporters Peltier and Maxwell overheard Joseph launch into a vicious attack on Shillingford: "You are representing white imperialists who want to deprive small, vulnerable societies of their traditional cultural pursuits."

Voices were raised, and the Caribbean press emptied the conference room to witness Joseph telling Shillingford that he should be ashamed to be a Rastafarian who puts white imperialist interests above those of his fellow Caribbean peoples. It got a lot of press, and it was becoming clearer that Japan was solidifying its mythical allegations that saving whales was a white eco-imperialist plot.

The IWC meeting closed with a summary statement that did not mention the Makah kill at all. A French delegation member told me, "The US can certainly twist some arms when it wants to."

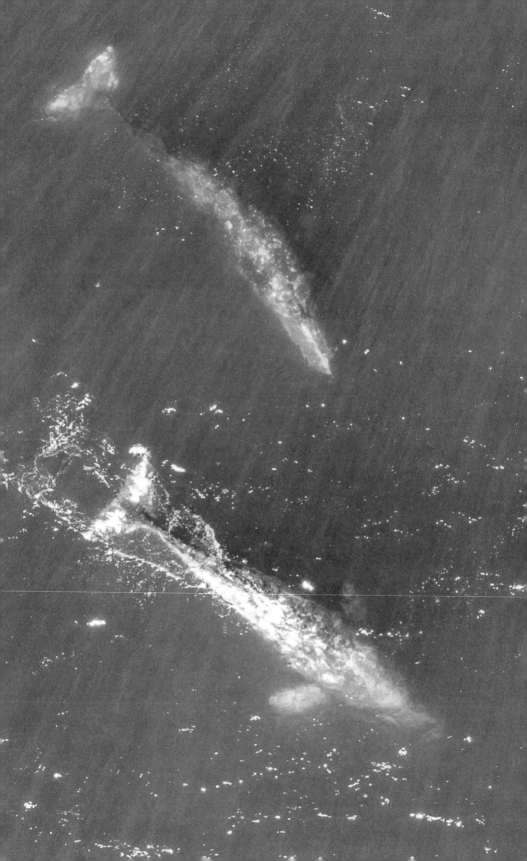

CHAPTER

Victory for the Whales

MAKAH BAY, 2000

I did not take my vessels to Makah Bay in the spring of 2000. Instead, we joined in the lawsuit to challenge the Makah's right to kill whales in the US Court of Appeals for the Ninth Circuit. The Sea Shepherd Conservation Society's primary reason for intervention was to prevent a precedent from being set that could be exploited by Japan and Norway. Thanks to the Makah whalers, the Japanese and the Norwegians got their precedent.

We would not have left if we had been the sole group opposing the killing. Fortunately, we were not. The Peninsula Citizens for the Protection of Whales would continue to oppose the plans of the whalers. Jonathan Paul had changed the name of SEDNA to Ocean Defense International and returned with a new boat, the *Avocet*. Bill Moss was returning with his group called the World Whale Police in his boat *Tiger*.

I looked to Chuck and Margaret Owens as the foundation for a continuing opposition to the whalers. It was their home, after all. And the courageous Makah elders never wavered in their defense of the whales, despite enormous peer pressure and threats. Jonathan Paul had demonstrated his commitment to effectively opposing whale killing.

I thought we could leave these whales in capable hands. As an international organization, we had other obligations in Iceland and

Norway, and, most importantly, we also had to deal with the illegal operations of the Japanese whaling fleet in the waters off Antarctica.

The Makah had played their part in the Japanese scheme to escalate whaling. The US as a top critic of Japanese whaling was muffled by the hypocrisy of advocating for whaling within the US while condemning whaling by other nations. I had to make the decision to focus on illegal Japanese whaling in the southern ocean, and toward that end, I began to prepare my ships for future campaigns in the waters of Antarctica.

The Makah did try to kill another whale, but effective interventions by Jonathan Paul and his crew prevented any whales from dying in 2000. The Coast Guard were far more aggressive in their defense of the whalers the third time around. Chief warrant officer Bob Coster saw an opportunity to beat up two female protesters during the opening days of the 2000 hunt. Erin Abbott of Ocean Defense International (ODI) successfully blocked the Makah whaling canoe with a Jet Ski but then a fast twenty-three-foot hard-bottomed Coast Guard inflatable moved in at high speed, slammed into her Jet Ski, and ran her over. Fortunately, she was unharmed by the props, but when she rose to the surface, she had cracked ribs and a broken shoulder. She was charged with violating the restricted area and told she was facing six years in prison and a possible $250,000 fine. Coast Guard admiral Paul Blayney justified the ramming by claiming the boat could not avoid hitting Erin Abbott. I asked Erin Abbott for her view of the events that day. She sent me this:

> I can remember parts of the day like it was yesterday, even though twenty years and a few months have passed since that day in 2000.
>
> It was still dark out when we woke and headed to the *Avocet*. The eight of us who were working with Ocean Defense International watched the sunrise on our long journey to Makah Bay from where we had been based and docked for several months in Sekiu, Washington.
>
> It was extra choppy when we set out that morning, and we didn't expect a hunt to happen. We patrolled almost daily, so it just became second nature to run through the routine regardless of the conditions. Unless there was a really bad storm, we were out there.

We heard over the radio that the tribe's plane had spotted a gray whale nearby. The mood shifted, and it was as if we couldn't get there fast enough. No one said much other than how much time had passed since they put up their flags, etc. We listened for all the rules that they needed to follow to be allowed to hunt in the first place, hoping to catch them in a fumble.

Standing on the back of the boat as we circled the moving exclusionary zone, I remember asking the Coast Guard to give us the line we couldn't cross and them not giving in to our simple request. I say "simple" because that's what the Coast Guard called it: simple. But it was a moving line in a giant body of water, changing every minute that the whalers moved. We had to stay behind it, with the Coast Guard trying to trip us up by going behind us, trying to push us farther back. There was the potential of a hefty fine and jail time if we crossed it, and certainly they would seize our boat in the process. We had two WaveRunners that we were okay sacrificing if need be, but we intended to keep *Avocet* out of harm's way.

Growing up in Florida, I used to drive WaveRunners all the time and was very comfortable doing that, so I volunteered to drive one of the two that we had to use. I knew how to operate it well and wanted to do my part to help save the whales with ODI. I was there to put another vessel in the water, be another set of eyes, and see the hunt from a different vantage point. We heard that a whale was spotted near the canoe and it was go time. I was on the WaveRunner, and, in some surreal world, I could hear the commotion on *Avocet* while also seeing the whale blow water into the air. I was two hundred yards away, and I could see it blow air through the choppy water. That's how massive the whales are. I saw one of the hunters stand up and move his arm into formation to throw his harpoon into the water.

I couldn't stand by and watch this happen. I zoomed toward where the canoe was and where the whale had just surfaced. I made that my path and stayed on it. I didn't know what *Avocet* was doing, nor did I know what the other WaveRunner rider was doing. I stood up and gassed the WaveRunner, full throttle. I needed to get in between the whalers and the whale, fast. I moved closer and closer, making eye contact with the hunters. I passed in front of their canoe and then moved alongside it. They proceeded to try to knock me off the WaveRunner with their outstretched oars. I was far enough away that they couldn't reach me, but I also moved farther away from them, toward the land. As I did that, a harmless spray of water crossed over the canoe, soaking the hunters. At this point, they were only focused on me and no longer pursuing the gray whale. I felt my job was nearly complete and successfully accomplished at that. I circled around the back of the canoe and, as I slowed down, I did a small turn to see if they were continuing to follow the whale. When I saw that they were not, I turned back toward the open water with my back to the whalers and the land.

That's when I was hit.

I never saw them coming until it was too late. The Coast Guard was right on top of me, hitting me across my back, and suddenly I was the one being hunted. I remember feeling the freezing-cold, clear green water; it felt like I was swimming in ice cubes. I pushed my broken body down and away from the engine that was almost on top of me. I was terrified. The boat hit me across my whole body, and I surfaced thinking that I might die. The same boat that ran me over was now in rescue mode and had to save me.

The hunters nearby laughed as I bobbed in the water for nearly five minutes. They found humor in the fact that a person could have died right in front of them. I couldn't breathe well and couldn't feel anything on the left side of my body. The hardshell, twin-engine boat that I was just underneath was now pulling up to get me out of the water. I told them I couldn't feel my left arm, and they proceeded to pull me up by my left arm anyway. A loud crack rang out and they dropped me back into the water. That's when they realized that my injuries were much more serious than they were allowing for.

Once they got me into the boat, I kept asking them why they ran me over. I wanted to hear them say it. I wanted them to admit it. I wanted to hear them say that they ran me over on purpose.

"Because you sprayed them with water," one man responded.

"Oh, you mean the water they grew up in? The water they are used to being around and are swimming in?" I asked.

"Yes, because you sprayed them with water."

I couldn't stop cursing at the men. I was so mad. Mad at their actions, their arrogance.

"What about the life of the whale?" I said. "That whale was swimming these waters long before you were here and will be here long after you're gone. What gives us the right to take that life from them?"

Insert more cuss words. I was really so mad. I don't think they knew what to do with a twenty-three-year-old wounded girl who couldn't stop cussing them out. It wasn't my finest moment. They got me onto a back-brace board, and we waited for a helicopter to arrive to take me to the ambulance. I needed to get to Port Angeles fast because of the intensity of my injuries.

I spent five days in the hospital with a collapsed lung, three broken ribs, hypothermia, and a broken scapula. Twenty years later, I still have issues resulting from my injuries. I was charged with gross negligent operation of a vessel while endangering myself. The state tried to get me to say I was endangering the whalers, but that simply wasn't true and I wouldn't stand for it. I took a plea deal because it was clear that I didn't have the right lawyers to battle this in court, and I didn't think that I'd do any good being in jail. I was honestly scared at the thought of jail. Again, I was just twenty-three and barely even had any traffic tickets on my record. To sign off on the plea deal, I had to agree to community service hours, though just how many hours escapes me all these years later. I know it took months for me to complete them all. I also had to agree to pay all of my hospital bills. I wasn't someone who missed a bill or skipped out on responsibility. They didn't know this about me, but they made assumptions and made sure to have me pay them in full. I wiped out my savings, but I did it.

At the trial, two of the Coast Guard agents were found guilty of perjury and were dismissed from the court. My lawyers missed a lot of things that in hindsight might have saved me all the money that I had to spend out of my own pocket. One simple thing that really stood out to me was that by law in Washington State if you see an endangered species being harmed you are supposed to intervene. I didn't know this until after my civil suit, which I also lost. So many things that I didn't know. But you are supposed to intervene to save the animal. Gray whales are endangered in Washington State. I was just doing my civic duty.

One of the Coast Guard agents lost his gun in the water that day, meaning he had it drawn and was ready to shoot me, if need be, solely because I sprayed some water and wanted to save a whale. I have no regrets. I saved the whale that day along with the rest of ODI, and it brought international attention to the case.

Many of the elders from the Makah tribe reached out to me afterward, thanking me. They didn't feel that hunting the whale was

part of their heritage anymore. Only two families were going to benefit from the hunt, and they didn't agree with it either. Alberta "Binki"
Thompson called me as I lay in my hospital bed, crying with happy
tears that the whale and I were okay. She was an elder in the tribe
and the most outspoken against the hunt. They killed her dog. They
kicked her family off the reservation. They threatened her life, but she
refused to be silenced. We should all channel a little Binki into our
lives and speak out when we see injustice in the world.

Another woman, Erin O'Connell, was arrested when she followed
Erin Abbott's lead and moved in to block the harpoon. She was not
injured. A third woman, a young Canadian named Julie Woodyer, was
on the water opposing the spring Makah hunt on April 17, 2000. She
had volunteered briefly in May 1999 and had crewed with Jonathan
Paul, where she was able to videotape the *Bulletproof* successfully
maneuvering between the whales and the harpooner. By the end of the
day on May 15, 1999, after preventing any whales from being struck,
the *Bulletproof* was seized by the Coast Guard and escorted back to
Neah Bay, where the crew was questioned by the FBI. Her efforts
frustrated, Julie returned to Vancouver along with the others whose
boats had been seized.

Two days later, Yabis was killed, and Julie was left feeling both sad
and helpless as she watched the whale writhing in pain while Wayne Johnson fired his big gun, sending .50 caliber rounds into the whale, ripping its
flesh apart and shattering vital organs. She decided to return in the spring
of 2000, and this time she crewed with Bill Moss on his boat *Tiger*.

On the opening day of the Makah hunt, Bill and Julie arrived at a
decoy hunt set up by the United States Coast Guard. Decoying for the
Makah whalers was not part of the Coast Guard's mission, but that was
what they were doing to deflect from the real hunt taking place to the
south. As Bill and Julie watched the decoy hunt, they noticed a helicopter
flying toward another location, so they decided to follow it.

As they headed toward the new location, the Coast Guard boat
followed and, without warning, sideswiped the *Tiger*, striking them
at a forty-five-degree angle. Bill Moss told them to stand down
and that his boat had suffered damages. The Coast Guard came at

them again, and this time Bill took off full speed toward where he thought the hunt might be taking place. The Coast Guard followed in pursuit.

Julie was leaning against the seat, filming with a video camera, as the thirty-ton Coast Guard vessel rapidly gained on them. Bill told her not to worry: the Coast Guard would not be foolish enough to collide with them at full speed. That was the last thing Julie remembered before losing consciousness.

The officer on board the Coast Guard vessel *Osprey* radioed headquarters in Seattle: "We had them decoyed for a while, but when they started to head toward the hunt, we popped them good, twice."

When Julie awoke, she was in handcuffs, and they had forced a life jacket over her head. There was broken glass in her hair, and the life jacket scraped the glass across her face. The cuts, however, were the least of her problems. Her lower spine was broken. She told them she was suffering severe pain in her lower back. They brought out a backboard and literally slammed her down on the board with her hands still cuffed. She screamed and went quiet, and one of the Coast Guard crew yelled that she was unresponsive. A medic boarded the Coast Guard boat to check on her, but instead of placing her in the helicopter, they took her back to port on the boat, and it was a rough ride.

The Coast Guard attempted to search her to find any video she had taken. She had placed the video between her thighs, and they did not force her to open her legs after she protested. She was not charged with any crime. She filed a civil suit against the Coast Guard, but the case was dismissed by the judge who insinuated that the Coast Guard was simply opposing an act of terrorism.

The United States Coast Guard, the so-called champions of safety at sea, had maliciously rammed the *Tiger*, inflicting Julie with serious spinal injuries that required her to endure a six-hour surgery and a five-year recovery, and pay thousands of dollars in medical bills.

On June 10, 2000, the Spokane *Spokesman-Review* reported that Erin Abbott had pled guilty to the charges. On the very same day, the US Court of Appeals rejected the environmental assessment that the Makah had used as their basis for resuming the killing of whales. The Ninth Circuit Court's two-to-one ruling dashed the Makah's plans to resume the hunt. Erin Abbott, Julie Woodyer, and Erin McConnell had something to show for their injuries and arrests. Their efforts had not been in vain.

CHAPTER

Twenty Years of Peace on the Cape

From the day that Yabis died until today, more than twenty years later, the Makah have not legally slain another whale. Yabis has been the only victim—and hopefully the last—of the so-called cultural revival, although the Makah tribe continues to lobby for permission to resume hunting.

The Makah have been unable to hunt whales because it was determined that they had neither an Environmental Impact Statement (EIS) nor a waiver to exempt them from the Marine Mammal Protection Act of 1972.

A 1997 federal lawsuit filed against the National Marine Fisheries Service demanded that an EIS and a waiver had to be granted before the Makah could legally kill a whale. The suit was won on appeal in 2000.

Since 2000, Sea Shepherd has opposed in the courts any and every effort to kill whales, and we will continue to do so at every opportunity. Our position is that this hunt is illegal and in violation of the rules of the International Whaling Commission pertaining to Aboriginal Subsistence Whaling—rules that remain valid.

The original intent of the Makah whalers was to kill five whales per year. Efforts to oppose this hunt have most likely saved the lives of about a hundred gray whales.

Regrettably, courageous elders such as Binki Thompson, Jesse Ides, and Charlie Claplanhoo have passed away. Sea Shepherd cannot actively oppose the whalers in Makah territory without an invitation from Makah elders. Will the elders today invite us back if the whalers triumph in their efforts to restore whaling? If they do, we will return; if not, we will continue our efforts in the courts to block the restoration of whaling for as long as we can, knowing that for every year we can stop the slaughter another five whales will live.

It was with great sadness that I heard that Binki Thompson passed away in April 2012. She remains one of the most courageous women that I have ever met and had the pleasure to work with. We are obligated to be true to our word that we cannot intervene in Makah waters without an invitation from the elders like the ones they gave to us in 1998 and 1999.

I met up with Makah whaler Wayne Johnson in late May of 2007 in Juneau, Alaska, at the fifty-ninth annual meeting of the International Whaling Commission. He was as cocky as ever and in my face about his rights to kill whales. When I told him we would block the whale hunt in court, he got angry.

"No one can tell us what to do. If we want to kill a whale, we will fucking kill a whale, and there is no white man's law that is going to stop us."

A few months later, he and four others illegally killed a whale.

In early September, Wayne appointed himself as a whaling captain, and he, along with Andy Noel, Frankie Gonzales, William Secor, and Theron Parker, set out to kill a whale. Theron Parker demonstrated that he did not learn much about whale hunting despite being the only Makah tribal member to have actually harpooned a whale before this illegal hunt organized by Wayne Johnson. The gray whale they targeted was in the Strait of Juan de Fuca heading seaward when they harpooned it, shot it sixteen times, and lost it. The whale was bleeding profusely and suffering for some time until it disappeared under the shroud of the sea, a noble life extinguished because of anger and pride.

The Makah tribal request to charge the five under Makah tribal law was rejected by the federal government. "We welcome the Makah tribe's statements that they plan to prosecute in tribal court as well," US attorney Jeff Sullivan said in a government statement. "However, those proceedings simply cannot replace federal prosecution of this killing that is clearly illegal under federal law."

The five were offered a deal: no jail time if they pled guilty and agreed to not kill a whale while on probation. They refused and said they would take their chances in a federal court.

In June 2008, the five were found guilty and sentenced. Wayne Johnson, as the whaling captain, was sentenced to five months in prison. Andy Noel was given a three-month prison sentence. Theron Parker, Frankie Gonzales, and William Secor were each given two years of probation and one hundred hours of community service.

In 2008, Micah McCarty, now the Makah tribal chairman, said that the Makah tribe was committed to whaling and that he hoped they could surmount the legal hurdles by 2010. As of 2020, they still had not secured their EIS or their waiver under the Marine Mammal Protection Act.

In 2018, a juvenile humpback whale was struck and killed by a ship. The carcass was towed into Neah Bay for a feast.

In 2019, with talk arising about the possible resumption of whaling by the Makah, I wrote the following letter to the *Seattle Times* in response to their pro-whaling editorial titled, "Honor Makah Treaty to Hunt Whales."

Sea Shepherd's View on Makah Whale Hunts

In 1995, Sea Shepherd Conservation Society was invited by a concerned group of Makah elders who requested that we help them defend and protect the whales. We agreed with those elders, whose invitation we honored, that having the right to kill whales does not mean that it is right to kill whales.

Sea Shepherd represents one of two opposing perspectives: the side of whale hunters who sought to kill whales and our side, including some Makah elders who sought to see the whales live. This remains a great concern, considering that hundreds of gray whales died this year from starvation, disease, ship strikes, and pollution.

Sea Shepherd opposes the killing of whales by anyone, anywhere, for any reason, without discrimination.

> Sea Shepherd is opposing Makah whaling in the courts, but we will only intervene directly, like we did in 1998 and 1999, if we are once again invited by Makah elders to do so.

DECEMBER 9, 2019

CAPTAIN PAUL WATSON, FOUNDER, SEA SHEPHERD CONSERVATION SOCIETY

After the confrontations in 1999, I took the *Sirenian* to the Galapagos Islands and donated the ship to the Galapagos National Park as a full-time patrol vessel for the Galapagos Marine Reserve.

We reregistered the *Sea Shepherd III* and renamed the vessel the *Ocean Warrior*. I took the ship back to Europe in 2000 to interfere with the killing of pilot whales in the Danish Faroe Islands. In 2002, I changed the registration again to the Canadian flag and renamed the vessel the *Farley Mowat*, after my friend, the author and naturalist Farley Mowat.

After clashes in 2002 with shark finners in the Pacific waters off Central America and in 2005 with seal hunters off Labrador in Canada, we crossed the Pacific to New Zealand to begin our lengthy campaigns against the Japanese whaling fleet in the Southern Ocean Whale Sanctuary, a fight that lasted until 2018, when we were finally able to drive the Japanese whalers out of the sanctuary for good. During that time, we produced a television series on Animal Planet called *Whale Wars*, and since then we have built up the Sea Shepherd fleet to fourteen vessels, operating worldwide in defense of marine species and habitats, and becoming the largest and most effective marine anti-poaching force on the planet.

The effort to stop the slaughter of whales that began for us in 1995 has resulted in a major conservation victory. A quarter of a century later, just two whales have been killed and the lives of up to a hundred whales have been saved. Those hundred lives are worth our struggles, including the accusations, the injuries, the charges, the fines, the loss of boats, and the time.

I wish I could say that I had sympathy for the Makah whalers, but I don't. I do have sympathy for the Makah people, however, especially for the elders who respected the whales. I wish the Makah every success in all things except for the killing of whales.

Looking back, I have no regrets for our actions. We did what we had to do to serve our clients: the whales. We did not injure anyone, and our ships operated within the boundaries of the law and practicality. Our strategy was aggressive nonviolence, and it was successful.

CHAPTER

The Death of a Myth

ith the death of Yabis, the scales of a perception that had guided and spiritually sustained me throughout my life fell from my eyes. I became aware of a form of racism that I had indeed practiced unknowingly for over four decades. I had felt betrayed by the Makah because they had shattered my myth. In fact, they had betrayed no one. It was my myth, not theirs.

Native Americans, Aboriginals, Indians, and the Makah were, after all, merely people, no different from me or any other member of our arrogant and ecologically ignorant species. It was not a welcome discovery. My myth had served to instill hope and feed my desire to believe that humanity could find redemption by learning from a people who revered the earth. My racism was in believing that the American Indian was superior to the European. My discovery at Makah Bay was that we were equals.

All of humanity's crimes throughout history are comparable. Europeans, Asians, Africans, Polynesians, Maoris, and North American Indians had all practiced genocide and specicide. They had all participated in slavery and were all capable of the same vices and virtues. Some cultures were more extreme than others due to their numbers and technology. Their instincts, however, tended to be the same.

By virtue of circumstantial technologies, Europeans and Asians held an early advantage over other anthropocentric cultures. This was the basis for Jared Diamond's book *Guns, Germs, and Steel: The Fates of Human Societies*. There is a perception that some cultures are superior, but when technologies are stripped away, the nature of humanity tends to be equal.

Biocentric cultures have a healthy relationship with nature. Unfortunately, biocentric cultures are becoming increasingly rare and tend to exist today only in Indigenous communities that have not been converted to anthropocentric indoctrination. The Makah community today is anthropocentric and, as such, cannot be compared to the relatively biocentric lifestyle of their ancestors. I had chosen to ignore the archaeological and anthropological evidence because it had previously compromised my faith. I could see it now.

The history of the subjugation of the tribes of the Americas was the same as the history of the subjugation of the tribes of Africa, Asia, and Europe. In all these cases, the oppressed either died or were assimilated by the oppressor. The European tribes were Romanized and, in a similar manner, the American tribes were Europeanized.

European values became American values, and thus the Indian became Christian. Even the language that was commonly used to describe the people and the land had become Europeanized, with the people taking the name from India and the land being named for a charlatan Italian.

At Makah Bay, I saw Europeanized people desperately trying to be what their ancestors once were. The gulf, however, was immense. People thinking like Europeans with Christian values and American culturalization can't even begin to glimpse reality as seen by their pre-Columbian forebears.

For the Makah to be what the Makah once were would be for me to be what my Scottish, Gallic, Viking, and Métis ancestors once were. We can't do it. We don't think like they did, nor do we experience reality as they did. The longboats ply the seas no more, and the Scots wear trousers now. The past has been swallowed by the changes that have led to the world we dwell within today.

Thus, we have Makah "warriors" dressed in wet suits, driving around in crafts with outboard motors, communicating by cell phones, armed with .50 caliber rifles, and receiving federal government subsidies to kill token whales.

Without the spirituality, without the sacrifices, without the hardships, and without the need, this hunt revived only one aspect of the tradition—the kill. The whalers chanting in traditional prayer would have been more convincing if they hadn't gone to church on Sunday to worship Jesus Christ. I could not help thinking that their culture could be better resurrected by destroying the churches on the reservation rather than the whales. But true to Christian tradition, nature would be scapegoated for the perceived need to be Makah. They would be patriotic, Christian, hamburger-eating, beer-drinking, four-wheel-driving, gun-shooting, pinball-playing, football-watching Americans all year round, but, by Jesus, they could still be Makah by killing a whale.

I suppose I could not blame them. The harpoon was an easy straw to be grasped in their quest for identity. I could almost accept their reasoning; I could almost understand why they were doing what they were doing. But I could not understand or accept the need to kill, to extinguish such a noble life, to destroy such majestic beauty just to mask reality.

The day after the kill, they were still what they were: a conquered people living within the paternalistic charity of the dominating US government, a people who gave thanks to Jesus Christ before their council meetings, a people whose real grievance was redirected from the government oppressor to an innocent whale. Custer may have died for the white man's sins, as Vine DeLoria Jr. once so eloquently wrote, but a whale had died for the sins of the Makah. And the sin of the Makah whalers is cowardice. The Makah whalers were cowards. They were afraid to face the real enemy, and so they slew the most convenient scapegoat. They killed a whale.

To drive a steel shaft into the back of a friendly whale, to blow it apart with high-velocity weaponry, and to follow this up by dancing upon the slain creature's back, flipping off reporters and whale protectors—this was a disgraceful act and the work of a people whose values were not those of their ancestors but instead the values of their oppressors.

My experience at Makah Bay forced me to re-examine everything I had believed about Native Americans. I realized that I had seen what I had wanted to see. I also realized this racial myth would always be a problem because people today are not what their ancestors once were. To believe this is so with Native peoples is to imprison them in a social limbo where they remain rooted in a myth and no longer can evolve within a living social reality.

I also realized that this myth served not only the Native Americans, but even more so the Euro-colonialist present-day inhabitants of the Americas. Keeping Native Americans locked in a segregationist myth of nations within a nation serves to keep them distracted and also serves to keep them as living museums to reflect a shadow of something that once existed.

The European invader had crushed a powerful and diverse Native American culture and replaced it with a weak and controllable shadow culture. This shadow culture could be relied upon to justify everything from the fur trade to whaling. Most importantly, it could be used to alleviate some of the guilt from a history of genocide. It gave the descendants of the oppressors a myth to support, and thus it was now safe, with the original cultures vanquished, not only to be supportive of the shadow culture but also to actually appear to feel inferior to this shadow culture. This inferiority was, however, simply a disguise for superiority because it was an inferiority that was chosen by the dominant culture as a means of appearing humble.

By simply championing the remnants of a conquered culture, the invaders could forgive their ancestors, clear their collective conscience, and be empowered to feel superior once again. This voluntary myth of inferiority was the perfect cover to mask the real and vicious crimes perpetrated against Native peoples: not just the genocide and the theft of land but also the horrific persecution of Native children in the residential schools, the sexual and physical abuse, the destruction of culture, and the denial of their languages. The complexity of this myth is that most non-Native Americans are also not European, African, or Asian. Most were born in North America, and the heritage of many goes back centuries within North and South America. Their ties to the land are in North America, not Europe, Asia, or Africa. In the case of African Americans, most did not even choose to come to North America. This was also the case for thousands of Europeans who found themselves shipped to the colonies as indentured servants, purchased brides, soldiers, or convicts.

It is easy for non-Natives to champion the return of the land to Native Americans. They can be fanatical about it. They can be adamant about it. It is a liberal cause that is easy to embrace and bestows righteousness upon the non-Native advocate of Native rights and claims. It is easy because it will never happen. Non-Native Americans will never give up their homes and property to scurry back to a

Europe, an Asia, or an Africa that would not accept them and that has no place for them.

There is one possible solution: self-government and absolute sovereignty over lands occupied by treaty to Native Americans. It would have to be more than an illusion, however. These nations should be real nations, governed 100 percent by their own citizens who would be allowed to carry real passports recognized by all other nations.

I would support a self-governing Makah nation with citizens completely independent of the United States. However, I would still oppose whaling in Makah waters, just as I now oppose whaling in the waters of Japan, Norway, Iceland, and the Danish Faroe Islands.

I do think it is possible for many of these Indigenous territories to campaign for and win real sovereignty. If they could, they would be able to determine the kind of society they wish for, and they would no longer be bound by the authority of the United States. One example is Eswatini, also known as Swaziland, which is a self-governing nation inside South Africa. There is no reason why many Native American communities could not achieve the same independent status.

The Americas have been lost to the Indians, not by the right of conquest but by reason of occupation by incredibly invasive numbers. Europe and Asia opened their spillways and the continent has been flooded with humanity, with the consequence of drowning the majority of the original inhabitants. Turtle Island is no more. The hunters of the plains are gone. The longhouses, wigwams, teepees, and totem poles have all become tourist attractions. A nonfunctional culture is no culture at all. It is simply a tease, an elaborate set for indulging the imagination, of reliving the past, of clinging to what is no more.

But the myth is embraced nonetheless by the occupiers, and toward this end, we have rewritten and romanticized Native American history to serve the allegory. A good example of this is the famous speech attributed to Chief Seattle.

In 1854, Isaac Stevens, the first governor of the new Washington Territory, started the treaty-making process with the tribes. Dr. David Maynard, an Indian agent and a friend of Chief Seattle, arranged a meeting between Stevens and the Duwamish chief. The meeting took place in Seattle, just north of where Safeco Field now stands.

Dr. Henry Smith attended this meeting and took notes. Smith could not speak the Suquamish dialect of the Lushootseed or the Salish language, but he could speak the Northwest trade language of Chinook, and the words of Chief Seattle were translated first into Chinook and then into English. He used these notes to reconstruct Chief Seattle's speech thirty-three years later for an article in the *Seattle Sunday Star* newspaper.

Smith was a poet, and he embellished the simple words of the Indian leader with his flowery style. Smith's record, however, is the only eyewitness account, and hidden beneath the ornate words is a glimpse of what Seattle actually said.

This is is Smith's text as it appeared in the *Seattle Sunday Star* on October 29, 1887:

Yonder sky that has wept tears of compassion upon my people for centuries untold, and which to us appears changeless and eternal, may change. Today is fair. Tomorrow it may be overcast with clouds. My words are like the stars that never change. Whatever Seattle says, the great Chief at Washington can rely upon with as much certainty as he can upon the return of the sun or the seasons. The White Chief says that Big Chief at Washington sends us greetings of friendship and goodwill. This is kind of him, for we know he has little need of our friendship in return. His people are many. They are like the grass that covers vast prairies. My people are few. They resemble the scattering trees of a storm-swept plain. The great, and, I presume, good, White Chief sends us word that he wishes to buy our land but is willing to allow us enough to live comfortably. This indeed appears just, even generous, for the Red Man no longer has rights that he need respect, and the offer may be wise, also, as we are no longer in need of an extensive country.

There was a time when our people covered the land as the waves of a wind-ruffled sea covers its shell-paved floor, but that time long since passed away with the greatness of tribes that are now but a mournful memory. I will not dwell on, nor mourn over, our untimely decay, nor reproach my paleface brothers with hastening it, as we, too, may have been somewhat to blame.

Youth is impulsive. When our young men grow angry at some real or imaginary wrong and disfigure their faces with black paint, it denotes that their hearts are black and that they are often cruel and relentless, and our old men and old women are unable to restrain them. Thus it has ever been. Thus it was when the White Man began to push our forefathers ever westward. But let us hope that the hostilities between us may never return. We would have everything to lose and nothing to gain. Revenge by young men is considered gain, even at the cost of their own lives, but old [men who stay] at home in times of war, and mothers who have sons to lose, know better.

Our good father in Washington—for I presume he is now our father as well as yours, since King George has moved his boundaries further north—our great and good father, I say, sends us word that if we do as he desires, he will protect us. His brave warriors will be to us a bristling wall of strength, and his wonderful ships of war will fill our harbors, so that our ancient enemies far to the northward—the Haida and Tsimshian—will cease to frighten our women, children, and old men. Then, in reality, he will be our father and we his children.

But can that ever be? Your God is not our God! Your God loves your people and hates mine! He folds his strong, protecting arms lovingly about the paleface and leads him by the hand as a father leads an infant son. But, He has forsaken His Red children, if they really are His. Our God, the Great Spirit, seems also to have forsaken us. Your God makes your people wax stronger every day. Soon they will fill all the land. Our people are ebbing away like a rapidly receding tide that will never return. The White Man's God cannot love our people or He would protect them. They seem to be orphans who can look nowhere for help. How, then, can we be brothers? How can your God become our God and renew our prosperity and awaken in us dreams of returning greatness? If we have a common Heavenly Father, He must be partial, for He came to His paleface children. We never saw Him. He gave you laws but had no word for His Red children, whose teeming multitudes once filled this vast continent as stars fill the firmament. No, we are two distinct races with separate origins and separate destinies. There is little in common between us.

To us, the ashes of our ancestors are sacred and their resting place is hallowed ground. You wander far from the graves of your ancestors and seemingly without regret. Your religion was written upon tablets of stone by the iron finger of your God so that you could not forget. The Red Man could never comprehend or remember it. Our religion is the traditions of our ancestors—the dreams of our old men, given to them in solemn hours of the night by the Great Spirit and the visions of our sachems and is written in the hearts of our people. Your dead cease to love you and the land of their nativity as soon as they pass the portals of the tomb and wander away beyond the stars. They are soon forgotten and never return. Our dead never forget this beautiful world that gave them being. They still love its verdant valleys, its murmuring rivers, its magnificent mountains, sequestered vales, and verdant-lined lakes and bays, and ever yearn in tender fond affection over the lonely hearted living, and often return from the happy hunting ground to visit, guide, console, and comfort them. Day and night cannot dwell together. The Red Man has ever fled the approach of the White Man, as the morning mist flees before the morning sun. However, your proposition seems fair, and I think that my people will accept it and will retire to the reservation you offer them. Then we will dwell apart in peace, for the words of the Great White Chief seem to be the words of nature speaking to my people out of dense darkness.

It matters little where we pass the remnant of our days. They will not be many. The Indian's night promises to be dark. Not a single star of hope hovers above his horizon. Sad-voiced winds moan in the distance. Grim fate seems to be on the Red Man's trail, and wherever he will hear the approaching footsteps of his fell destroyer and prepare stolidly to meet his doom, as does the wounded doe that hears the approaching footsteps of the hunter.

A few more moons, a few more winters, and not one of the descendants of the mighty hosts that once moved over this broad land or lived in happy homes, protected by the Great Spirit, will remain to mourn over the graves of a people once more powerful and hopeful than yours. But why should I mourn at the untimely fate of my people? Tribe follows tribe, and nation follows nation, like the waves of the sea. It is the order of nature, and regret is useless. Your time of decay may be distant, but it will surely come, for even the White Man whose God walked and talked with him as friend to friend cannot be exempt from the common destiny. We may be brothers after all. We will see.

We will ponder your proposition, and when we decide we will let you know. But should we accept it, I here and now make this condition that we will not be denied the privilege without molestation of visiting at any time the tombs of our ancestors, friends, and children. Every part of this soil is sacred in the estimation of my people. Every hillside, every valley, every plain and grove has been hallowed by some sad or happy event in days long vanished. Even the rocks, which seem to be dumb and dead as they swelter in the sun along the silent shore, thrill with memories of stirring events connected with the lives of my people, and the very dust upon which you now stand responds more lovingly to their footsteps than yours because it is rich with the blood of our ancestors and our bare feet are conscious of the sympathetic touch. Our departed braves, fond mothers, glad, happy-hearted maidens, and even the little children who lived here and rejoiced here for a brief season will love these somber solitudes and at eventide they greet shadowy returning spirits. And when the last Red Man shall have perished and the memory of my tribe shall have become a myth among the White Men, these shores will swarm with the invisible dead of my tribe, and when your children's children think themselves alone in the field, the store, the shop, upon the highway, or in the silence of the pathless woods, they will not be alone. In all the earth there is no place dedicated to solitude. At night, when the streets of your cities and villages are silent and you think them deserted, they will throng with the returning hosts that once filled them and still love this beautiful land. The White Man will never be alone. Let him be just and deal kindly with my people, for the dead are not powerless.

The words of Chief Seattle were considered relatively unimportant at the time. Governor Stevens did not express amazement or surprise at the translation he received. He just wanted the chief to agree to take his people to the reservation and was satisfied that the chief had agreed to do just that.

It is interesting that Chief Seattle was made to refer to the British as King George. In fact, Queen Victoria had been on the throne for years at the time of the speech. This was because British traders shrewdly portrayed King George as continuing to reign: they knew that a woman as leader would not garner the same respect from these particular tribes as a king. Seattle's people in the Northwest were not advocates of feminism, no matter what the modern myth suggests.

In 1976, Earth Day celebrations honored Chief Seattle's speech as an example of just how in tune the Indian spirit was with the protection of the environment. Copies of the speech were widely distributed. I remember being very impressed with Seattle's early foresight. This chief was a visionary and truly a father of environmentalism, a contemporary of Henry David Thoreau. I viewed the speech as an inspiration, and it cemented my conviction: there needed to be an alliance between Native American culture and the environmental movement.

Unfortunately, the text was quite different from what was recorded by Dr. Henry Smith. This is because in the winter of 1971–72, Ted Perry, a screenwriter working for the Southern Baptist Convention Radio and Television Commission, reworked Chief Seattle's speech into the script for *Home*, an ecology film. The producer wanted to depict an American Indian chief delivering a speech of concern for the earth.

It was a great inspirational speech, and Ted Perry should have been given credit for it, but it was not a speech given by Chief Seattle, nor did it even come close to the words that Dr. Smith had written. Perry expected to be given credit for writing this in the film script, but he made the mistake of including the chief's name in his text. According to Perry, the producer didn't credit him because he thought the film might seem more authentic without a "written by" credit. Since then, Perry's environmental text has been widely circulated as a prophetic ecological statement by Chief Seattle himself.

Michael Her Many Horses, executive director of the Oglala Sioux tribe on the Pine Ridge Reservation in South Dakota, remembered the first time he doubted the speech's authenticity. He had seen a TV program about the Northwest rainforest. In it the narrator presented the nineteenth-century Suquamish leader's plea for living in harmony with nature.

"My reaction was that here's a guy that understood what the environment could provide for his people," recalled Her Many Horses in 1976. "But somehow the chief's words didn't ring true. It made me feel good, but it seemed too perfect."

Perhaps I should have seen this also, but I wanted to embrace the sentiments in the speech so much that I ignored the contradictions. Chief Seattle had never seen a buffalo, let alone herds of buffalo rotting on the plains. He had never been to the plains, nor had he ever ridden in or seen a train or telegraph wires. There were no trains across the plains in 1852.

Ted Perry is today a professor of theater and arts at Middlebury College in Vermont. He has tried many times to set the record straight but has expressed frustration at the continued evolution of the myth.

"Why are we so willing to accept a text like this if it's attributed to a Native American?" he asks. "It's another case of placing Native Americans up on a pedestal and not taking responsibility for our own actions."

The following is the Perry text, and it can be readily seen how it had been changed to a Christian-influenced modern speech, environmentally aware and politically correct:

How can you buy or sell the sky, the warmth of the land? The idea z strange to us. If we do not own the freshness of the air and the sparkle of the water, how can you buy them? Every part of the earth is sacred to my people. Every shining pine needle, every sandy shore, every mist in the dark woods, every clear and humming insect is holy in the memory and experience of my people. The sap which courses through the trees carries the memory and experience of my people. The sap which courses through the trees carries the memories of the Red Man.

The White Man's dead forget the country of their birth when they go to walk among the stars.

Our dead never forget this beautiful earth, for it is the mother of the Red Man. We are part of the earth and it is part of us. The perfumed flowers are our sisters; the deer, the horse, the great eagle, these our brothers. The rocky crests, the juices in the meadows, the body heat of the pony, and the man, all belong to the same family.

So, when the Great Chief in Washington sends word that he wishes to buy our land, he asks much of us. The Great White Chief sends word he will reserve us a place so that we can live comfortably to ourselves.

He will be our father and we will be his children. So, we will consider your offer to buy land. But it will not be easy. For this land is sacred to us.

This shining water that moves in streams and rivers is not just water but the blood of our ancestors.

If we sell you land, you must remember that it is sacred blood of our ancestors. If we sell you land, you must remember that it is sacred, and you must teach your children that it is sacred and that each ghostly reflection in the clear water of the lakes tells of events in the life of my people. The waters murmur is the voice of my father's father.

The rivers of our brothers, they quench our thirst. The rivers carry our canoes and feed our children. If we sell you our land, you must remember to teach your children that the rivers are our brothers, and yours, and you must henceforth give the rivers the kindness that you would give my brother. We know that the White Man does not understand our ways. One portion of land is the same to him as the next, for he is a stranger who comes in the night and takes from the land whatever he needs. The earth is not his brother but his enemy, and when he has conquered it, he moves on. He leaves his father's graves behind, and he does not care. He kidnaps the earth from his children, and he does not care.

His father's grave and his children's birthright are forgotten. He treats his mother, the earth, and his brother, the same, as things to be bought, plundered, sold like sheep or bright beads. His appetite will devour the earth and leave behind only a desert.

I do not know. Our ways are different from yours. The sight of your cities pains the eyes of the Red Man. But perhaps it is because the Red Man is a savage and does not understand.

There is no quiet place in the White Man's cities. No place to hear the unfurling of leaves in spring, or the rustle of an insect's wings. But perhaps it is because I am a savage and do not understand, the clatter only seems to insult the ears. And what is there to life if a man cannot hear the lonely cry of the whippoorwill or the arguments of the frogs around a pond at night? I am a Red Man and do not understand. The Indian prefers the soft sound of the wind darting over the face of the pond and the smell of the wind itself, cleansed by a midday rain or scented with the pinon pine.

The air is precious to the Red Man, for all things share the same breath—the beast, the tree, the man, they all share the same breath. The White Man does not seem to notice the air he breathes.

Like a man dying for many days, he is numb to the stench. But if we sell you our land, you must remember that the air is precious to us, that the air shares its spirit with all the life it supports.

The wind that gave our grandfather his first breath also receives his last sigh. And if we sell you our land, you must keep it apart and sacred, as a place where even the White Man can go to taste the wind that is sweetened by the meadow's flowers.

So we will consider your offer to buy our land. If we decide to accept, I will make one condition: the White Man must treat the beasts of this land as his brothers. I am a savage and do not understand any other way. I have seen a thousand rotting buffaloes on the prairie, left by the white man who shot them from a passing train. I am a savage and do not understand how the smoking iron horse can be made more important than the buffalo that we kill only to stay alive.

What is man without the beasts? If all the beasts were gone, man would die from a great loneliness of the spirit. For whatever happens to the beasts, soon happens to man. All things are connected.

You must teach your children that the ground beneath their feet is the ashes of our grandfathers. So that they will respect the land, tell your children that the earth is rich with the lives of our kin. Teach your children what we have taught our children, that the earth is our mother. Whatever befalls the earth befalls the sons of the earth. If men spit upon the ground, they spit upon themselves.

This we know: the earth does not belong to man; man belongs to the earth. All things are connected like the blood which unites one family. All things are connected.

Whatever befalls the earth befalls the sons of the earth. Man did not weave the web of life; he is merely a strand in it. Whatever he does to the web, he does to himself.

Even the White Man, whose God walks and talks with him as friend to friend, cannot be exempt from the common destiny. We may be brothers after all. We shall see.

One thing we know which the White Man may one day discover— our God is the same God. You may think now that you own Him as you wish to own our land, but you cannot. He is the God of man, and His compassion is equal for the Red Man and the White.

The earth is precious to Him, and to harm the earth is to heap contempt on its creator. The Whites too shall pass, perhaps sooner than all other tribes.

But in your perishing you will shine brightly, fired by the strength of the God who brought you to this land and for some special purpose gave you dominion over this land and over the Red Man.

That destiny is a mystery to us, for we do not understand when the buffalo are slaughtered, the wild horses tamed, the secret corners of the forest heavy with the scent of many men, and the view of the ripe hills blotted by talking wires. Where is the thicket? Gone. Where is the eagle? Gone. The end of living and the beginning of survival.

I do not know what Chief Seattle thought, nor do I know how he perceived the world. I do know now that he did not perceive it in the way Ted Perry or even Henry Smith did. Our perceptions of Chief Seattle are based on a white man's very generous embellishment of another white's man's flowery version of what he understood or wanted the speech to be.

Were Native Americans inclined to live more harmoniously with nature than Europeans? Technologically, yes. As Canadian writer Farley Mowat once told me, "It was pretty easy to love nature when you didn't have a gun."

Given the gun, the average Indian demonstrated a ruthlessness on par with the average white man. It is technology that allows us to hold dominion over nature. The more efficient the technology, the more efficient is that dominion. As an example, consider Australia. There were incredible creatures that once lived and foraged in the wilds of Australia more than fifty thousand years ago. They have since vanished. They were victims of widespread fires set by the first human inhabitants, the ancestors of modern-day Aboriginals. The fires were set to burn the brush, either to assist in hunting or to clear the land. Whatever the reason, the fires were devastating and the result was a massive extinction of species, primarily the majority of the continent's incredible megafauna.

The entire ecosystem of Australia some fifty millennium ago was disrupted and transformed by humans. Fires wiped out food sources for browsing animals like the two-hundred-pound flightless bird called the Genyornis *(Genyornis newtoni)*. Marsupials the size of grizzly bears were obliterated. Also destroyed were tortoises twice the size of those in the Galapagos today and snakes and lizards in excess of twenty-five feet. In all, about 85 percent of the megafauna was removed because of human intervention.

According to research by scientists at the University of Colorado, the Australian National University, and the University of Washington, the analysis of organic material in about seven hundred fossil eggshells laid over centuries by the enormous Genyornis revealed that the birds lived among an abundant array of vegetation that suddenly became very scarce. This scarcity coincided with the period of colonization of Australia by humans from Indonesia.

"It was systematic burning that caused the catastrophic collapse of the largest animals," said Gifford Miller in an interview at the Australian National University in Canberra. He continued:

The widespread fires altered the environment so drastically that what had been forest turned into a dry landscape of small, scrubby shrubs and grasses where smaller animals that could thrive on much more varied diets were able to survive while the megafauna vanished. It can happen anywhere at any time. Humans are a part of any ecosystem, so when you introduce people into the system, they're bound to alter it—often so rapidly that other parts of the ecosystem don't have any time to adjust. The result is extinction.

The same holds true for the Americas. Many species became extinct when hominids first colonized the New World. In fact, the rate of extinction of species was uniform, relevant to the introduction and growth of human populations in all continents.

The myth is well entrenched, and even today many Indigenous people believe it as well.

Terry Williams, the commissioner of fisheries and natural resources for the Tulalip Tribes, called me a racist at Neah Bay. "There has never been an Indigenous people that has ever put another species in danger," he said. "I challenge Watson to name just one species."

Okay. The cave bear, the woolly rhinoceros, the mammoth, the saber-toothed tiger, the giant sloth, the horse and camel in North America, and I have already cited the extinctions caused by Indigenous peoples in Australia.

Williams continued. "They ought to be ashamed, people like Sea Shepherd, to target a race and call it environmentalism."

I responded to Williams by saying it would be racist of our group not to oppose the Makah hunt when we would oppose a similar undertaking by whites. I have spent nearly fifty years protecting whales, and for nearly five decades the whalers have hurtled that accusation at me. *All* the whalers. I have been called a racist by the Japanese, Native Americans, Russians, Norwegians, Danes, Mexicans, Icelanders, and Spaniards. The one thing they all have in common is that they all kill whales. If protecting whales is racist because some of the whalers are of a different race, then I guess I must plead guilty to racism. But the truth is, I deal with all whalers equally. I oppose them equally.

Georg Blichfeldt of the Norwegian High North Alliance called me a racist because, according to Georg, the only opponents of whaling are Anglo-Saxons. Talk about racial generalizations!

I haven't got a trace of Anglo-Saxon in me. I can't be anti-Danish because my grandfather was born in Copenhagen and his name was Larsen. And I don't think that I am anti-Asian because my daughter is half Chinese. And I am also Acadian Métis.

I have a long record of actions in support of Native American rights and I have Native American ancestors. So being called anti-Indian does not wash with me much, and I refuse to be guilted into supporting an illegal whaling activity by such coercion.

We had never before waged a campaign for whales in the territory of the United States, so we were somewhat surprise by the vehement accusations of racism hurtled against us. Saving whales and dolphins has always been as progressive as supporting civil rights, but now, for the first time, we found our defense of the whales to be grounds for condemnation as "racist" and "ethnocentric imperialists." The accusations did not come from the public at large but primarily from media people. Whereas before we could always count on the media to back the cause of whale protection and conservation, we were now finding the media championing the cause of the men with the harpoons and the guns based solely upon their race. If these were white men gunning for the whales, the media would have been solidly in our court.

The Japanese certainly knew what they were doing. They had done their homework, and they had discovered that harnessing white liberal guilt was easier than shooting a docile resident baby whale with an antitank gun.

For this reason, I would like to state my position on the issue of racism and whaling. I should note that I am doing so simply to clarify where I stand, but I really could not care less what people think or accuse me of.

I think that racism is a despicable form of behavior, and I have never condoned, nor have I ever participated in, the victimization or discrimination of any person based on race or ethnic origins. I want to get something straight, however. The killing of that innocent young whale was a barbaric and savage act committed by people raised in a culture that glorifies violence. It was not the Makah culture. It was our modern, media-influenced, good old American culture that those whalers in Makah Bay adhered to. It was the kill without the personal sacrifice, without traditional methods, and without respect. It was about killing, and as whaling captain Wayne Johnson noted, it was about revenge. The whalers were not people who practiced traditional Makah culture. They were instead a people who watched television; ate cheeseburgers; played and watched football; attended Christian churches; observed Thanksgiving, Christmas, and Easter as their spiritual holidays; and did not even think about killing a whale until they received a visit from a few men from Japan with a great idea about how they could regain their identity by simply becoming whalers again. And down the road, there would be money in it.

The race that killed the whale on May 17, 1999, was a cruel race, a ruthless race, and a barbaric and ecologically insensitive race. The man who threw that harpoon was a member of that savage race. The man that blasted the whale with the big gun was also a member of that race. The reporter who gleefully reported the kill to her wire service and the television anchor who excitedly covered the butchering of the whale were members of the same race. The US Coast Guard officer who joyfully pronounced it a great day when he received an award for his support in the slaughter was of the same race. You and I, all of us, are also of that race.

In a world in which millions of species are exploited without mercy, where ecosystems are pillaged without shame, where death is traded as a commodity, and where human trivialities dominate and shape an anthropocentric reality, there is only one species that takes while all others must give. That species is composed of one race: the human race.

There is very little difference in the physical and absolutely no difference in the moral, emotional, spiritual, and intellectual makeup and capabilities of any segment of the human species that embraces the conceit of anthropocentrism. Anthropologically, the four major subdivisions of humans—Asian, Australoid, Black, and white—are defined not by color but by characteristics that allowed for adaptation to different geographic regions, climates, and terrain.

East Indians are considered white and specifically Indo-European, although the skin of some Asians is darker than the skin of many Black individuals. American Indians are not a race unto themselves but are part of the group of humans indigenous to Asia.

More complex differences have developed over the last twenty millenniums, such as language, culture, religion, and politics. The fact is, though, not one of these groups is more moral than the others, despite the claims by some that they are. Not one is more inclined to vice or savagery than another. Our collective history demonstrates that all of us descended from the same background of tribal warfare, deception, cruelty, territorial thievery, vice, virtue, and appetites.

The tribes of Europe were culturally obliterated by so-called civilized Romans. They in turn were vanquished by the Gaels, Huns, and Vandals. The Irish, the Gaels, and the Germans weren't much different from Amerindians before they were conquered. Some of the imperialistic exploits of the Aztec in Mexico, the Thule conquest of the Dorset people of Labrador in pre-Columbian times, rival the Romans for sheer ruthlessness. Even the Makah had driven their war canoes across from Vancouver Island to wage a bloody war of extermination against the Ozette peoples hundreds of years before Europeans arrived. They took the land by Cape Alava prairie by conquest. There are no Ozette people left to reflect on that injustice.

In the first decade of the twentieth century, a war party of the Makah slaughtered hundreds of Clallam people. The US government actually ignored the slaughter because there was little interest in becoming involved in what was considered a cultural dispute among the Indians.

The truth is that neither the Europeans nor the Asians had to teach genocide or land stealing to the Indians or the Africans. Europeans did not introduce slavery to Africa; they simply exported it for their own use. Europeans bought Black people from other Black people and transported them to plantations. Slavery had been an institution in Africa for hundreds of years before Europeans arrived. Slavery was also a practice of early Europeans and Asians, and it was a well-documented practice among Native American and Polynesian tribes.

It is interesting that the Makahs, who champion cultural whaling, were lauded by some African Americans, despite the fact that slavery was just as important to the traditions of the Makah as whaling. The Makahs held slaves right up until they abandoned whaling earlier in the last century. In fact, I recall once again how Makah tribal council member John McCarty is on record as saying that the people in the tribe who were critical of whaling had no right to an opinion because they were descendants of slave families, and slave families had no right to criticize elite whaling families.

Political correctness is a strange ideology. It allows acceptance of hierarchy, killing, and discrimination as long as the package is championed by a culture that is in political favor.

For example, it is quite all right to some people that the Afghan Taliban or the Saudi Arabian royalty have a cultural and religious right to silence women in accordance with their traditional and religious beliefs, and, therefore, we should not be surprised to find people defending the right of the Makah to silence their anti-whaling elders for speaking their opinions. Tradition has been utilized to justify all sorts of barbarities and human rights violations. American media quite rightly condemned the white South African Boers for the slaughter of Black people at Sharpeville, for the murder of Stephen Biko, and for disenfranchising non-whites. The same media ignored the mass murder of the Ndebele people by the Shona people of Zimbabwe. It apparently was more politically correct for Black people to be killed by Black people than by whites.

It is my opinion that all people are equal and should be treated equally and fairly under the law. The fact is that the International Whaling Commission does not recognize the Makah whale hunt as a legitimate Aboriginal hunt. It does not meet the criteria of subsistence necessity and unbroken tradition. If we were to allow the Makah to violate the IWC regulations unopposed because they are Native American, we would be guilty of racial discrimination.

The Sea Shepherd Conservation Society deplores and condemns racism, and we will not allow ourselves to be coerced into a racist decision by the dictates of political correctness. If the hunt is illegal as defined by the IWC, the culture, race, or nationality of the whalers is irrelevant.

From a biocentric viewpoint, racism is ridiculous. With tens of millions of diverse species and millions threatened with extinction, we cannot discriminate against any one group of the *Homo sapiens* species: one group is neither better nor worse than any other group. We are all guilty. If you've been born, you are guilty of contributing to the diminishment of the diversity of life on this planet. If you recognize that this is so, that *Homo sapiens* are the problem, then any solution is guaranteed to be perceived as unacceptable or anti-humanity by those who exploit the natural world.

Being a conservationist means saying and exposing things that are unpopular, and it means taking actions that are unpopular. The plain fact of the matter is that protecting nature from Man—any man, meaning any male, female, race, creed, or behavioral trait of the species *Homo sapiens*—is a revolutionary act against the dominant paradigm of anthropocentrism. We must be prepared to suffer the slings and arrows of those who would denounce us with anthropocentric values that they believe are paramount over the reality of the natural paradigm.

Racism, sexism, class differences, and religious differences are all important issues within the collective cultures of our one species, but they pale into insignificance compared to the laws of ecology, such as the law of biodiversity, the law of interdependence of species, and the law of finite resources. Without a diverse ecosystem to support humanity, all anthropocentric values are meaningless and, soon enough, extinct.

Thus, it is absurd to accuse a biocentric conservationist of racism for opposing the slaughter of a species of whale or for opposing the destruction of a rainforest being slashed and burned by Natives in Madagascar. The survival of a species or an ecosystem takes precedence over any culture or any belief.

It is true that some are more culpable, more aggressive, and more ruthless than others. The burning of the rainforest by Natives in Madagascar is relatively minor in comparison to the destruction by oil and coal companies, but it is not insignificant in the eyes of lemurs and other nonhuman species whose home is being destroyed. In other words, it is not above criticism. When we intervene to stop turtle poaching on the island of Mayotte, we do so because it is in the interest of the survival of a species, and that takes precedence over the fact that the poachers are Native or poor. The right of a species to survive takes precedence over all other human priorities.

I believe this is a responsible position. Although I am philosophically opposed to the killing of all whales by any group of people, I would not set myself up as a judge of morality. Instead, I recognize as a foundation the rule of law as established by legitimately recognized marine conservation authorities, such as the International Whaling Commission (IWC) or the Convention on International Trade in Endangered Species of Wild Fauna and Flora (CITES).

I do not see Makah, Norwegian, or Japanese whalers; I see whalers. I do not see Hispanic loggers in New Mexico; I see people who clear-cut. I do not see Somali elephant poachers; I see poachers. I do not see the color of the skin or the dress of the whaler who throws the harpoon or fires the gun. I am blind to the justification and to the public relations posturing of those who kill whales in violation of international marine conservation law.

PUBLIC INTEREST ENVIRONMENTAL LAW CONFERENCE
UNIVERSITY OF OREGON SCHOOL OF LAW

I knew when we became involved with the Makah whale hunt that the Sea Shepherd Conservation Society would be subject to anger and harsh criticism for the stand that we would be taking. We accepted this, and thus we have not been surprised by the viciousness of the attacks in which we have been called a racist organization and I have been accused of being both a liar and a racist.

On March 2, 2001, I was one of the keynote speakers at the Public Interest Environmental Law Conference hosted by the Land Air Water Environmental Law Society at the University of Oregon. I delivered a presentation on conservation, media, and the law that was well received. I was followed by Ward Churchill, who represented the American Indian Movement.

Churchill wasted this opportunity to speak to a large crowd about real concerns when he decided to devote his speech to a personal attack on me. He said that I had not been at Wounded Knee, and that I had not been a part of the occupation. He told them that in opposing the Makah whale hunt that I was a racist. He also said that if I had any commitment to Native rights that I would have supported the Makah in an effort to regain land. Churchill even suggested that it was hypocritical of me to oppose the Makah treaty with the United States and that I was bound to uphold it since it was a treaty with the United States.

In response, I took the stage and stated that I had indeed been a medic at Wounded Knee during the occupation and that I opposed the whale hunt for the same reason that I have opposed any whale hunt—because it is illegal. I also told him that we had, in fact, initiated the idea to approach Congress for the purpose of arranging a swap of whaling rights for the return of lands. He called me a liar again. But I could leave the stage feeling good. The truth is the truth and it cannot be changed by revisionist statements from those who simply have a political agenda to deny the truth.

What Ward Churchill and a few members of the American Indian Movement may think of me is irrelevant. Sea Shepherd and I were in Makah Bay to protect whales. I was not a citizen of the United States, and thus a treaty between the Makah and the United States had no binding effect on me.

The next day, there was a panel discussion on International Whaling made up of Jonathan Paul of Ocean Defense International, Makah lawyer John Arum, and me. Jonathan and I concentrated on the illegality of the hunt, and Jonathan presented documentation proving that the Makah's intent was commercial whaling. Some people (mostly white) in the room loudly denounced us as racists. One woman stood up and demanded that we respect the sacred tradition of whaling, and I answered that there was nothing sacred about killing a whale and that the Makah had demonstrated gross disrespect for the death of Yabis when they kicked the whale and did backflips off the whale's body.

A man wearing dark sunglasses and a baseball cap with "NATIVE" stenciled on it stood up and proclaimed himself an elder. He launched into a monologue punctuated with ten to twenty seconds of silent, stone-faced stares at me. I stared right back at him.

"We are not people. We are the two-legged ones," he said. "I know where I come from. My people go back a thousand generations, and I know every one of them. I see disrespect here today. You whites cannot know the true way. We, the two-legged ones, speak to our brethren in the wild, and our brethren give themselves to us."

He carried on. He was not saying anything new. It was simply the same old myth-speak, the same old tired rhetoric. If you say something often enough it becomes the truth.

In all honesty, I felt sorry for him. He believed in the shadow myth that kept him where he now was—an angry man desperately searching for an enemy to respond to him.

"Yabis did not give herself to anyone. She was slain with an anti-tank gun," I said.

I thanked him for his opinion and summarized that our opposition was simply a question of law.

"What law? Whose law?" someone demanded.

"The international laws protecting whales," I answered.

"We don't recognize those laws," someone else answered. "The Makah have a treaty, and that is the law."

"Yes, indeed it is," I answered. "The treaty is between the United States and the Makah. The International Whaling Commission is an international body whose regulations take precedence over bilateral treaties."

"Says you," someone yelled angrily.

"I do say so, and there are Makah elders who agree," I responded.

A white woman wearing feathers and beads spoke up. "Native Americans are all much wiser environmentalists than you. Humane respect for animals is a part of their spirit. They are one with nature, one with the Creator. If they wish to take a whale, it is not your place to deny them."

"And what of those Native Americans, those Makah, those elders who oppose the killing of whales? Do their voices not count, or are they simply to be drowned out by the demands of those who wish to kill a whale?" I answered.

I left the conference wondering where there was a shred of evidence to demonstrate that the Aboriginal peoples of the Americas today are more humane, more environmentally conscious, more attuned to nature, and more respectful of life and the natural world than the Africans, Asians, or Europeans?

The pattern of human behavior weaves a similar tapestry throughout all human cultures. In each there can be found murder, territorial warfare, religious intolerance, abject cruelties, ritualized slaughter, subjugation of people because of gender, sexual orientation, ethnicity, or political differences, or just because they feel like being hostile. I see a history that echoes the same vices and the same crimes across all continents.

Hernán Cortés did not take Tenochtitlan—a city with a population of 250,000 and defended by tens of thousands of Aztec warriors—with just nine hundred Spanish soldiers. Nor was the defeat of Montezuma accomplished because the Spaniards had guns, horses, a few cannons, and armor. Sheer Aztec numbers could have easily overrun the terribly inefficient harquebuses and the cumbersome cannons. Spanish weaponry could have breached the Aztec battle lines, but unless there were numbers to invade that breach, complete victory would be frustrated.

But the Spanish *did* have the numbers to breach those battle lines. In the final battle, Cortés deployed three armies of only two hundred Spanish soldiers. However, each of the three armies was backed up by twenty to thirty thousand warriors of the Totonacs, the Tlaxcalans, and Choluteca.

The empire of the Aztecs fell at the hand of the tribes that had suffered under brutal Aztec rule for so long. These were the people who had been the victims of blood sacrifices and forced to pay tribute to the Aztecs, the ones who had stolen their land.

In North America, many tribes allied themselves with the invader to punish rival tribes. My own ancestors, the Mi'kmaq, eagerly volunteered to go to Newfoundland to exterminate Beothuk for the bounty the British put on their heads. The Crow rode with Custer. Tribes betrayed tribes. The great Chief Kamehameha, so revered by the modern-day Hawaiians, is a part of the myth. They forget that he waged bloody war on and subjugated the other islands and that he welcomed the Europeans and sold them the farm—literally. Kamehameha was no friend to the Hawaiians. He was the white man's tool and the white man's ideal. They romanticized him and, as such, he prospered; his place was reserved in the revisionist history where he is now honored by his own people for betraying them.

The media shapes our perception of the Indian, shapes it for Natives and non-Natives alike. The perceptions change as the media portrayals change them from bad guys to good guys, from ruthless savages to nature- and peace-loving gurus.

Hollywood has defined the Indians and redefined them and then redefined them again. Hollywood has also defined and redefined the Europeans and the Americans.

In *Dances with Wolves*, we cheered as the Lakota killed the American soldiers, and our enthusiasm was genuine. The plot of that film dictated that we like these particular Indians, just as we all loved chief Dan George in *Little Big Man* and *The Outlaw Josey Wales*. Yet we cheered with an equal passion when the Lakota dispatched the Kiowa warrior in *Dances with Wolves*. He was a bad Indian. Ironically, it was Kiowa land that both the Lakota and the whites had encroached on.

We loved Graham Greene in *Thunderheart* and *Dances with Wolves*. Yet I feel his best movie was *Clearcut*, a film that died at the box office within days because it didn't feed the myth. It was too close to reality. In *Clearcut* we saw the myth exposed. We saw the liberal white man show his true colors when presented with the reality of what the Indian truly wanted. Content to posture support for Native rights and environmental protection, the white guy turned on the Indian for not being the Indian that the myth dictated he should be.

At the same time that we have bad Indians and good Indians, we have bad whites and good whites. George Armstrong Custer was a bad white, mainly because he was a loser. If not for Little Big Horn, may have become president of the United States.

We have even incorporated reality into the myth by enlisting Native American activists to perform in the movies. John Trudell was righteously wonderful in portraying a radical Indian in *Thunderheart*. It was brilliant casting. Who better to depict a radical American Indian Movement activist than a radical American Indian Movement activist?

And Russell Means, who I have always respected as an inspirational leader, was truly inspirational in *The Last of the Mohicans*. How absolutely ironic that it was the voice of Russell Means as the father of Pocahontas in the Disney animated story of one of the great enduring romantic myths of the Americas. In *Pocahontas* we see the myth in all its glory. It's a romantic tale of a beautiful Native American princess who falls in love with a handsome English soldier named John Smith. With their marriage comes peace between the English and the Indians, and the couple and their respective peoples live happily ever after.

The real story, of course, was less than romantic. The girl was named Matoaka, and she was the daughter of Wahunsenacawh, a chief of the people known by the English as the Powhatans. She was married not to John Smith but to John Rolfe. In Rolfe's own words, it was hardly a romantic relationship. In a letter to his superiors, Rolfe wrote that he "sought the marriage not out of the unbridled lust desire of carnall affection, but for the good of this plantation, for the honour of our Countrie . . . and for the converting to the true knowledge of God and Jesus Christ, an unbelieving creature."

In other words, with her father seeking peace, Matoaka was thrown in as a peace offering. She was only twelve or thirteen at the time. She was taken to Gravesend, England, on the banks of the River Thames, where she died of smallpox at about age twenty-one.

Her husband returned to Jamestown, where, in 1618, he was slaughtered by his wife's people and his body was cut into pieces. The English retaliated and massacred thousands of Powhatans, effectively removing them forever. The miserable life of Pocahantas became an embellished legend to feed the myth. I had to laugh when I saw the posters for the Disney movie. Unknowingly, Disney was marketing a children's animated movie with a very racy, pornographic title.

Pocahantas was a nickname Matoaka had acquired. It is from the Algonkian word *pocohaac*, which can be translated as the "privities or secret of a man." It can also be translated more directly as "penis," and used in the context of a nickname by this maiden, it would literally have meant "cock teaser."

As a child, I believed the fable just as many children believe it today, thanks to Disney's version of history. Just another story reworked once again in the ever-evolving mythology of the Americas.

Today we see the exploitation as invasive miners, loggers, and farmers push into the Amazon. Dams are erected and the rainforest is slashed and burned as Native peoples continue to suffer and die.

Since 2000, some fifteen thousand conservationists have been murdered, and the majority of the victims have been Indigenous peoples. All over the world, Indigenous cultures move steadily toward extinction, with languages disappearing and biocentric lifestyles discouraged. Their land continues to be stolen, and the history books continue to be Orwellian: manipulated and censored.

Perhaps when anthropocentric civilization collapses, there will be a resurfacing of biocentric values and, perhaps, just perhaps, the Indigenous cultures will be resurrected and freed at last from the restrictive colonialist myth that was constructed to keep them imprisoned within a system that, from the beginning, had the goal of absolute assimilation or obliteration. When that day should arrive, there will be no need to sacrifice a whale for the pretense of resurrecting our cultures.

The Makah elders that I had the honor to speak with, people such as Alberta Thompson and Jesse Ides, represented the strength that is needed for that resurrection. They understood that the people need to be intimately connected and a part of the natural world. The whales that once sustained them with flesh could now sustain and guide them toward a better future—when humans respect rather than harpoon them. In the not-so-distant future, when modern society collapses, as it most certainly will, the Makah canoes may venture onto the water with a true understanding of a world now forgotten.

And this holds true for all who will survive and who seek a better and more meaningful relationship with the "others"—those species whose existence is essential for the survival of us all. A world without whales, without fish, without trees, without insects, without plankton is not a world that can sustain our species. The only thing that will sustain us will be humility and a respect for our relationship to all our relatives in the sea and upon the land—both animal and plant—within diverse ecosystems.

PRINCIPALS IN THE CONFLICT AT NEAH BAY

Listed in alphabetical order (only names that appear in this book are included).

Principal Anti-Whaling Forces

Abbott, Erin . . . . Ocean Defense International

Anderson, Will . . . . Progressive Animal Welfare Society

Brooks, Lorena (pseudonym) . Sea Shepherd staff member

Brown, Peter . . . . First mate of the Sea Shepherd vessel *Sirenian*

Conway, Jake . . . . Crew member with SEDNA

Cousteau, Jean-Michel . . . Oceanographic explorer and environmentalist

Christie, Andrew . . . . Sea Shepherd director of information

Cook, Janet . . . . Sea Shepherd photographer

Calvert, Brian . . . . San Juan County port commissioner

Chamblin, Dottie . . . . Makah elder, attended IWC meetings in Aberdeen and Monaco

Claplanhoo, Ruth . . . . . . Makah elder

Dick, Simon (Tanis) . . . . . Kwakiutl spirit dancer and carver

Dutton, Steph . . . . Sea kayaker and member of In the Path of Giants

Elissat, Dinah . . . . Sea Shepherd crew on *Sirenian*

Hall, Anna . . . . Spokesperson for the West Coast Anti-Whaling Society

Harper, Josh . . . . Crew member with SEDNA

Ides, Jesse . . . . Makah elder, attended IWC meeting in Monaco

Johnson, Viola . . . . Makah elder

Ides, Isabell . . . . Makah elder

Irving, Margaret . . . . Makah elder

Jennings, Dave . . . . Sea Shepherd observer to the IWC meeting in Aberdeen

Kundu, Michael . . . . Director, Sea Shepherd Pacific Northwest

Lance, Allison. . . . . *Sirenian* crew member, arrested on May 17, 1999

Lawson, Matt. . . . . Captain of the *Sea Shepherd*

Marining, Rod . . . . Crew member, Sea Shepherd vessel *Sirenian*

McKee, Lena. . . . . Makah elder

Metcalf, Jack . . . . United States congressional representative

Moore, Angela. . . . . Sea Shepherd observer to the IWC in Dublin

Moss, Bill . . . . World Whale Police

Mowat, Farley . . . . International chair of Sea Shepherd

Munson, Don. . . . . Chief engineer on Sea Shepherd vessel *Sirenian*

Nichols, Ken. . . . . Crew member, Sea Shepherd vessel *Sirenian*

O'Connell, Erin . . . . Ocean Defense International

O'Conner, Kate . . . . Whale and Dolphin Conservation

Owens, Chuck . . . . Peninsula Citizens for the Protection of Whales

Owens, Margaret. . . . . Peninsula Citizens for the Protection of Whales

Rorabeck-Siler, Cheryl . . . Jet Ski operator charged with disrupting whale hunt

Paul, Jonathan . . . . Leader of Sea Defense Alliance (SEDNA)

Robinson, Carla. . . . . Administrative director, Sea Shepherd

Siler, Bret. . . . . Jet Ski operator charged at Neah Bay skirmish

Smith, Mabel . . . . Makah elder, attended IWC meeting in Monaco

Spong, Dr. Paul . . . . Whale scientist, founder of OrcaLab

Thompson, Alberta. . . . . . Makah elder and anti-whaling voice

Tiura, Heidi . . . . In the Path of Giants

Vogel, Carroll. . . . . Sea Shepherd board member

Watson, Captain Paul. . . . President of the Sea Shepherd Conservation Society

White, Ben . . . . Leader of People for the Makah and Whales

Woodyer, Julie . . . . Campaign Director of Zoocheck Canada

Principal Whalers and Makah Whale Hunt Supporters

Ahdunko, Lionel . . . . Makah tribal police chief

Alexander, Andrea. . . . . . Makah tribe general manager, 1995

Arum, John. . . . . Attorney for the Makah tribe

Coster, Bob . . . . US Coast Guard

Dailey, Denise. . . . . Director, Makah Whaling Commission

Felleman, Fred . . . . Pro-whaling whale biologist

Greene, Dan . . . . Makah fisherman and pro-whaling advocate

Happynook, Tom Mexis . President, World Council of Whalers

Johnson, Ben . . . . Makah tribal chairman (1998 and 1999)

Johnson, Eric . . . . Captain of the Makah whaling crew in 1998

Johnson, Keith . . . . President, Makah Whaling Commission

Johnson, Wayne . . . . Captain of the Makah whaling crew in 1999

Lucas, Jerry . . . . Makah tribal spokesperson

McCarty, Micah . . . . Member of the Makah whaling crew

McGimpsey, Joe . . . . Makah tribal member

Nakamura, Tadahiko . . . . Japan Whaling Association

Parker, Marcy . . . . Makah tribal council member, 1998

Parker, Theron . . . . Makah harpooner

Sones, Dave . . . . Assistant director of Makah Fisheries, 1995

Svenson, Eric . . . . Makah tribal police officer

Swan, Don . . . . Member of the Makah whaling crew

Ward, Helma . . . . Elder critical of Alberta Thompson

Watters, Lawrence . . . . Instructor, Lewis and Clark College

Watts, George . . . . Spokesperson for the Tseshaht Band

Media

Anderson, Peggy . . . . Reporter for the Associated Press

Blore, Shawn . . . . Reporter for the *Georgia Straight*

Hall, Neal . . . . *The Vancouver Sun*

Henifin, Jacob . . . . Photographer, Associated Press

Hunter, Robert . . . . Reporter for Citytv; author of *Red Blood*

Mapes, Linda . . . . Reporter for the *Seattle Times*

McMahon, Patrick . . . . . . Reporter for *USA Today*

Nilsen, Terje . . . . Reporter for Norwegian television

Russell, Dick . . . . Author of *Eye of the Whale*

Scigliano, Eric . . . . Writer for the *Seattle Weekly*

Shukovsky, Paul . . . . Reporter for the *Seattle Post-Intelligencer*

Tizon, Alex . . . . Reporter for the *Seattle Times*

Government Authorities

Campbell, Gordon . . . . . . BC Liberal Party leader, 1998

Cashore, John . . . . BC minister for Aboriginal Affairs

Cull, Elizabeth . . . . BC Environment, Lands and Parks minister, 1998

Hayes, Margaret . . . . Attorney for the National Marine Fisheries Service

Howe, Joe . . . . Clallam County sheriff

Locke, Gary . . . . Democratic governor of Washington State

Martin, Joe . . . . Undersheriff of Clallam County

Slaminski, Jerry . . . . Port Angeles US Customs chief officer

Swartz, Steve . . . . National Marine Fisheries Service scientist

Tillman, Michael . . . . Deputy US commissioner to the IWC

NOTES CONCERNING SOURCES FOR QUOTES

All quotes by people mentioned in this book were derived from documented media sources, including newspapers, magazines, television, radio, and filmed interviews. No quotes have been taken from the internet without citing a reference to specific publications or broadcasts as a primary source unless the quote is from a person whose individual or corporate website has specifically posted it. Quotes from email were used only if the text was available from a message sent directly from the person quoted.

The sources for the quotes used are listed in the media references that follow. The only exceptions are quotations by people the author interviewed directly or heard in a conversation. If there are any disputes regarding my use of a quote, the author will supply the specific source in the form of a photocopy, tape, or videotape on the condition that the inquiry includes costs for duplication and postage. To validate a quotation in which the author is the source, he will provide a notarized affidavit. This will require the cost of the notary public plus postage.

REFERENCES AND SOURCES
General References

The author has drawn upon the following publications and sources with regard to references to Makah spirituality, traditional whaling practices, modern whaling practices, treaty rights, and history.

1. The Treaty between the United States of America and the Makah Tribe of Indians, January 31, 1855, ratified April 18, 1859, signed by president James Buchanan.

2. Elizabeth Colson, *The Makah Indians: A Study of an Indian Tribe in Modern American Society* (University of Manchester Press, 1953).

3. Robert Hunter, *Red Blood: One (Mostly) White Guy's Encounters with the Native World* (McClelland & Stewart, 1999).

4. Albert Irvine, *How the Makah Obtained Possession of Cape Flattery* (Indian Notes and Monographs, No. 6).

5. James G. McCurdy, *By Juan de Fuca's Strait* (Metropolitan Press, 1937).

6. Dick Russell, *Eye of the Whale: From Baja to Siberia with the World's Largest Mammal* (Simon and Schuster, 2001).

7. Robert Sullivan, *A Whale Hunt: Two Years on the Olympic Peninsula with the Makah and Their Canoe* (Scribner, 2000).

8. T. T. Waterman, *The Whaling Equipment of the Makah Indians* (University of Washington Press, 1920).

9. Lawrence Watters and Connie Dugger, "The Hunt for Gray Whales: The Dilemma of Native American Treaty Rights and the International Moratorium on Whaling," *Columbia Journal of Environmental Law* (vol. 22:319, 1997).

The following publications were sources for material on the history of the conflict over Aboriginal whaling:

The Sea Shepherd Log, spring/summer edition, 1999.

The logbooks of the *Sea Shepherd* and the *Sirenian* are the sources for dates of events.

CHAPTER 1

THE SPIRIT OF AUMANIL

1. The title name for the first chapter is Aumanil. This is the name of the friendly Inuit deity that controls the movements of whales.

2. The quote from chief Simon Baker that begins Chapter 1 is taken from his dedication to the author of *Our Elders Speak*. The dedication is written on page 36 of the copy in Paul Watson's possession. This dedication was written in August 1992 at Harrison Hot Springs in British Columbia.

3. During the summer of 1999, there was much discussion on Native American internet chat sites saying that Paul Watson did not participate in the occupation of Wounded Knee. Evidence that he was a participant at Wounded Knee in March 1993 can be found in reports filed to and published in the *Vancouver Sun*. Specifically, these reports, written by Robert Hunter, were published on March 14, 1973, and on March 23, 1973. Both Paul Watson and David Garrick (who was also a participant in the occupation) wrote and published accounts of their experience at Wounded Knee in the Vancouver weekly newspaper the *Georgia Straight*.

   In the book *Voices from Wounded Knee 1973* by Akwesasne Notes (published by the Mohawk Nation in Rooseveltown, New York, 1974), Paul Watson is pictured on page 65, the second person from bottom left, wearing a Cowichan woolen sweater, seated with his chin resting on his right hand. Watson is also pictured on page 76, in the upper right corner, last person in the row of people marching, wearing a Cowichan sweater and hat. Page 201, he is center rear of picture, wearing a Cowichan hat. He appears between a woman in a long coat and man with a cowboy hat. Page 245, David Garrick appears (first person on the left, standing with walking stick).

4. The conversation between Dr. Paul Spong and Farley Mowat is taken with permission from *Song of the Whale* (the dramatic story of Dr. Paul Spong, founder of the Greenpeace Save the Whales movement, and his startling discoveries about whale intelligence). Authored by Rex Weyler, the book was published by Anchor Press/ Doubleday in 1986.

5. Information on the family history of Paul Watson comes from family archival letters, photos, and birth, marriage, and death documentation papers.

6. A more detailed account of the voyage to oppose the Columbus reenactment voyage can be found in *Red Blood* by Robert Hunter (McClelland & Stewart, 1999).

7. The history of Greenpeace can be found in *Warriors of the Rainbow: A Chronicle of the Greenpeace Movement* by Robert Hunter (Holt, Rinehart, and Winston, 1979). Reference to the Wounded Knee involvement by Paul Watson and David Garrick is found on page 155.

8. Another excellent history of Greenpeace is the book *Greenpeace* by Rex Weyler (Raincoast Books, 2004).

CHAPTER 2

A HARPOON TO SLAY ONE THOUSAND WHALES

1. Iron Eyes Cody was the star of a famous TV commercial of the seventies that featured an Indian paddling a canoe and turning a bend to see a factory polluting a river. Iron Eyes Cody was later revealed to be of Italian descent.

Sources for this chapter are listed under Notes on Media References below, May 1995 through November 1995.

CHAPTER 3

IDI:GAWÉ:SDI

1. Quote from Paul Watson taken from the *Christian Science Monitor* article by Mark Trumbull (July 25, 1995).

2. Chamblin and Claplanhoo quotes.

3. Dan Greene's quote from "Whaling: B.C. Will Talk, Gov't Replies to Native Bid," by Don Hauka (*Vancouver Province*, May 24, 1995). The quote was also in "Native Plan to Hunt Whales," by John Bermingham (*Vancouver Province*, May 23, 1995).

4. Extracted from "American Indians Apply to Resume Whale Hunting," by Nick Nuttall (*London Times*, June 1, 1995).

5. "Whaling Group Criticised," by John Mooney (*Irish Times*, May 30, 1995).

6. Extracted from "Traditional Whaling" (*Echo*, Dublin, May 31, 1995, vol. XLVII #3, page 2).

7. Quotes from tribal members taken from "The Accidental Whale," by Paula Bock (*Seattle Times Pacific NW* magazine, November 26, 1995).

8. Extracted from "Take that Harpoon . . . and Keep It Where the Sun Doesn't Shine," by Mike Roberts (*Vancouver Province*, May 25, 1995).

9. Source for quotes from John and Ginger McCarty, "Seeing a Future in the Past," by Roberta Ulrich (*Oregonian*, June 5, 1995).

CHAPTER 5

A WHALE OF A CRAPSHOOT IN MONTE CARLO

1. *Fishing News* (September 5, 1997).

2. Michael Kundu of Sea Shepherd drafted the wording for the congressional letter condemning the US proposal to allow whaling in US waters.

3. Letter from Peter Bridgewater to Michael Kundu.

CHAPTER 7

THE DEATH OF YABIS

1. Written account directly from Cheryl Rorabeck-Siler. Cheryl was thirty-two years old at the time of the incident and was a high school teacher in Tillamook, Oregon. She and her husband, Bret Siler, live in Nehalem, Oregon. Cheryl and Bret spent months at Neah Bay.

2. Reference to a letter from Roy Kline.

CHAPTER 8

VICTORY FOR THE WHALES

1. Conversations from 2020 with Will Anderson, Erin Abbott, Erin O'Connell, Jonathan Paul, Julie Woodyer.

2. Transcript of United States District Court Western District of Washington at Tacoma: Julianne Woodyer, Plaintiff v. United States of America. Docket # 04-35338.

CHAPTER 10
THE DEATH OF A MYTH

On February 22, 2001, the author called Middlebury College in Vermont and confirmed that Ted Perry was on the faculty in the Department of Theatre.

Ward Churchill's accusations against the author were made on March 2 at the Public Interest Environmental Law Conference hosted by the Land Air Water Environmental Law Society at the University of Oregon School of Law, where he and the author were keynote speakers. Both speeches were videotaped by the law school.

The source for the information on the extinctions in Australia is David Perlman, science editor (*San Francisco Chronicle*, January 8, 1999). The source for the information on Cortés and his Meso-American allies is *Aztec Warfare: Imperial Expansion and Political Control* and *Mexico and the Spanish Conquest*, both by Ross Hassig, professor of anthropology at the University of Oklahoma.

Two sources were used for the historical information on Pocahontas. The first is *Wilderness at Dawn: The Settling of the North American Continent* by Ted Morgan (Simon & Schuster, 1993). The other source is *The Conquest of Paradise* by Kirkpatrick Sale (Alfred A. Knopf, 1990).

During the controversy, there was some dispute as to the racial affiliation of the Ainu. Supporters of the whale hunt insisted that the Ainu are a non-white tribe native to Japan. *Webster's Dictionary of the English Language* describes the Ainu as "members of the Aboriginal race of the northernmost islands of Japan, having Caucasoid features, light skin, and hairy bodies." "Caucasoid" is defined as a subspecies of mankind, including the light-skinned peoples of Europe, North Africa, Eastern Asia, and India, and their descendants in other parts of the world. Linguistically, the Ainu language is related to Finnish and Hungarian.

SUMMARY OF MAKAH WHALING PROCEDURAL HISTORY

June 16, 1994: The Eastern North Pacific (ENP) gray whales are delisted from the Endangered Species Act (ESA).

May 5, 1995: The Makah tribe (hereafter referred to as "the tribe") formally notifies the US government of the tribe's interest in resuming its alleged "ceremonial and subsistence" harvest of ENP gray whales under the Treaty of Neah Bay, asking the Department of Commerce to represent it in seeking approval from the International Whaling Commission (IWC) for an annual quota.

October 13, 1997: NMFS enters into an agreement with the tribe to pursue a quota at the IWC.

October 17, 1997: NMFS issues a final Environmental Assessment (EA) and finding of "no significant impact" (FONSI) after conducting an environmental review under the National Environmental Policy Act (NEPA). The EA determines whether or not a federal action (here, NMFS's approval of the hunt) has the potential to cause significant environmental effects. If there is a finding of significant impact on the environment, an Environmental Impact Statement (EIS) must be prepared.

October 18, 1997: The IWC sets a catch limit of 620 ENP gray whales for 1998 through 2002. The Russian Federation (acting on behalf of the Chukchi people for a total of 600) and the US (acting on behalf of the Makah for a total of 20 whales) submit "needs statements" to the IWC.

April 6, 1998: NMFS allocates a quota to the tribe for hunts in 1999 under the Whaling Convention Act.

September 21, 1998: The United States District Court for the Western District of Washington grants summary judgment for NMFS in a lawsuit filed in October of 1997, ruling that the tribe can resume whaling.

May 17, 1999: The tribe hunts and kills an ENP gray whale.

June 9, 2000: Metcalf v. Daley (214 F.3d 1135), Court of Appeals for the Ninth Circuit reverses and remands the district court's September 1998 opinion, holding that NMFS failed to take a "hard look" under NEPA at the proposed whale hunt.

July 12, 2001: NMFS issues a final EA with a preferred alternative granting the tribe the IWC quota of five whales a year for alleged "ceremonial and subsistence purposes."

December 20, 2002: Anderson v. Evans (314 F.3d 1006), Court of Appeals for the Ninth Circuit rules that (1) NMFS must prepare an EIS and (2) the tribe must comply with the Marine Mammal Protection Act (MMPA) by seeking a waiver authorizing a "take" of marine mammals otherwise prohibited by the MMPA moratorium.

February 14, 2005: The tribe issues a request to NMFS for a waiver of the MMPA's take moratorium.

September 8, 2007: Five members of the tribe illegally hunt and kill a gray whale in the Strait of Juan de Fuca.

May 9, 2008: NFMS announces a draft EIS on the tribe's request for a waiver.

May 21, 2012: NMFS withdraws its draft EIS due to new scientific evidence potentially supporting the classification of the Pacific Coast Feeding Group (PCFG) gray whales as a separate "stock" from ENP gray whales. PCFG gray whales would be the most vulnerable to a tribal hunt. NMFS begins a process to develop a new draft EIS.

March 2015: NMFS announces a new draft EIS. The DEIS considers a new set of alternatives from those assessed in 2008.

April 5, 2019: NMFS announces a proposed waiver of MMPA take prohibitions and the commencement of a formal rule-making process before a Coast Guard Administrative Law Judge (ALJ) to decide if the proposed waiver satisfies the MMPA.

November 14–21, 2019: ALJ George J. Jordan holds a public, formal administrative hearing under the MMPA in Seattle. The administrative hearing is conducted in a trial format. Sea Shepherd Legal, on behalf of itself and SSCS, participates as a party to the proceeding to oppose the waiver. Sea Shepherd is joined by the Animal Welfare Institute and the Peninsula Citizens for the Protection of Whales. The Makah participate as a party to support NMFS's proposed waiver.

February 27, 2020: NMFS announces its intent to prepare a supplemental draft EIS to assess (1) new (since preparation of the 2015 draft EIS) scientific information related to the currently declared ENP gray whale unusual mortality event (UME), and (2) the effect of the proposed composite even/odd year hunt scheme (which was not presented in the 2015 draft EIS) on gray whales.

Next Steps: At the time of publication of this book, the ALJ's recommended decision on the proposed waiver to the acting administrator of NMFS is substantially overdue and the timing remains uncertain, even though it is entirely within the control of the ALJ. Once a decision is issued, the acting administrator will take it into consideration in making a final determination on the waiver. Before making a final decision, NMFS is required by law to provide the public with a twenty-day comment period on the ALJ's recommended decision. At some time (not specified in the rules) following this comment period, NMFS will issue its final decision on the waiver. We anticipate that a waiver will likely be granted, but that decision can be challenged in federal court on a broader range of legal grounds (e.g., the ESA) than in the MMPA administrative waiver proceeding.

To date, a final decision has not been made by scientists as to whether PCFG gray whales should be declared a separate stock from ENP gray whales. If they are declared a separate stock, that declaration would have a serious negative impact on whether the Makah hunt could ever go forward. Of course, the delay also affects (and angers) the tribe, which was likely hoping to commence a hunt in July 2021, under the "even/odd year" hunt scheme selected by NMFS. The further delay and anticipated new legal challenges following the ALJ's decision make the possibility of any such hunt taking place highly unlikely.

NOTES ON MEDIA REFERENCES

Media references are listed when they refer to a specific quote, incident, or event used in the book.

May 23, 1995: *Vancouver Province*, "Natives Plan to Hunt Whales," headline story by John Bermingham.

May 24, 1995: *Vancouver Sun*, "Indian Whaling Ships 'Will Be Sunk,'" by Neal Hall. Quotes from BC Liberal Party leader Gordon Campbell and Diane Lake, media officer with the federal Department of Fisheries and Oceans in Vancouver.

May 24, 1995: *Vancouver Province*, "Whaling: B.C. Will Talk, Gov't Replies to Native Bid," by Don Hauka.

May 25, 1995: *Vancouver Province*, "Take That Harpoon . . . and Keep It Where the Sun Doesn't Shine," by Mike Roberts.

May 25, 1995: *Seattle Times*, "The Whale Hunt: Listen to the Case for the Makahs," by Don Hannula.

May 26, 1995: *Vancouver Province*, "Lineup for Whale Kill," by John Bermingham. Quotes from chief George Watts.

May 27, 1995: *Globe and Mail* (digest), Greenpeace spokesperson Catherine Stewart states that the Greenpeace Foundation was opposed to reopening a Makah whale hunt.

May 28, 1995: *Peninsula Daily News*, ad sponsored by PAWS featuring seven Makah elders stating their opposition to a Makah whale hunt.

May 30, 1995: *Irish Times*, "Whaling Group Criticised," by John Mooney. Sea Shepherd critical of the IWC.

May 31, 1995: *Guardian*, "Illegal Trade Evidence Hits Japan's Case for Whaling," by Paul Brown.

June 4, 1995: *New York Times*, "Tribe's Hope in a Whale Hunt Worries US," by Timothy Egan.

June 4, 1995: *Seattle Times*, "Makah Tribe Seeks Return to Tradition of Whaling," by Timothy Egan.

June 5, 1995: *Oregonian*, "Seeing a Future in the Past," by Roberta Ulrich.

June 6, 1995: *Seattle Post-Intelligencer*, "Makah Whale Hunt Plans Alarm Animal Activists," by Paul Shukovsky. Quotes taken from Paul Watson, Dave Sones, Andrea Alexander, Fred Felleman, Steve Swartz, John Cashore, and Elizabeth Cull.

June 8, 1995: *Seattle Post-Intelligencer*, "The Makah's Case for Whale Hunting," editorial.

June 10, 1995: *Seattle Post-Intelligencer*, "Conservation Society Will Do Its Best to Intervene," letter to the editor by Captain Paul Watson.

July 5, 1995: *Seattle Weekly*, "Last Stands," by Eric Scigliano.

July 17, 1995: Associated Press, "Gray Whale Dies in Makah Net."

July 18, 1995: *Peninsula Daily News*, "Makah Fishing Leader Netted 10-Ton Whale," by Christina Kelly. Quotes from tribal general manager Andrea Alexander.

July 25, 1995: *Christian Science Monitor*, "Indians Hope to Harpoon New Whale-Hunting Rights," by Mark Trumbull. Quote from Makah tribal council member Jerry Lucas.

August 2, 1995: *Los Angeles Times*, "Makah Tribe Seeks to Take to the Seas on the Trail of the Whale," by Kim Murphy. Quote from Dan Greene.

November 26, 1995: *Seattle Times Pacific NW* magazine, "The Accidental Whale," by Paula Bock.

August 5, 1996: *Philadelphia Inquirer*, "Dispute Spears Whaling Revival," by Carol Morello. Quotes by Dan Greene calling elders Thompson and Chamblin "traitors." Quotes from Makah tribal member Helma Ward. Quotes from Alberta Thompson from Aberdeen, Scotland.

June 27, 1996: *Seattle Times*, "Makahs' Whaling Bid Raises Passions," by Danny Westneat. Quote from Alberta Thompson from Aberdeen, Scotland. Quote from Rep. Jack Metcalf.

June 29, 1996: *Pocono Record*, "Whale Hunt: A Fish Story," editorial.

September 4, 1996: *Seattle Weekly*, "Whale Hunt: The Makah Tribe, Coast Guard, and Sea Shepherd Skirmish at Sea," by Eric Scigliano.

September 26–October 3, 1996: *Georgia Straight*, "Whaling Nation," by Shawn Blore.

August 5, 1997: *Peninsula Daily News*, "Whale Hunt Protest Possible; Sea Shepherd May Meet Indian Canoes In Port Angeles," by Brad Lincoln.

August 7–14, 1997: *Georgia Straight*, "Watson Expects Whale of a Confrontation with Makah."

September 4, 1997: *Victoria Colonist*, "Activists Denounce Aboriginal Whaling," by Judith Lavoie.

October 10, 1997: *Seattle Times*, "Anti-whaling Crusade Heats Up, Metcalf to Attend Monaco Meeting," by Danny Westneat.

May 14, 1998: *Seattle Post-Intelligencer*, "Whale Hunt Concerns Aired, Task Force Hopes to Prevent Violence," by Paul Shukovsky.

May 17, 1998: *Aftenposten* (Norway), "Watson Is Moving the Whale War to USA," by Jan Gunnar Furuly.

May 19, 1998: *Seattle Times*, "Whaling Protesters, Police Plot Strategy," by Jim Simon.

May 20, 1998: *Peninsula Daily News*, "Lawmaker Wants Tribe to Watch Whales," by Christina Kelly.

May 28, 1998: *Seattle Post-Intelligencer*, "Makahs Say Animal Rights Group Is Lying About Whale Meat Deal," by Paul Shukovsky.

June 28, 1998: *Peninsula Daily News*, "Tribal Rift Kills Whaling Effort," by Christina Kelly. Quotes from Kate O'Conner and James Baker.

July 23, 1998: *Seattle Times*, "Buffer Zone Set for Whalers," by Jim Simon.

July 24, 1998: *Seattle Post-Intelligencer*, "Whaling Confrontation Shapes Up," by Paul Shukovsky.

July 25, 1998: *Seattle Times*, "Arrival of Anti-Whaler's Ship Sends Neah Bay Into Tizzy," by Alex Tizon.

July 26, 1998: *Peninsula Daily News*, "Makah Whale Hunt Rationalization Doesn't Ring True," by Marlene Davis.

August 9, 1998: *New York Times*, "Permission Granted to Kill a Whale. Now What?" by Robert Sullivan.

August 12, 1998: *Peninsula Daily News*, "Makah Plan Protest Defense," by Jesse Hamilton.

August 12, 1998: *Seattle Times*, "Makahs to Expand Festival Security," by Alex Tizon.

August 12, 1998: *Seattle Post-Intelligencer*, "Makah Hunt for Whaling Heritage."

August 13, 1998: *Seattle Post-Intelligencer*, "Makah Whale Hunt Bitterly Opposed," by Paul Shukovsky.

August 21, 1998: *Seattle Post-Intelligencer*, "Locke Weighs Sending Troops to Makah Celebration," by Paul Shukovsky.

August 23, 1998: *Seattle Times*, "Makah Manifesto," by Keith Johnson.

August 25, 1998: *Seattle Times*, "Harpoon Locke's Plan to Use National Guard," editorial.

August 26, 1998: *Olympian*, "Makah Get Unwanted Attention," by Chester Allen.

August 27, 1998: *Los Angeles Times*, "All Not Whale in Hunting Dispute," by Kim Murphy.

August 28, 1998: *South County Journal* (Kent, Washington), "Makah Should Reconsider Hunt for Gray Whale," editorial.

August 28, 1998: *Vancouver Sun*, "Clashes Feared Over Whale Hunt."

August 28, 1998: *Seattle Post-Intelligencer*, "Makah Fear Anti-Whaling Violence," by Paul Shukovsky.

August 29, 1998: *Seattle Times*, "Tribe Accuses Media of Disruption," by Christine Clarridge.

August 30, 1998: *Olympian*, "Soldiers Idle at Makah Days," by Chester Allen.

Fall, 1998: *Akwe:kon's Journal of Indigenous Issues*, "Fighting for Native Rights," by Beth Hege Piatote.

September 1, 1998: *Seattle Post-Intelligencer*, "Makah Guarding an Expensive Call," editorial.

September 5, 1998: *London Times*, "Whaling Wall: The Makah Do Not Have a 'Special Case' for Hunting," editorial.

September 9, 1998: *Sequim Gazette*, "Makah Days Cost Clallam County $26,000 for Law Enforcement," by Robert Whale.

September 20, 1998: *Seattle Times*, "The Whale Hunt," by Alex Tizon.

September 24, 1998: *Peninsula Daily News*, "Makah, Foes Square Off," by Jesse Hamilton.

September 30, 1998: *Everett Herald*, "Makahs Can Still Decide Not to Look Backward," editorial.

October 2, 1998: *Globe and Mail*, "Makah Whalers Dodge Opponents, Delay Attempt to Revive Hunt," by Sarah Schmidt. Refers to "Watson Goes Ashore at Neah Bay for Interviews."

October 2, 1998: *Seattle Post-Intelligencer*, "Day of Reckoning at Hand for Whale Hunt," by Paul Shukovsky and Mike Barber. Refers to Keith Johnson comments on Sea Shepherd. Information and reference to SEDNA.

October 2, 1998: *Bremerton Sun*, "Neah Baywatch," by Christopher Dunagan. Refers to Norwegian producer Terje Nilsen.

October 2, 1998: *USA Today*, "Whale Hunt Draws Flotilla of Protest," by Patrick McMahon. Refers to Greenpeace statement that they do not oppose the hunt.

October 3, 1998: *Oregonian*, "Makah's Whale Hunt Still Floundering Ashore," by Peggy Anderson, Associated Press.

October 4, 1998: *Los Angeles Times*, "Aspiring Whalers Practice, Proselytize Their History," by Peggy Anderson, Associated Press. Refers to erroneous report of Makah whalers practicing.

October 4, 1998: *Peninsula Daily News*, "Makah Have Chance for Secret Whale Hunt," by Jesse Hamilton. Refers to quote from Ben Johnson.

October 4, 1998: *Los Angeles Times*, "Elders Opposed to Whaling Find Resistance at Home, Reverence Outside," by Peggy Anderson, Associated Press.

October 5, 1998: *Ottawa Citizen*, "Whale Hunt Sparks War on West Coast," by Greg Middleton.

October 5, 1998: *Globe and Mail*, "Whale Quest Loses Harpoonist as Weather Keeps Crew in Port," by Sarah Schmidt.

October 6, 1998: *Tacoma News Tribune*, "Reporters, Activists Mark Time While Makahs Play it Coy," by Leslie Brown.

October 7, 1998: *Peninsula Daily News*, "Are the Makah Whaling Today?" by Jesse Hamilton.

October 8, 1998: *Seattle Times*, "The Whale-Waiting Game," by Lynda Mapes.

October 8, 1998: *Seattle Weekly*, "Wait and Switch," by Eric Scigliano.

October 9, 1998: *Peninsula Daily News*, "Makah Foes Slash at Sea," by Jesse Hamilton.

October 10, 1998: *Globe and Mail*, "Makah Hunt Helps Industry Undermine Ban on Whaling," by Sarah Schmidt.

October 11, 1998: *Peninsula Daily News*, "No Whale Hunt After 11 Days," by Jesse Hamilton.

October 12, 1998: *Peninsula Daily News*, "Makah Patiently Wait for Right Conditions," by Brad Lincoln.

October 12, 1998: *Los Angeles Times*, "Whale Hunt Amid Sea of Discontent," by Kim Murphy.

October 12, 1998: *Peninsula Daily News*, "Makah Can Still Decide Not to Look Backward," editorial.

October 16, 1998: *Seattle Post-Intelligencer*, "Makah Asks Protesters of Whaling to Take Their Boats Elsewhere," by Peggy Anderson, Associated Press.

October 17, 1998: *Washington Post*, "As Tribe Pursues Whales and a Way of Life, Conflict Grows," by Rene Sanchez.

October 20, 1998: *Peninsula Daily News*, "Media Play Waiting Game for Makah Tribe's Whale Hunt," Associated Press.

October 20, 1998: *Bellingham Herald*, "Community Debates Makahs' Tribal Right to Hunt for Whale," by Carolyn Nielsen.

October 22, 1998: *Peninsula Daily News*, "Sea Shepherd Posts Reward for Advance Notice of Hunt," by Jesse Hamilton.

October 24, 1998: *Globe and Mail*, "Documents Show Makah Eyed Commercial Whaling," by Sarah Schmidt. Refers to US Federal government documents. Quotes from Denise Daily.

October 25, 1998: *Peninsula Daily News*, "Another Thing to Protest: Sea Shepherd Disputes PA Customs Ruling," by Jesse Hamilton.

October 26, 1998: *Seattle Times*, "Will Gun Kill Whale Quickly?" by Lynda Mapes.

October 30, 1998: *Seattle Times*, "Some Makahs Oppose Hunt," by Lynda Mapes.

November 1, 1998: *Seattle Times*, "Standoff at Makah Border Gets Ugly," by Lynda Mapes.

November 1, 1998: *Seattle Times*, "My Job Is to Rock the Boat," by Alex Tizon.

November 2, 1998: *Seattle Times*, "Rock Throwing and Jeers in Battle Over Whaling," by Lynda Mapes.

November 2, 1998: "Whaling Protesters, Makah Indians Clash in Neah Bay, Washington," by Peggy Anderson, Associated Press. Anderson reports in this article that an AP photographer was struck with a rock thrown by the Makah.

November 2, 1998: *Seattle Post-Intelligencer*, "Four Protestors Arrested in Shoreline Set-to with Whalers," by Paul Shukovsky.

November 3, 1998: *Seattle Times*, "Lead Stuntman in Anti-Whaling Drama Is One Seasoned Actor," by Erik Lacitis.

November 4, 1998: *Seattle Post-Intelligencer*, "Tribe Considers Charges Against Elder," by Mike Barber. Quote from Ben Johnson concerning possible charges against Alberta Thompson.

November 4, 1998: "Tribal Foe of Whaling in Hiding," by Peggy Anderson, Associated Press.

November 6, 1998: *Seattle Post-Intelligencer*, "Cousteau Son Asks Makah Not to Whale," by Paul Shukovsky and Mike Barber. Quotes from Jean-Michel Cousteau.

November 12, 1998: *Globe and Mail*, "Day 45 in Wait for Makah Whale Hunt," by Sarah Schmidt.

November 12, 1998: *Sault Star*, "Makah Tribal Leaders Want Environmentalists Out," by Peggy Anderson, Associated Press.

November 17, 1998: *Peninsula Daily News*, "Tribal Election Could Change Makah's Stance on Whaling," by Jesse Hamilton.

November 18, 1998: *Seattle Post-Intelligencer*, "Key Figure in Whale Hunt Loses Makah Vote," by Associated Press.

November 18, 1998: *Anchorage Daily News*, "Tribal Family Feuds Delay Resurrected Whale Hunt," by Paul Shukovsky.

November 19, 1998: *Seattle Weekly*, "Blowing It: Why Neither Side is Winning the Makah Whaling War," by Eric Scigliano.

November 27, 1998: *Corvallis Gazette-Times*, "Sea Shepherd Pulls Out of Neah Bay," by Peggy Anderson, Associated Press.

November 19, 1998: *Seattle Times*, "Whale-Hunt Foes Exit Neah Bay; Talks Planned," by Peggy Anderson, Associated Press.

November 23, 1998: *Seattle Post-Intelligencer*, "Makah, Activists Plan Lunch Meeting Today," by Peggy Anderson.

December 1, 1998: *Seattle Times*, "Deadliest Part of Whale Hunt Is the Long Wait," by Alex Tizon.

Spring 1999: *Amicus Journal*, "Tribal Tradition and the Spirit of Trust: A Makah Elder Speaks Out for the Gray Whale," by Dick Russell.

March 1999: *Saturday Night*, "The Media, the Makah, and the Missing Whale: A Really Big Fish Story," by Sarah Schmidt.

March 31, 1999: *Journal of the San Juan Islands*, "Commissioners Object to Gray Whale Hunt," by Stacy D. Stumbo.

April 1999: *Journal of the Japanese Institute for Cetacean Research*, "The Makah and Whale: A Tale of True Ecoterrorism," by John Beatty.

May 11, 1999: *Seattle Post-Intelligencer*, "Makah Harpoon Misses Whale," by Scott Sunde, Paul Shukovsky, and Mike Barber.

May 11, 1999: *Seattle Times*, "First Harpoon: a 'Magic' Miss," by Lynda Mapes.

May 20, 1999: *Globe and Mail*, "A Whale for the Killing," by Margaret Wente. Quotes from Charlie Claplanhoo.

May 24, 1999: Opening statement by the High North Alliance to the fifty-first annual meeting of the IWC.

May 28, 1999: IWC final press release from Grenada.

June 1999: Newsletter of the World Council of Whalers. Report on the second international meeting of the WCW.

June 3–10, 1999: *Georgia Strait*, "Red Tide," by Bob Hunter.

June 14, 1999: *Globe and Mail*, "Whaling Lobby Gets Federal Cash, PR Assistance. Commercial Whalers Told References to Natives Could Help Win Over 'Emotional' Support," by Sarah Schmidt.

Quotes from chief Tom Mexis Happynook, professor Milton Freeman, and Brian Roberts at WCW meeting in Iceland.

April 12, 2000: *Seattle Times*, "Protesters Are Back as Whale Hunt Nears," by Criag Welch and Keiko Morris.

April 21, 2000: *Seattle Post-Intelligencer*, "Whaling Protest Ends in Injury," by Paul Shukovsky and Michael Barber.

June 10, 2000: *Los Angeles Times*, "Ruling Allowing Whale Hunts by Makah Tribe Rejected," by Kim Murphy.

September 24, 2000: *Vancouver Province*, "One Whale of a Hunt for 'Research,'" editorial.

Feb 7, 2001: *Peninsula Daily News*, "Anti-Whaling Group Targets Weaponry," by Austin Ramzy. Cites reference to ballistics expert Roy Kline on the use of .50 caliber rifles. Quotes from Chuck Owens and Brian Gorman.

May 1, 2002: *Seattle Times*, "Anti-Whaling Activists Ask Judge to Stop Hunt," by Elizabeth Murtaugh, Associated Press.

Sept 9, 2007: *Spokesman-Review*, "Dead Whale Was Shot, Harpooned."

January 13, 2008: *Bellingham Herald*, "Makahs Hope to Hunt Whales by 2010."

March 25: *Longview Daily News*, "Whale Hunters Reject Plea Deal at Last Minute."

June 29, 2008: *Spokesman-Review*, "Makah Whalers to Be Sentenced."

July 1, 2008: *Bellingham Herald*, "Two Makahs Get Jail Time for Hunt."

August 26, 2018: *Spokesman-Review*, "Whale Killed by Ship Now a Harvest Celebration as Makah Prepares Rare 'Emotional' Feast."

November 17, 2019: *Spokesman-Review*, "After 20 Years, State Tribe Hopes to Hunt Whales Again."

December 9, 2019: *Seattle Times*, "Sea Shepherd's View on Makah Whale Hunt."

DOCUMENTS LISTED BY DATE

December 7, 1997: Memorandum from Joe Martin, Clallam County undersheriff to the members of the law enforcement whaling task force. Announcing a meeting for 10:00 a.m. on December 18 at the US Coast Guard base in Port Angeles.

January 7, 1998: Memorandum from Joe Martin, Clallam County undersheriff to the members of the law enforcement whaling task force. Announcing the next meeting for 10:00 a.m. on February 18 at the Clallam County Court House in Port Angeles.

May 27, 1998: Memorandum from Joe Martin, Clallam County undersheriff to the members of the whaling committee. Announcement of change in venue of the meeting to the Makah tribal council site and a notification that the tribe will provide lunch. No mention of date in the document, just the time of 10:00 a.m. The date is believed to be June.

June 9, 1998: Memorandum from the Makah tribal council to the law enforcement whaling task force from Patty Manuel, the Makah operations director. Another change of meeting place for the June 17 meeting announced this time to the Makah Community Hall. The reason for the change was the large number of participants expected to attend. The tribe provided lunch and a tour of the tribal museum.

July 9, 1998: Memorandum from Joe Martin, Clallam County undersheriff, to the members of the law enforcement/intelligence committee. Announcement of a meeting of the committee to be held on July 21 at the El Cazador restaurant in Sequim at 11:00 a.m.

MEDIA SOURCES FOR EVENTS AT WOUNDED KNEE, SOUTH DAKOTA
MARCH 1, 1973, TO MAY 9, 1973

Thursday, March 1, 1973: *Vancouver Sun*, "Senators Fly in to Talk With Indians," page 3.

Monday, March 5, 1973: *Vancouver Sun*, "Wounded Knee Indians Reject Talks, Say They'll Turn to Guns, Violence," page 3.

Friday, March 9, 1973: *Vancouver Sun*, "At Wounded Knee, Agreement Nears in Sit-In," page 5.

Saturday, March 10, 1972: *Vancouver Sun*, "Indian Murder Sparked Sit-In," page 3.

Sunday, March 11, 1973: *Tampa Tribune*, "US Quits Wounded Knee, Militants Expect Charges," page 2.

Tuesday, March 13, 1973: *Vancouver Sun*, "US Officials Threaten to 'Starve' Out Indians," page 3.

Wednesday, March 14, 1973: *Vancouver Sun*, "Negotiations at Wounded Knee Stalled by Severe Snowstorm," page 3.

Wednesday, March 14, 1973: *Vancouver Sun*, Robert Hunter column, page 44.

Saturday, March 17, 1973: *Vancouver Sun*, "Belly Down at Wounded Knee, City Man Joins the Protest," page 6.

Monday, March 19, 1973: *Vancouver Sun*, "Ultimatum Drawn up by Militant Indians," page 8.

Friday, March 23, 1973: *Vancouver Sun*, Robert Hunter column, page 32.

Saturday, March, 24 1973: *Vancouver Sun*, "City Men Make Trek for Aid," page 4.

Tuesday, March 27, 1973: *Vancouver Sun*, "Marshal Wounded at Wounded Knee," page 5.

Thursday, March 29, 1973: *Vancouver Sun*, "Split Stalls on Indian's Siege," page 6.

Friday, April 6, 1973: *Vancouver Sun*, "AIM Leader Taken to Capital for Talks," page 3.

Monday, April 16, 1973: *Victoria Times*, "Colonists' Medicine Blocked," page 16.

Saturday, April 21, 1973: *Vancouver Sun*, "Residents Threaten Shoot-out," page 38.

Thursday, April 26, 1973: *Honolulu Advertiser*, "Wounded Knee's First Battle Death," page 2.

Sunday, April 29, 1973: *Austin American*, "Conflict Looms over Burial of Wounded Knee Defender," page 2.

Wednesday, May 9, 1973: *Vancouver Sun*, "Wounded Knee Clean-Up Begins," page 3.

ANCESTRAL LINEAGE

CHIEF HENRI MEMBERTOU (1490–1560)
AND CAPTAIN PAUL WATSON

Chief Henri Membertou (1490–1560), twelfth great-grandfather and father to Henricus Chief Kiisaqmaw Memberou Shaman Maupeltuk (1507–1611)

> father to Marie Anne Membertou (1599–1699)

> mother to Catherine LeJeune (1633–1672)

> mother to Jeanne Savoie (1658–1735)

> mother to Anne Pellerin (1683–1727)

> mother to Anne Brun (1708–1764)

> mother to Catherine Admirault (1735–1817)

> mother to Judith Blanchard (1780–1857)

> mother to Jerome Boudreau (1801–1891)

> father to Luc Bourdreau (1838–1875)

> father to Mathilde Belle Boudreau

> mother to Joseph Watson (1895–1982)

> father to Antonio Joseph Watson (1928–1999)

> father to Paul Franklin Watson (1950–)

INDEX

Christopher Columbus reenactment voyage and, 16–18
conservationism and, 1, 23, 59, 208, 209, 214
early life of, 1–2
extremism view of, 122
forestry clearcutting fight and, 18–19
Greenpeace and, 8, 86
as "Grey Wolf Clear Water," 6
harpoons/harpooning and, 13, 14, 61, 74, 99, 122, 128, 162, 191, 205
Iceland deportation and, 36
Ides, Jesse, and, 214
IWC reinstatement and, 53
as journalist, 3, 4–5, 92
Kayapo warriors and, 14
Makah's Custer charge and, 143
Mowat, Farley, and, 186
myth/mythology about Indians and, 189–193, 212–213
Native Indians/Native Americans and, xvi–xvii, 1, 3, 143, 204
Oglala Nation of Wounded Knee citizenship and, 6
Paiakan, Chief Paulinho, and, 14–15
poem given by, on Norwegian whaler, 43
poverty and, 2
racism/racism accusations and, vii, 18, 29, 123, 144, 189, 203, 204–205, 209
radicalness charge and, 143
Seattle Post-Intelligencer quote and, 58–59, 61–62
Seattle Times profile and, 143
Smith, Mabel, and, 91
Squamish blessing upon, 1
Taillefer, Clotilde, and, 90, 93
terrorism accusations and, 32, 33–34, 36, 39, 144
Thompson, Alberta ("Binki"), and, 91, 184, 214
tribal support/connections and, 1, 6, 15–16, 18
US Coast Guard and, 205
Valentine, Sophie, and, 90
Vestri, René, and, 90, 91
vision quest and, 6–7, 9
wasicu designation of, 6, 9
whale intimacy experiences and, 9–14, 38, 123

wicasa wakan (holy man) and, 6
as wildlife conservationist, 1
wolves' extermination plan and, 18
Wounded Knee experience and, 4–9
Yabis's death and, 189, 205
Avocet (boat), 175, 176, 177
Ayukawa, Japan, 108
the Aztecs, 206, 211

B

Baird's beaked whales, 108, 170
Baja, California, 121, 122
Baker, Chief Simon (Khot-La-Cha), 1
Baker, James, xv, 66, 67–68
Banks, Dennis, 7
Barbuda, IWC and, 101
Barrett, Dave, 32
BBC (British Broadcasting Corporation), 27, 30–31, 172
BBC Caribbean, 172
BC Liberal Party whale hunting position, 51
Beatrix, Queen, 88
Belany, Anahareo, 2
Belany, Archie, 2
Belize, 137, 138
Bella Bella, British Columbia, 11
the Beothuk people, 211
Bering Sea, 103, 118
Bernard, Prince, 85
BIA (Bureau of Indian Affairs), 4, 5, 8, 58, 146
Biko, Stephen, 207
biocentrism, 190, 207, 208, 214
Birnie, Patricia, 56
Bissonette, Pedro, 7–8
Black Elk, Wallace, 6, 7
Black Harvest (documentary), 31
Black people, 205, 207
Blair, Linda, 85
Blayney, Paul, 176
Blichfeldt, Georg, 57
Bloom, Susan, 155
Blore, Shawn, 24
blue whales, xv, 107
bluefin tuna fishery proposal, by the Japanese, 102–103
the Boers, 207
Borg, Sten, 33, 34
bowhead whales, 104–105
Brave Heart, Dewey, 4, 8
Brave Heart family, author's acceptance in, 6

Brazil, 14–15, 97, 104, 108, 127, 137, 170
BREACH, 125
The Breakers restaurant (Washington), 147
Bremen, Germany, author's arrest warrant and, 84
Bremerhaven, Germany, *Sea Shepherd III* in, 84, 89
Bridgewater, Peter, 104
Bristol, England, 31
Britain/the British (the English)
America and, 40
author's arrest warrant and, 84
the Beothuk and, 212
bureaucracy and, 40
Chief Seattle and, 197
fish product boycott, Faroese government and, 31
media corporation (BBC), 27, 30–31, 172
navy/warships and, 40, 87
piracy and, 40
slave trade comparison and, 87
Smith, John, and, 213
whale support and, 23, 31, 114
British Broadcasting Corporation (BBC), 27, 30–31, 172
British Columbia Association of Non-Status Indians, 3
British Columbian government, whaling position and, 51
Bronson, Suniva, 18
Brooks, Lorena, 140, 142, 146, 157, 161
Brosnan, Pierce, 85
Brown, Peter, 16, 139, 140, 141–142, 148, 149
Brown, Ronald, 135
Brownell, Robert L., xiv
the Brulé people, author and, 6
Brundtland, Gro Harlem, 55, 56
Buddy (resident whale), 132, 133
Bulletproof (boat), 139, 155–156, 157, 161, 162, 163, 180
Bureau of Indian Affairs (BIA), 4, 5, 8, 58, 146
Burke, William, 108
Busch, Marc, 71, 72, 73
Bychkov, Vladimir, as guide, in Provideniya, Russia, 75–77, 78, 79

C

Calico, South Dakota, 4, 6, 8

Ingling, Allen, and, 118
lawsuit against, 183
the Makah and, xiv, 25, 59, 61, 63,
118, 128, 135
Sea Shepherd and, 59, 63, 122
Seattle Post-Intelligencer editorial
and, 59
Swartz, Steve, and, 61
Yabis and, 158, 159
National Marine Mammal Laboratory
(NMML), 118
National Oceanic and Atmospheric
Administration (NOAA), 135
Native Americans (American Indians)/
Native Indians. *See also* specific
names of tribes
Amazon rainforest exploitation and,
214
author and, xvi–xvii, 1, 3, 5, 7, 143,
189–193, 204
conservation and, 23
as environmentalists, 210
Europeans and, 92, 190, 202
genocide/specicide practiced by,
189
Greenpeace and, 51
Hollywood's portrayal of, 212
Home (film) and, 198
human species and, 205
opposition to whale killing and, 211
Perry, Ted, and, 198–202
politics and, 49, 60
racism/racial stereotyping and, xii,
189, 203
rights and, 3, 22, 123, 192, 209,
212
Sea Shepherd and, vii–viii, 134,
207
Seattle, Chief, and, 194–198, 202
sovereignty and, 193
Thunderheart (film) and, 212–213
Turtle Island and, 193
the Navajo people, 146
the Ndebele people, 207
Neah (resident whale), 132
Neah Bay, Washington, the Makah gray
whale hunt (1995/1998)
Ahdunko, Lionel, and, 142, 145,
146, 147, 148
American culture and, 131–132
Associated Press and, 141
author and, 123–124, 148, 153
Brown, Peter, as stand-in for author
and, 148–149

Bulletproof and, 139
Canadian Coast Guard and, 128
canoe practice and, 130
Cousteau, Jean-Michel, and, 147
dead whale report and, 128
E. coli poisoning and, 150
family dissension/feuds and,
150–151
FBI and, 129, 136, 146
Freedom of Information Act and,
134–136
the Gitxsan people and, 148, 149
gray whale killing in, xi–xvii, 24–26
Greenpeace USA and, 129
"harassment" incidents and,
133–134, 136–137
helicopter landing and, for meeting
with the Makah, 149
"Ishmael" reference and, 153
Japanese/IWC and, 47–52
KOMO-TV and, 150
Los Angeles Times and, 111
Makah Manifesto and, in Seattle
Times, 114–121
media and, 127–129, 130, 132–
133, 135–136, 139, 141, 142,
144–145, 146, 151, 152–153
(See also specific media)
Metcalf, Jack, and, 146
migrant whale vs. resident whale
and, 128
NMFS and, 128
organizations/groups campaigning
against and, 124–126
Ottawa Citizen and, 130
Peninsula Daily News and, 126,
134, 137, 144
Prince of Whales Zodiac boats and,
139
reward and, for advance warning of
hunt, 134
ritualized/symbolic hunt suggestion
and, 147
Sea Shepherd III and, 111–114,
122–123, 126–127, 133,
136–138, 139–142, 147, 151
Sea Shepherd's reactions to Makah
Manifesto and, 121–122
Seattle Post-Intelligencer and,
58–63, 126
Seattle Times and, 111–112,
114–121, 126, 138–139, 143,
144, 145
Seattle Weekly and, 144

Sirenian and, 122–123, 126, 127,
133, 134, 136, 137, 138, 139,
141, 142
stolen land and, 153
Svenson, Eric, prosecution and, 153
tensions during, 138–144
Thompson, Alberta ("Binki"), and,
140, 142, 145, 146, 147, 151
tribal council and, 151, 152
"U People tribe" and, 148
US Coast Guard and, 128–129, 133,
136, 137–138, 140, 142, 151,
152
US Customs and, 136–137
US marshals and, 147
US State Department and, 129
USA Today and, 129
Vancouver Sun and, 129
whale-naming tactic and, 132
whale petting and, 122
whale-watching boats and, 139
Netherlands, 54, 84–89, 104, 108
Nevada, Lionel Adhunko's scandals
and, 146, 147
New Brunswick, Canada, author in, 2
New Chaplino ("Novoye Chaplino"),
Russia, Sea Shepherd and, 75–76,
77, 79
New York City, New York, Cleveland
Amory eulogy in, 147–148
New Zealand, 102, 104, 106, 108, 186
Newfoundland, Canada, 49,211
NGOs (nongovernmental organiza-
tions), 98–99, 100
Nice-Matin (French newspaper), 95–96
Nichols, Ken, 141–142, 146
Nieuwe Revu (Dutch magazine), 85
Nilsen, Terje, 128
Nimpkish Band, 129
Nina replica ship, 16
NMFS (National Marine Fisheries
Service). *See* National Marine
Fisheries Service (NMFS)
NMML (National Marine Mammal
Laboratory), 118
NOAA (National Oceanic and Atmo-
spheric Administration), 135
Noel, Andy, 184, 185
Nome, Alaska, *Earth Undercover*
television program and, 75, 80
nongovernmental organizations
(NGOs), 98–99, 100
Nootka language, of the Makah people,
153

GROUNDSWELL BOOKS
SOLUTIONS FOR A SUSTAINABLE WORLD

For more books that inspire readers to create a healthy,
sustainable planet for future generations, visit
BookPubCo.com

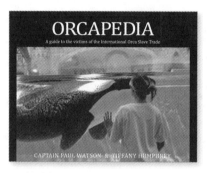

Orcapedia:
A Guide to the Victims of the
International Orca Slave Trade

Captain Paul Watson and Tiffany Humphrey

978-1-57067-398-6 • $24.95

Dark Side of the Ocean:
The Destruction of Our Seas, Why It Matters,
and What We Can Do About It

Albert Bates

978-1-57067-394-8 • $12.95

Transforming Plastic:
From Pollution to Evolution

Albert Bates

978-1-57067-371-9 • $9.95

Cooking' Up A Storm:
Sea Stories And Vegan Recipes

Laura Dakin

978-1-57067-312-2 • $24.95

Purchase these titles from your favorite book source or buy them directly from:
Book Publishing Company • PO Box 99 • Summertown, TN 38483 • 1-888-260-8458

Free shipping and handling on all orders